Meeting the Need Children with En Additional Langu.

Drawing on the latest research into how young children learn, this book considers how early years practitioners can best meet the needs of children with English as an Additional Language. It examines the factors that influence children's learning including parents and the family, the environment, health and well-being, curriculum, play and relationships and aims to challenge misconceptions, assumptions and stereotypes.

Featuring case studies and reflective questions, the chapters explore a range of important topics including:

- Language learning for children with EAL
- The historical concept and modern reconceptualisation of EAL
- How to develop and use Culturally Appropriate Pedagogy
- Regulation and performativity, and their implications for children with EAL
- Leading learning for children with EAL

Meeting the Needs of Young Children with English as an Additional Language is essential reading for students and practitioners wanting to promote an inclusive culture where different languages, cultures and religions are accepted and celebrated.

Malini Mistry is Senior Lecturer in Education at the University of Bedfordshire, UK.

Krishan Sood is Senior Lecturer in Education at Nottingham Trent University, UK.

Meeting the Needs of Young Children with English as an Additional Language

Research Informed Practice

Malini Mistry and
Krishan Sood

Routledge
Taylor & Francis Group

LONDON AND NEW YORK

First edition published 2020
by Routledge
2 Park Square, Milton Park, Abingdon, Oxon OX14 4RN

and by Routledge
52 Vanderbilt Avenue, New York, NY 10017

Routledge is an imprint of the Taylor & Francis Group, an informa business

© 2020 Malini Mistry and Krishan Sood

British Library Cataloguing-in-Publication Data
A catalogue record for this book is available from the British Library

Library of Congress Cataloging-in-Publication Data
A catalog record has been requested for this book

ISBN: 978-0-367-20762-5 (hbk)
ISBN: 978-0-367-20763-2 (pbk)
ISBN: 978-0-429-26339-2 (ebk)

Typeset in Palatino
by Wearset Ltd, Boldon, Tyne and Wear

Contents

Acknowledgements

Malini said to me one summer day, I need to do 'something' with this PhD research and reading I have done. This 'something' was to write this book arising from research, practice, experience and reflections by both of us. It sounded so easy when we thought about it on that summer day. We had forgotten how difficult a task it was when we wrote our first book five years ago. One soon forgets the pain!

As ever, there are million thank you's to be made to all who helped us shape this book as we offer it to you to enjoy, read, reflect and open spaces for debate. These are our thoughts borne out of many years of practice as teachers, leaders and university lecturers. We know that any errors in this book are of our making and offer our apologies unconditionally.

Our heartfelt thank you goes to our editor Annamarie Kino for her timely feedback and encouragement. To Ramesh and Vimla Mistry for their unconditional love and support during this process – especially the endless snacks and chai that appeared to help sustain us. To Yvonne and Roza for reading earlier drafts and giving their critical feedback to improve our ideas and thinking.

A very special thank you to Roshan Mistry, Presha Mistry and Jasmine Jones who very kindly illustrated the front cover of this book – their enthusiasm and excitement was awesome. Maybe this will inspire all of them to write a book in the future!

Finally, we would like to dedicate this book to all the children with EAL who are the real inspiration for writing this book. We hope the book enthuses the leaders, governors, practitioners, academics, policy makers and learners to take the messages within the text that will help them become better teachers, counsellors and gurus and in turn, impact outcomes for their learners.

Malini said to me one summer day, 'I need to do something' ... – after this book, you must be joking!

'Life is a song – sing it. Life is a game – play it. Life is a challenge – meet it.
Life is a dream – realize it. Life is a sacrifice – offer it. Life is love – enjoy it.'
(Sri Sathya Sai Baba (Brainy quote, 2013))

1

Introduction – structure of the book

Introduction

Rising immigration to England since the 1960s, particularly from the commonwealth countries, has led to an increased number of children in Early Years settings and primary schools, many of whom come from a range of backgrounds with a plethora of different languages other than English. The 2018 school census clearly shows consistently rising numbers of immigrant children since 2006 with 21.1 per cent of children exposed to a language other than English as their first or home language (DfE, 2018: 10). In this context, English as an Additional Language (EAL) can be defined as those children who speak English in Addition to their home or first language(s) (Mistry and Sood, 2015). Furthermore, the DfE (2018) emphasise that children with EAL consistently have access to, and regularly use a language other than English at home or with their family. This implies that other language(s) are used instead of English as the main form of communication outside the setting. It also suggests that many of these bilingual and multilingual children are well immersed in different languages and have what we call the three C's, capacity, capability and competencies of good communication skills, which settings should be aware of. Therefore, settings need to capitalise on these rich living experiences such diversity brings to them regardless of whether they are mono-cultural or multicultural.

Children with EAL can also be referred to or labelled in different ways such as: bilingual children, pluralingual children, multilingual children, and children with English as a Second Language (ESL). Each of these labels has a different meaning (defined and discussed in Chapter 5) which needs to be understood in relation to the Early Years context. The number of children with EAL varies between Early Years settings depending on their geographical location (Strand *et al.*, 2015). We consider Early Years settings to include: toddler groups, nurseries, sure start centres, and reception classes in primary and infant schools. Generally, these Early Years settings follow the Early Years Foundation Stage (EYFS) framework (DfE, 2017) guidance for children aged birth to five to help support children's learning experiences. To aid transition, in some schools this Early Years phase extends to Year 1 classes within the National Curriculum.

What this book is about

We believe that this book is the first of its kind that looks critically at the roots of provision and practice associated with children who have EAL. This book goes beyond identifying a range of quick fix strategies aimed at short term solutions in meeting the needs of children with EAL. Rather, it is about focusing on a deeper philosophical and theoretical understanding of how children learn and more importantly how learning needs to be adapted for young children with EAL. This is because all children with EAL do not have the same needs all the time. It explores controversial, contested issues like categorising children by labelling them and the effect of this on children's learning and willingness to learn when they also have EAL. There are also references to policy contexts, various educational acts, and documentation that have influenced changes in the Early Years sector and therefore provision and practice. We believe that with a strong foundation of understanding how children with EAL grow, learn and develop, practitioners are much better placed in meeting the needs of this diverse group of children without relying on random strategies for a short term solution.

What this book covers

This book covers two key concepts. First, children with EAL and second, the Early Years phase. A range of philosophical and theoretical understandings associated with these concepts are presented to heighten awareness of what it means to meet the needs of children with EAL in your setting regardless of personal and societal assumptions (Mistry and Sood, 2010). More importantly, this book focuses on the context of Early Years and how this context has changed over time to become a distinct learning phase in its own right, alongside government intervention and control which has an impact on provision.

A multitude of issues are deconstructed and explored within the chapters, such as philosophy and theory related to school readiness, theory associated with language learning and how this is applicable to children learning EAL, and the impact of categorising children through labelling them whilst they try to assimilate and learn in a socially just environment. Additionally, this book covers how theory can link to current practice in order to better understand the roots of learning. This book is a deeper and more rooted version of our previous book *English as an Additional Language in the Early Years: Linking theory to practice.*

Structure and organisation

This book is organised into ten chapters which are progressive in time and nature. Chapter 1 is the introduction which sets the structure for this book.

Chapter 2 sets the scene through a brief historical context which mentions a range of issues that are discussed in later chapters in more detail.

Chapter 3 starts at the beginning in terms of looking at what philosophers and theorists perceive about the way in which children learn best, and how their ideology can be linked to meet the needs of children with EAL to ensure they make progress.

Chapter 4 explores the educational regime that children with EAL have had in the past and currently have, and the factors that have influenced this. This chapter also looks at the impact of various policies and educational acts that have informed the way in which education for children with EAL is perceived and translated into provision and practice.

Chapter 5 aims to reconceptualise what is meant by the term EAL and the associated debate with terminology. This chapter investigates various terms associated with children who have EAL and the notion that these terms are used interchangeably to suggest that they all mean the same, implying that all children with EAL have the same needs.

Chapter 6 investigates a range of language learning theory which is essential for all practitioners working with young children. How these theories are translated into practice can be debated, especially if evidence suggests fluency in one language can support learning in a new language. We argue that transference of skills from different languages with different sounds and symbols to the English language may not happen.

Chapter 7 investigates the importance of culturally responsive pedagogy and how this is particularly relevant for children with EAL to ensure they make progress.

Chapter 8 charts the historical changes that have taken place within the Early Years sector from no government intervention to a culture of control and surveillance to ensure children achieve certain targets in core areas of learning, regardless of their well-being.

Chapter 9 looks at the notion of performativity in the Early Years. This is particularly important with Ofsted (Office of Standards in Education) continuously monitoring standards and targets in settings which are used to illustrate how effective practitioners are in relation to improving children's outcomes.

Finally, Chapter 10 brings together the themes of this book by looking at being an effective strategic Early Years leader because they have the power to change and make a difference for children with EAL through leading by example.

Who is this book for?

This book is aimed at all those who work in the Early Years and the primary sector. It is particularly useful for leaders, teachers, teaching assistants, nursery nurses, key workers, bilingual assistants, students, trainee teachers, and parents working in settings. Additionally, it can be a set reader for students studying at undergraduate and post graduate level on a range of different courses that involve working with children both QTS and non QTS. This book is also aimed at all those who support children with EAL within and beyond the Early Years phase.

What this book aims to achieve

We have written this book to give a deeper conceptual understanding regarding not only the roots of learning, but also how children with EAL can be different in terms of their learning needs (especially if they have language learning needs). We want to encourage our readers to move away from the notion that because Early Years is developmental, no effort needs to be made to help children access learning as they will eventually assimilate and learn. Rather, it is about seeing each child as a unique, special human being with a range of strengths that inform their character and personality regardless of their English language skills. More importantly, we hope this book helps to support the reader in terms of how practice and provision can be adapted to meet the different needs for children with EAL for long term gain. Finally, we hope to give readers a depth of understanding and critical reflection in addition to some suggested strategies.

The inspiration and passion for this book stemmed from the various perspectives and experiences of the authors who are multilingual practitioners themselves and want to share their knowledge from different cultural perspectives to support the practice of others for their EAL children.

In summary

In summary, this book aims to show that philosophical and theoretical thinking should inform practice for all children. Children with EAL in Early Years do not require one single strategy that will be the golden thread to enable them to become fluent in the English language overnight or to open up access to learning. It is many different strategies that all pull together over time to encourage children to make connections in their learning to broaden their understanding of the world to help them be successful. The emphasis here is on the importance of good teaching based on research informed practice regardless of whether a child has EAL or not, through having a secure theoretical foundation of how children learn, develop and grow.

References

Department for Education (DfE) (2017) *Statutory framework for the early years foundation stage: Setting the standards for learning, development and care for children from birth to five.* London: DfE.

Department for Education (DfE) (2018) *Schools, pupils and their characteristics: June 2018.* Available at: https://assets.publishing.service.gov.uk/government/uploads/system/uploads/attachment_data/file/719226/Schools_Pupils_and_their_Characteristics_2018_Main_Text.pdf (Accessed September 2018).

Mistry, M. and Sood, K. (2010) English as an Additional Language: Challenges and Assumptions. *Management in Education*, 24 (3), July (1–4).

Mistry, M. and Sood, K. (2015) *English as an Additional Language in the Early Years: Linking theory to practice.* London: Routledge.

Strand, S., Malmberg, L. and Hall, J. (2015) *English as an Additional Language (EAL) and educational achievement in England: An analysis of the National Pupil Database.* Oxford: University of Oxford Department of Education.

2

Historical context

When you have finished reading this chapter you will

- be aware of how the changing historical and political climate has had an impact on the provision for children with English as an Additional Language within the context of Early Years
- understand the impact of categorising and labelling children with EAL

Chapter outline

This chapter will set the scene for the rest of the book by beginning with a historical overview of children with EAL followed by a short discussion on the impact of rising numbers of children with EAL. There will then be an overview of the context of children with EAL and how increased immigration has led to categorisation and labelling. The focus then moves onto how Early Years education in England has gone through a complete change from non-existent intervention from the government to current regulation with key emphasis on marketisation and performativity (discussed in Chapter 8) through a goal orientated curriculum. The current inclusion agenda implies that the needs of all children should be met including those children with EAL, but how and to what extent these needs are met can be contested and debated. Finally, this chapter concludes with a brief overview of some of the challenges associated with meeting the needs of children with EAL.

Historical overview of children with EAL

Children who have EAL can come from a variety of different backgrounds ranging from asylum seekers to economic migration, as well as migration for other reasons. It is important to note that children with EAL can also include those children who are born and raised in England with a different first language(s) other than English. For example, a family could fluently use a different language at home other than English, especially if a child is part of an extended family or the family decide that they would prefer to use their mother tongue rather than English.

After the end of World War II the rebuilding of the British economy required immigrant workers, but this appeal for workers was directly aimed at white migrants from Europe who had generally dominated migration to Britain. Post war migrants from the commonwealth countries like India, Pakistan and the Caribbean also began to increase especially from the 1960s. This was partly due to the British Nationality Act of 1948 which enabled people of commonwealth countries to have the right to live and work in the UK implying they were not subject to the same rules of immigration controls as those from outside the commonwealth (BBC, 2014).

After Britain joined the European Union in 1973 there was greater freedom of movement between European countries. Hence, migration to England from these countries increased and therefore different first languages became more evident. According to Drummond (2014) some of the most common first languages today include: Polish, Romanian, Portuguese, Spanish, Italian and French in addition to Punjabi, Urdu, Bengali, Gujerati, and Mandarin Chinese. Historically, this variety of first or home languages was not as evident as it is today suggesting the group of children now termed as having EAL has become very diverse. Therefore, the misconception that children with EAL generally come from a few selected countries around the world, has now been dispelled.

Rising numbers of children with EAL

The number of children with EAL in English settings is over one million and rising (Drummond, 2014). This means that with approximately a fifth of the child population speaking a different language(s) (as indicated in the introduction), practice in Early Years settings and primary schools need to adapt to the changing needs of children especially in relation to strategies used for English language learning. In Early Years practitioners need to make sure learning is cognitively demanding but not linguistically demanding to enable children with EAL to participate in order to help them access learning to make progress.

Children with EAL come from a different range of backgrounds and situations each with their own particular ways of life. For example, a child with EAL could be a new arrival from employment associated migration, to a child from a refugee camp, to a child from a war-torn country seeking asylum. Although in the 1960s migration to England was mostly from the commonwealth countries, from the late 1990s onwards, this trend was taken over from Eastern European countries. Reasons for migration to England are varied and, in some cases, complicated. Today, the pattern of migration is dynamic and changing and children with EAL do not just come to England from a only few select countries around the world anymore, and the trend is more localised in that there is no set pattern across England as to which countries migration is dominated from. This means that as different languages and cultures resulting from migration began to increase in Britain, the non-white population also began to increase and become more visible in society. This increase in different people in society has led to categorisation, labelling and even racism.

Context of children with EAL in Early Years

Early Years is a crucial phase of learning for children because in this stage the foundations are set for building future learning. Early Years (EY) is the age phase for pupils aged birth to five. The Early Years Foundation Stage (EYFS) framework (DfE, 2017) is government guidance for registered EY settings in England. These settings include young children's groups, play groups, nurseries, sure start centres, and primary schools with nursery and reception classes, all of which play a critical role in shaping pupils' identity as learners (Bruner, 1996). Starting in Early Years, high quality education (DfE, 2016) can open up learning opportunities and enhance life experiences. How children learn is often influenced by the home and setting culture, thus knowledge of this is critical for leaders and practitioners in ensuring planning and provision is effective in meeting needs including for those children with EAL.

With rising migration to England, some children with EAL can have very little, or no English language fluency when starting Early Years provision. This does not mean that these children have no language skills at all, or that they do not understand, it simply means that they can be perceived to be at a slight disadvantage compared to their monolingual peers in terms of accessing the opportunities created from the EYFS framework because these are in English. Therefore, children with EAL need extra effort and support to help them catch up to their peers especially in terms of early English vocabulary associated with speaking. According to Hulstijn and Bossers' (1992) young children's vocabulary can be a good predictor of reading comprehension but we know that this may not always be the case as some children with EAL can read English fluently without actually understanding meaning. Furthermore, early experiences through play with phonological awareness can have an impact on children's decoding skills (whereby print is translated to sound). For children with EAL this means that they will need time and adjusted learning to catch up to their monolingual peers in terms of the English language. Gregory (1996) argues that phonological skills from home language(s) in the pre-school can transfer to learning English in the setting environment. However, we argue that this may not always be the case as this can be dependent on the home language in use. For example, languages like Mandarin, Urdu and Arabic have very different letter shapes and sounds and therefore there is no direct comparison or correspondence to letters and sounds in the English alphabet, meaning phonological skills transfer can be problematic. This is further supported by Brisk and Harrington (2000) who suggest that although vocabulary development is important within Early Years, children with EAL may not have the background knowledge that gives clues to the meaning of text especially if the same words can be used in different contexts with different meanings.

Most importantly, just because children with EAL are not speaking much (or any English) it does not mean that they are not absorbing the language and learning taking place around them. In this respect, the knowledge and experiences provided in an Early Years setting are crucial in ensuring young children have access to learning English in a variety of different ways especially though play and modelling.

Why and how children with EAL are categorised

All young children, including children with EAL have the same right and entitlement to access a broad, balanced and varied curriculum regardless of their proficiency in the English language. In many settings today children can be grouped according to ability especially for literacy and numeracy to aid differentiation in learning. This can also be evident within the context of some Early Years settings for group activities in areas of learning like early number and phonics. Although we can argue that grouping ideally should not take place in Early Years, we are aware that even discreetly, some form of grouping may take place in relation to children's ability.

One assumption that can be made about children with EAL is that these children do not understand or that they do not have any language skills especially if they are not fluent in English (Mistry and Sood, 2010). If this is the case, then children with EAL could be placed either in the lowest ability group or the special needs group suggesting a disregard for the knowledge and skills they already have and placing these children at a direct disadvantage. Furthermore, there could be a situation whereby practitioners have so much pressure from Key Stage 1 in terms of key skills that young children need to acquire by the end of the reception year that they do not have time to make the effort to meet the needs of children with EAL, who may require personal adaptations in learning.

The key point here is that children with EAL should be grouped according to their cognitive ability and potential rather than their proficiency in the English language including reading, writing, speaking and listening. A number of suggestions are offered for this:

- Adults in the setting need to model aspects of language correctly especially spoken language including tense and grammar
- Young children need good role models to observe and learn from and this may be more evident with more confident and more able children

- Use of words and pictures to help support connections in children's thinking
- Making the context of learning clear so that children with EAL can see how similar words can have different meanings in different contexts
- Promote higher order thinking skills such as the use of gentle effective questioning to understand children's reasoning

The strategies above need to be carefully thought through in relation to how groupings or pairs for learning through play are constructed. Perhaps it may not be effective to withdraw young children with EAL for intensive phonics or number interventions just to meet the required Early Learning Goals (ELGs) all the time (DfE, 2018). We also agree that, as suggested by Vygotsky (1978) the social nature of learning through play in the Early Years needs greater emphasis to ensure that children with EAL do not feel excluded from their peers in relation to learning.

In addition, it is important to recognise that children with EAL do not form one homogenous category (discussed later) and therefore there are differences within the EAL group which need to be first, recognised and second, understood so that provision is matched accordingly. Each sub group under the umbrella of EAL has different characteristics and needs which in turn influence how this group of children is categorised and even labelled.

Labelling of children with EAL

Children who speak a different language or languages can be labelled in different ways like bilingual, multilingual, pluralingual, and EAL. Sometimes the issue here is that all these terms are assumed to have the same meaning, when in fact they are all very different, as discussed in Chapter 5. As mentioned earlier, EAL is defined as children learning English in addition to their own language(s), but the issue here is that by labelling children as EAL immediately implies that these children have a learning problem associated with the English language. Here, labelling a child as having EAL focuses our mind on the issues associated with helping them to learn or acquire English rather than looking at the child as a human being and everything positive they bring into the setting. Additionally, the implication here is that before any labels are applied, we need to be aware of what individual children are capable of, because sometimes children with EAL can be very fluent in all aspects of English but they do not want to share this knowledge with practitioners yet.

This theory of labelling stems from Becker (1963) and is associated with social constructivism which aims to explain the reasons for certain types of behaviour by individuals in society towards others. In the context of education, this theory is about how practitioners can apply labels to their children in terms of their academic ability, educational need or behaviour. Furthering the labelling theory is the theory of regenerative shaming by Braithwaite (1989) which explores the difference between the individual being stigmatised and regenerative shaming without being labelled. Although these theories have the clearest links to the field of criminology, they can also be connected to children who are labelled as having EAL in education as these children can be made to feel ashamed of being different so all they want to do is to be the same as their dominant monolingual peers. This is illustrated by the following case study.

Case study 2.1

Ram was a 3-year-old boy in a nursery with Bengali as his first language. Although he was not a new arrival, he only knew a few limited words in English as English was not used at home. However, with word picture cues, he was rapidly picking up key words in the nursery like toast, jam, apples – the words used during snack time. In addition, he was also picking up a range of other words like play time, snack time, choosing, reading time which determined a particular routine.

Despite his rapid English language development, he was labelled 'the EAL boy' by the practitioners in the nursery and was also referred to as 'the EAL boy' by practitioners when discussions took place. During a play activity in the water tray he was referred to by other children as 'Ram the EAL boy' because they had overheard Ram being addressed in this way by staff. One child asked Ram 'what does EAL mean? does it mean brown?' Ram had no idea or the English language skills to formulate an answer so he just shrugged his shoulders. As the year progressed, Ram tended to copy what others were doing rather than choosing activities himself because he did not want to be different from the others.

Key point

- The terminology applied by practitioners towards the child has also transpired to being used by other children without understanding exactly what it means, leading to shaming the child or the child feeling embarrassed about their differences.

Although the application of labels can be useful in determining the support required for particular needs of children in the context of education, the continued use of labels can be contested. One implication of labelling is that once a label is applied to a child, they may be treated in accordance with the label by others. Furthermore, as suggested by Rosenthal and Jacobson (1968) children with EAL may also associate themselves with the label in terms of their identity and self-worth as they may feel that they will always have issues with the English language.

In Early Years if a child is labelled, then there is a danger that the label can stick regardless of the growth and development of the child. This means that early labelling can be harmful and in some cases children can have a label attached to them throughout all of primary education. Sometimes, this EAL label can be used as a reason for children with EAL not achieving in line with the rest of their peers. Children with EAL could be fluent in one or more other languages, therefore at times it takes them time to process in their mind how to translate what they want to say, or how to say what they want to in the correct way in English as illustrated by the following scenario:

Case study 2.2

Ria was a 4-year-old girl in a reception class. She was fluent in Gujerati at home and knew some words and phrases in English. After starting school her mother noticed that during their conversations at home, Ria would use English words for anything she did not know a Gujerati word for. Ria would use the same strategy at school whereby she would use Gujerati to gain the teachers attention. After being told by the teacher to only speak in English, Ria became quiet and reserved, only choosing to speak with other children during play and away from the teacher's earshot. This meant that every time the teacher asked Ria to speak, she would clam up trying to think about how to say what she needed to in the correct way in English so that her teacher would not be angry with her. As a result of this thinking or processing time that Ria took, she was labelled as an underachiever as she was slower in her communication.

Two years later, Ria was one of the most able children in her class in all subjects and was noted as one of the top achievers in the school.

The danger of attaching a label to a child without really knowing their needs is that different kinds of needs could be overlooked such as issues with hearing or a disability. However, it can also be argued that attaching a label means that practitioners may find it easier to differentiate learning. The important point here is that if children are labelled, then this needs to be used in a positive way to support them rather than the case of Ria.

Key points

- Find out what children can do first rather than focusing on the problems or extra effort associated with teaching them English.
- Not all children require support for learning English, therefore, for these children the term EAL is simply as per the definition.

Norwich and Koutsouris (2017) argue in favour of replacing the language of labelling with the capability approach, which is more positive. They suggest the need to focus on the capability of individuals not on their identity, which is a much more ethical way to behave and act. So, language can be a powerful ideological tool that can express assumptions, stigmatise people and can also exclude people.

How Early Years has changed

Education is constantly changing and Early Years is no exception to this. For many years Early Years education in England has been ignored by government intervention with the assumption that young children should be seen and not heard. Historically, little government intervention in Early Years education has existed. Hence, regimes of truth were originally dependent on individual philanthropists until regulation following the 1988 Education Reform Act, whereby the introduction of a focused market-orientated approach to education led to a greater degree of central regulation focusing on performance and on-going debates between key founders who favoured a more child centred approach and policy makers focusing on school effectiveness through directed learning (Woodhead, 1989), measurement of progress, targets and competition between institutions.

However, with the aim of improving quality and raising standards the British government began to intervene in the Early Years sector through first, the introduction of the desirable learning outcomes in 1996 (SCAA, 1996), which was a set of learning goals to help gain some consistency in the Early Years sector. Those desirable learning outcomes were later revised several times to what we now know as the seventeen Early Learning Goals (DfE, 2017) which implies a goal orientated curriculum that young children must achieve.

Since its introduction, the Early Years framework has been in constant debate between policy makers who believe that education is about school effectiveness and standards, and those philosophers, theorists and pioneers who believe that Early Years education should be child centred and should focus on children's well-being and development rather than a performing towards a goal orientated curriculum (discussed in more detail in Chapter 9). As Early Years provision in England is rooted in the socio-political context of any one point in time, this may mean the diversity of children such as those with EAL poses a challenge to provision and practice when, for example, there is a one size fits all approach to policy in terms of the EYFS framework with the emphasis on early number and early reading and associated practice in education, as is at present.

What does the inclusion agenda mean for pupils with EAL?

Before discussing what the inclusion agenda means in practice for children with EAL, it is important to be clear about what inclusion means because it is more than just including all children. Essentially, the term inclusion is linked to the concepts of equality and equity whereby it is not just about providing children with equal opportunities within their learning, but it is about making the extra effort to ensure that there is parity of fairness in every situation to enable all children to achieve (Mistry and Sood, 2014). Here, the concepts of equality and equity are about the principles, values, beliefs and morals that determine how each child should be treated. Namely, fairly and with respect regardless of their race, ethnicity, background, religious denomination, disability and gender.

With increasing migration, our Early Years settings and schools have to meet a greater range of learning needs for children including those children who are refugees, asylum seekers, gypsy roma and traveller children as well as those with specific learning needs, like children with EAL. It is not enough just to be aware of inclusion and the key factors of how inclusion is demonstrated in practice, inclusion needs to be rooted in the process of learning.

Booth and Ainscow (2011) summarise how inclusion can be embedded in learning through:

- Putting inclusive values into action
- Increasing participation for children and adults in learning and teaching activities
- Reducing exclusion, discrimination and barriers to learning
- Fostering mutually-sustaining relationships between schools and surrounding communities
- Restructuring cultures, policies and practices to respond to diversity in ways that value everyone equally

For children with EAL, this means that time and extra effort is needed to ensure that they have a level playing field in terms of the opportunities they have to help them achieve their potential. Very often, the assumption is that by using the same resources all children have equal opportunities. But the key factor is how resources are adapted, or how the use of language is differentiated, or how the experiences provided are linked to real life situations which are different ways in which extra effort is made.

Challenges of meeting the needs of children with EAL

It is important to recognise that a blind and uncritical approach could exist for some children with EAL. This is when the needs of children with EAL are ignored with the view that these children will eventually assimilate into the setting culture so time should not be wasted and no effort is required to help meet their needs. Confused communication can also be a challenge. We are not saying that there is a lack of communication as both the child and adult could be very effective communicators in their own respective language(s) and context, but in a strange environment each person can be unclear as to whether their interpretations and expectations have been understood or not.

Time for meeting the needs of children with EAL is one of the biggest issues (Mistry and Sood, 2012, 2013, 2015). Sometimes strategies personalised for children with EAL could be viewed as ideas of good practice to be used for all children including those with special needs. There is also the challenge of not having enough of a range of strategies for meeting the needs of children as a result of a lack of opportunities of working with these children. Here, the emphasis needs to be on a range of small personalised strategies (that we do naturally) that all pull together over a period of time to help meet the language and other needs of children with EAL. The focus should be to develop a range of personalised strategies that achieve the following outcomes:

- To ensure children feel safe and secure
- To ensure children feel comfortable and happy
- To respect the background and culture of children with EAL
- To use their background, culture, and current knowledge as starting points for learning
- To make learning through play as comfortable and enjoyable as possible
- To give children time to develop the confidence to contribute
- To allow children with EAL to talk in whichever language they feel comfortable (because it is better to hear their voice in their chosen language than not hear their voice at all)

Many of the strategies above could be applied to all children in Early Years, but the key point is that when young children in a setting feel comfortable to contribute, they should not be judged for their lack of fluency in the English language. Instead, we should celebrate their confidence and enthusiasm to try to have a go.

Key reflection points

- Children who have EAL are not all the same and therefore require different strategies to meet their needs.

- To be aware that children with EAL already have knowledge and understanding of concepts.

- To change our mindsets to ensure that children are not labelled for any longer than necessary.

In summary

In summary, this brief historical context will inform deeper discussions in the rest of this book. The aim being that this book is not about having a checklist of strategies to use with children who have EAL, but rather having a better awareness of the historical and political context over time which has led to certain decisions being made about the provision and practice for children with EAL. As you read through this book you will see critical debates between those who suggest the best way in which young children learn and the political priorities in education of the given time. This historical understanding is important in understanding some of the strategies we employ in our Early Years and primary settings today that have no form of critical reflection.

References

Becker, H. (1963) *Outsiders; studies in the sociology of deviance*. London: Free Press of Glencoe.

Booth, T. and Ainscow, M. (2011) *Index for inclusion developing learning and participation in schools*. Bristol, UK: Centre for Studies on Inclusive Education.

Braithwaite, J. (1989) *Crime, shame, and reintegration*. Cambridge: Cambridge University Press.

Brisk, M. E. and Harrington, M. M. (2000) *Literacy and bilingualism: A handbook for all teachers*. Mahwah, NJ: Lawrence Erlbaum Associates.

British Broadcasting Cooperation (BBC) (2014) *History*. Available at: www.bbc.co.uk/history/familyhistory/bloodlines/migration.shtml?entry=british_nationality_act&theme=migration (Accessed January 2019).

Bruner, J. (1996) *The culture of education*. Cambridge, MA: Harvard University Press.

Department for Education (DfE) (2016) *Educational excellence everywhere. The schools' white paper 2016*. London: DfE. Available (online) at: www.gov.uk/government/uploads/system/uploads/attachment_data/file/508447/Educational_Excellence_Everywhere.pdf (Accessed September 2016).

Department for Education (DfE) (2017) *Statutory framework for the early years foundation stage: Setting the standards for learning, development and care for children from birth to five*. London: DfE.

Department for Education (DfE) (2018) *Schools, pupils and their characteristics: June 2018.* Available at: https://assets.publishing.service.gov.uk/government/uploads/system/uploads/attachment_data/file/719226/Schools_Pupils_and_their_Characteristics_2018_Main_Text.pdf (Accessed September 2018).

Drummond, C. (2014) *How can UK schools support young children learning English.* British Council. Available at: www.britishcouncil.org/voices-magazine/how-uk-schools-support-young-learners-english. (Accessed February 2020).

Gregory, S. (1996) *Bilingualism and the Education of Deaf Children.* Available at: www.leeds.ac.uk/educol/documents/000000306.htm (Accessed September 2017).

Hulstijn, J. H. and Bossers, B. (1992) Individual differences in L2 proficiency as a function of L1 proficiency. *European Journal of Cognitive Psychology, 4* (4): 341–353. doi:10.1080/09541449208406192 (Accessed January 2019).

Mistry, M. and Sood, K. (2010) English as an Additional Language: Challenges and Assumption. *Management in Education*, 24 (3), July (1–4).

Mistry, M. and Sood, K. (2012) Raising standards for pupils who have English as an Additional Language (EAL) through monitoring and evaluation of provision in primary schools. *Education 3–13: International Journal of Primary, Elementary and Early Years Education.* 40 (3): 281–294.

Mistry, M. and Sood, K. (2013) Permeating the social justice ideals of equality and equity within the context of Early Years: Challenges for leadership in multi-cultural and mono-cultural primary schools. *Education 3–13: International Journal of Primary, Elementary and Early Years Education.* 43 (5): 548–564.

Mistry, M. and Sood, K. (2014) Permeating the social justice ideals of equality and equity within the context of Early Years: Challenges for leadership in multi-cultural and mono-cultural primary schools. *Education 3–13: International Journal of Primary, Elementary and Early Years Education.* iFirst Article (1–13).

Mistry, M. and Sood, K. (2015) *English as an Additional Language in the Early Years: Linking theory to practice.* London: Routledge.

Norwich, B. and Koutsouris, G. (2017) *Addressing dilemmas and tensions in inclusive education.* Oxford: Oxford University Press.

Rosenthal, R. and Jacobson, L. (1968) *Pygmalion in the classroom: Teacher expectation and pupils' intellectual development.* New York: Holt, Rinehart, & Winston.

School Curriculum Assessment Authority (SCAA) (1996) *Desirable outcomes for children's learning.* London: SCAA and Department for Education and Employment.

Vygotsky, L. (1978) *Interaction between learning and development.* (Trans. Cole, M.) Cambridge, MA: Harvard University Press.

Woodhead, M. (1989) School starts at five … or four years old? The rationale for changing admission policies in England and Wales. *Journal of Education Policy*, 4 (1): 1–21.

3

How children learn – key founders

When you have finished reading this chapter you will

- understand the fundamental principles of the way in which young children learn
- be aware of the principles and key beliefs from key Early Years founders that have an impact on provision and practice
- be able to critically evaluate the perspectives of key founders in relation to provision and practice for children with EAL

Chapter outline

This chapter begins with a rationale for the term 'key founders' through differentiating the very fine line between our perceptions and understandings of philosophers, theorists and pioneers. Following this, there will be a brief discussion about the key beliefs each group of people have and how they have contributed to the field of Early Years education, alongside how some of their ideology can be adapted for children with EAL. Next, there is a discussion on why the ideals of key founders are important in Early Years education today in terms of how children learn. There is a critical debate between the revolutionary thinking of key founders and their influence on shaping Early Years practice in the current climate, where emphasis is on children's performance through the goal orientated EYFS framework (DfE, 2017).

Key words: philosophers, theorists, pioneers, key founders, performative culture

Introduction

Children learn in different ways and a number of key founders have given their views on how they think young children learn best. Before we discuss how children with EAL learn best, it is crucial to have a solid understanding of how children learn as a foundation. Regardless of the age phase, ethnicities, gender, ability/disability or sexuality of the children, all practitioners working with children need to have a secure foundation of how children learn in order to inform their thinking and practice. Without this base of theoretical understanding, the planning and associated teaching taking place will not fully meet needs of children beyond a superficial level. Furthermore, although the focus of this chapter is in relation to children in Early Years, knowledge of this theory informed foundation is essential for all those who work with children regardless of their age phase. This chapter focuses on perspectives of key philosophers, theorists and pioneers associated with how they view children learn best in Early Years and the allied transition into primary education. There are a number of factors that influence children's learning which can include parents, family, the environment, health and well-being, curriculum, play and relationships which have been considered by key founders to a greater or lesser extent. Finally, this chapter considers how controversy can exist between what the theory is suggesting in terms of how children learn best and the current performative educational culture through the EYFS (DfE, 2017).

Rationale for terminology

There is an element of confusion in terms of exactly who are Early Years philosophers, theorists, pioneers and founders. We have found that these people are termed differently in the variety of texts and sources which has meant different people in education may perceive these individuals in different categories – hence causing further confusion in terms of interpretation. In some cases, the individuals that have had an impact on Early Years education are referred to as theorists in general, which again causes confusion.

Task 3.1 – Understanding terminology

- Make a list of who you think are philosophers, theorists and pioneers associated with Early Years education.
- What do you think is the difference between them? Give reasons for your answer.
- Can you identify any issues of confusion between your understandings of these three groups of individuals?

This task is to illustrate that even though we work with young children there can be confusion in understanding what theoretical perspectives mean. This confusion can lead to differences in practice and provision so we have attempted to clarify the terminology through grouping selected key founders who have influenced Early Years understanding in Table 3.1.

In the context of education we need to be clear about the contributions of each group of individuals and the links between them. The term philosophy originates from the Ancient Greek word 'philosophos' which means someone who loves wisdom/knowledge or in other words, people who are key thinkers. Philosophical perspectives are worldviews that define the nature of the world, the individual's place in it and the possible relationships to that world and its parts (Schuh and Barab, 2007: 68). Philosophers are concerned with explaining how knowledge in a particular field is interconnected and what the underlying meaning of knowledge is, which in this case is how children learn best. Furthermore, academic definitions of philosophers are more concerned with the nature of knowledge, the existence of knowledge and the reality of knowledge. Here, learning and instructional theories are developed with respect to a particular set of assumptions regarding what it means to know and learn (ibid.: 68). In the case of this book, philosophy is about a particular way of thinking associated with Early Years practice. It is about what practitioners believe to be the key beliefs and values in meeting the needs of young children, including their well-being.

Generally speaking, the link between philosophers and theorists is that theorists build on the idea(s) suggested by philosophers in order to explain it in a different way linked to their field (Early Years). Pioneers can also build on the

TABLE 3.1 Showing key founders associated with learning in Early Years

Philosophers and key belief(s) about how children learn	Theorists and key belief(s) about children in Early Years	Pioneers and key belief(s) about children in Early Years
Aristocles Plato (427 BC–327 BC) – children have innate knowledge	Friedrich Froebel (1782–1852) – children construct meaning through play and experiences	Johann Pestalozzi (1746–1827) – focused on the whole child
John Amos Comenius (1592–1670) – matching pedagogy to early childhood development	Lev Vygotsky (1896–1934) – social interaction is essential to cognitive development	Robert Owen (1771–1858) – founder of the first nursery in Great Britain
John Locke (1632–1704) – children are born with a blank mind	Jean Piaget (1896–1980) – stages of cognitive development	Maria Montessori (1870–1952) – children learn by doing
Jacques Rousseau (1712–1778) – childhood is a golden age	John Bowlby (1907–1990) – importance of relationships linked to attachment theory	Margaret McMillan (1860–1931) – emphasised social reform
John Dewey (1859–1952) – children learn best by doing	Jerome Bruner (1915–2016) – language as a tool for thought	Susan Isaacs (1885–1948) – child centred learning
Rudolph Steiner (1861–1925) – importance of children moral and spiritual development	Luis Moll (1947 – present day) – funds of knowledge	Margaret Donaldson (1926 – present day) – decentred thinking

ideas of others, but essentially it is about how their ideas based on the suggestions of others shape practice in a given field. In one respect, pioneers can have more influence in a field than philosophers because they can be more well-known or better linked to specific aspects of Early Years pedagogy, such as the environment, play and the role of the adult. However, the nature of learning needs to be understood first because only then will there be a comprehensive understanding of how theorists have expanded the ideas of others and how pioneers have taken this even further to shape practice. We are also aware that there can be a cross over between theorists and pioneers depending on personal perspective, and that theorists can also be deemed to be pioneers in terms of influencing practice, but we argue that whether a theorist is a pioneer or not depends on which aspect of young children's development is the focus. Therefore, to be clear, we have referred to all in the table as key founders because to a greater or lesser extent, they have all had an influence on the way in which children learn and have subsequently shaped Early Years. Once we have a clearer understanding of these various perspectives, we are better placed to meet the needs of all children, but especially those with EAL.

How children learn from a philosophical perspective

There are many different educational philosophies aimed at trying to explain the social and academic growth and development of children. Early Years education is a socially and historically constructed concept therefore philosophical 'interest in Early Years has a long history' with regimes of truth offering a variety of discourses on how young children learn best (Woodhead, 2006: 5). A range of perspectives suggesting how young children learn which influences policy and practice are discussed next.

Plato

The Greek philosopher Plato (427–347 BCE), (Brickhouse and Smith, 1995) was influenced by the teaching of Socrates and believed that young children naturally have knowledge within them from birth and more importantly, it is through play that education begins, 'in that way you can better discern what each is naturally directed towards' (Perrin, 2015). This is because play is innate to a child in the fact that they learn naturally through play. Plato further claims that forced knowledge such as learning facts and figures out of context holds no bearing on the mind, which in turn has an impact on the way in which we organise our learning in Early Years. In his writings, Plato describes different stages of education associated with a specific curriculum for each stage which is different to Piaget's developmental stages. With his educational stages, Plato perceived education should be progressive, from informal in the Early Years to formality as children become older, which is something that resonates in our education system today.

Comenius

Czech philosopher Comenius (1592–1670) outlined a staged school system which today translates to Early Years, primary, secondary and higher education, which was also endorsed by the 1944 Education Act (see Chapter 8). This is because he believed that education should be viewed as a series of life stages (from birth to death) which is similar to Plato, but he disagreed with some of the teaching approaches of his time. Like Plato, he suggested that memorising facts and figures serves no real purpose and is not conducive in helping children understand meaning, especially in isolation. Furthermore, Comenius suggested that the structured approach to learning grammar in his time also did not help learning, which can have some resonance to children with EAL today especially when trying to learn specific aspects of grammar linked to sentence construction. Similar to Plato, he believed all children should have the right to an equal education regardless of their background, which in one sense was revolutionary for that time when only the children of the privileged attended any form of education. Furthermore, he believed young children should be educated in their native language till the age of six (Bowers, 2013), which today could have huge implications for settings that have a high proportion of children with EAL alongside monolingual practitioners. Another challenge to his thinking is that his views were based on a Christian foundation which can pose issues for today's multicultural society (ibid.: 2013).

Locke

Locke (1632–1704), the British philosopher, emphasised that when children are born their minds are a blank slate (also known as the tabula rasa perspective) which is in contrast to Plato's view. He perceived that children learn though a range of experiences provided to support their individuality. Locke also focused on the importance of moral education to enable children to be good human beings, which in some way can be linked to the current focus on moral education in the EYFS through personal social and emotional development (DfE, 2017). Furthermore, he suggested that a standard from of instruction for learning like aspects of the current curriculum we have today is detrimental to children developing naturally. Again, Locke's ideals were revolutionary for his time, where the traditional 'chalk and talk' approach was the only way in which learning took place.

Rousseau

The Swiss philosopher Rousseau (1712–1778) emphasised childhood as a golden age in which children should be free to be children through play and natural learning without the pressure of mastering skills in certain subjects within a given timeframe, as demonstrated through his passion in the arts. He emphasised the importance of the expressive arts and nature in young children's learning. Similar to Locke, he implied all children are born good and wholesome and stay innocent, but the actions of society can and do corrupt children and their natural pathway of learning. This suggests tensions can exist between how a child should learn best and the expectations of society in terms of what children should learn and by when. In current education, the ideology of Rousseau can be identified in parts through the EYFS framework (DfE, 2017) whereby the top down pressure to achieve certain standards in early number and phonics through the prime areas can override in-the-moment opportunities and learning through play. One criticism of Rousseau's works is that complete freedom in life does not always exist as we are all bound by certain laws and regulations as well as different responsibilities. With the increasing use of social media by young children, they can be vulnerable to interpretation of what is deemed to be right or wrong, especially when situations such as doing the wrong thing for the right reason can occur. Additionally, children are constantly faced with news of wrongdoings and disasters around the world through the media. These experiences and different interpretations can also be deemed to corrupt young children.

Dewey

Dewey (1859–1952), an American philosopher, introduced the notion of progressive education in that experimental learning was the best way in which young children learn. He believed in child centred approaches to learning which is evident in today's Early Years settings. Furthermore, his beliefs go on to suggest that learning for young children is not just about the transference of knowledge from adult to child, rather, it is about understanding the experiences children already have and bring with them, which is similar to Moll's (1992) funds of knowledge. Through child centred environments and interactions with the community, Dewey believed young children would be better prepared for living in a democratic society which, in one way, links to the current British values (Young Citizens, 2018). However, Dewey's perspective has encountered criticism. One criticism is that experimental learning implies concepts should be learned when children are ready, but Hirsch (2013) argues that children must learn concepts such as key vocabulary within a predetermined timescale otherwise specific subject related vocabulary may not be learned until much later in education. For children with EAL, this means that they may not have enough time to catch up to their monolingual peers if instruction has to wait until they have overcome the English language barrier. Furthermore, Hirsch (2013) implies classroom instruction is essential for children to learn and make progress which goes against the Dewey way.

Steiner

The Austrian philosopher Steiner (1861–1925) suggested specific stages for children to develop socially, emotionally and physically, which is similar to Comenius's and Piaget's stages. The emphasis here is not on the formal focus of literacy and numeracy, but rather on child and practitioner led learning through play and experiences. Here, he does not imply that literacy and numeracy is not important, but that these skills can be taught in a more discreet way through play in a secure creative indoor and outdoor environment which is evident in many Early Years settings. But the criticism with his stages is that with greater emphasis on children's well-being, academic learning and skills can take a back step which in turn does not concur with the expectations of the EYFS framework (DfE, 2017) or transition to the National Curriculum (DfE, 2014). Another concern is that interventions associated with key skills and knowledge maybe overlooked if emphasis is on well-being only.

To summarise this section, one common feature from many of the philosophers discussed is that they believe in some sort of educational or life stages implying that education should be compartmentalised with different requirements at different ages or stages of life. This compartmentalisation may not work for all children because they develop differently and have different needs at different times, which is particularly the case for children with EAL. But the key point is that all the philosophers were revolutionary thinkers of their time in terms of their ideals, especially if you take into consideration the way education was structured and for whom in their day.

Impact of philosopher's beliefs on children with EAL

With greater diversity in English settings, a re-examination of philosophical perspectives about how children learn is timely. This is because it seems that some philosophers' ideology and beliefs are incompatible in some ways with the current educational approach, derived since the 1988 Education Act (HMSO, 1989) from neo-liberalism and a marketised framework.

Plato suggested that young children have innate knowledge and the role of play is central to this process. This means the key way of learning in Early Years is through play and for children with EAL, it is the only way to understand the knowledge and skills they bring with them through a meaningful approach. Comenius extends this further by suggesting that memorising knowledge is not conducive to learning, which we argue is the case for children with EAL, who need contextual meaning rather than isolated facts which do not support connections in learning at a later date. Additionally, Comenius' implies all children should be entitled to an equal education through a standardised curriculum which is partly reflected in the EYFS framework (DfE, 2017) in that the needs of all diverse children including those with EAL should be met. However, the issue here is how to help children with EAL gain access to their entitlement when some practitioners lack the knowledge and understanding in making the extra effort needed. One challenge associated with Locke's philosophy is the assumption that children are born as blank slates, which we know is not true especially when considering the impact of neuroscience. In addition, for some children with EAL, it can be assumed that they have very little knowledge in terms of setting structures and routines if they are new arrivals or have little knowledge of the English language, when in fact they have greater knowledge than that perceived. More importantly, it is about recognising that their knowledge is linked to a different language and culture other than English.

Dewey, through his notion of progressive learning, believed the experiences a child has are important to their learning. This is particularly the case for children with EAL who already have a range of experiences which can be very different to other children in the setting. Through freedom in play these children are able to demonstrate their knowledge and understanding, which otherwise may be very challenging. This is also supported by Steiner, who focuses on the importance of children's social, emotional and physical development as the foundation for other learning, which in one respect can be linked to the prime areas in the current EYFS (DfE, 2017). For children with EAL the implication is the need to have opportunities to develop socially and emotionally first with different children and without the burden of skills and knowledge associated with phonics and early number. They need time to feel safe and comfortable in their environment and with the other children and practitioners surrounding them before they are in a position to learn specific literacy and numeracy skills. But this approach of putting the child at the heart of the learning process may not always be evident in Early Years, especially with the top down pressure of performance related outcomes (discussed in Chapter 9).

How children learn from a theoretical perspective

Theorists have different approaches to education (cognitive, behaviour, psychosocial, ecological), this section will focus on the key beliefs of theorists associated with how children grow, develop and change in the context of Early Years through a cognitive approach. In addition, key beliefs of theorists will be compared and contrasted against other theorists to help develop critical thinking (which will also be explored in more detail in the rest of the book).

Froebel

Froebel believed that whilst in play, young children begin to construct their understanding of the world. He is most well-known for the introduction and implementation of kindergartens through his belief that play is the only form of child development. He emphasised that Early Years is a stage within its own right not a preparation stage for Key Stage 1, education in general, or adulthood, which contests the notion of school readiness (discussed in Chapter 9). In addition, he suggests that quality education in Early Years a combination of first the child, second the context in which learning takes place, and third the knowledge and understanding, which is how the child develops and learns (Bruce, 2001), and adults are central to this process. However, the ideology of Froebel can be criticised by those who believe that a more formal form of instruction is required in Early Years in comparison to play alone, which can be evidenced within the EYFS (DfE, 2017).

The thinking here is that if young children have an earlier start in learning key skills associated with certain subjects like literacy, then this would place them in a better position for learning as they grow older. However, this can be criticised because we know that this is not the case, especially when children in England start formal school in the term after their fourth birthday and yet children in some European countries like Finland and Sweden start school around seven and achieve much higher results than our children in the Programme for International Student Assessment (PISA) results even though they have had less time for formal instruction than the children in England (PISA, 2018). We need to recognise that different countries adopt different approaches to their Early Years education which we cannot directly transplant into England, but we can look at aspects of good practice demonstrated by them and consider if any adaptations can take place in personal practice to suit the needs of our children with EAL.

Vygotsky

The social constructivist Vygotsky emphasised that children learn best within a socially and culturally relevant environment to help understand meaning, and that the level of learning taking place is scaffolded by More Knowledgeable Others (MKO) which can be both practitioners and other children (1978). This is extended further through his notion of the Zone of Proximal Development (ZPD), which is the zone in which a child can potentially achieve more with the help of another more able than on their own. He emphasised that learning does not happen alone or in isolation, which is why the role of the adult is so important in helping children with their constructions of the world in a social and cultural context. In addition, he suggested that although thought and language are initially a separate parts of a child's thinking, they do merge to form inner speech – which is very evident in Early Years when children are observed in play talking to toys quietly. However, Piaget has criticised Vygotsky's view of learning socially in that if children are not ready to learn in collaborative activities then the views of others could influence children's individual thinking, which we argue can be more evident with children who have EAL because of their different experiences and cultural understanding. In addition, the ZPD is unclear in terms of exactly what the child's needs are or the process of development (Chaiklin, 2003: 42–46).

Piaget

Piaget is well-known for his specific stages of cognitive development. Contesting Locke's tabula rasa perspective, he suggested children construct mental images of the world through interaction with the environment indicating that the mind already has a range of complex cognitive structures to help learning. Although there is some similarity to Vygotsky, Piaget's views are different in that he assumed that cognitive development is a progressive reorganisation of mental processes resulting from biological maturity and experiences encountered. Vygotsky also disagreed with Piaget's view in that experience with physical objects is not the only method of raising cognitive development. He suggests that other factors supporting cognitive development need careful consideration, such as the role of culture and language in the learning process. A further criticism is that not all children will progress developmentally through Piaget's stages at given age points, because all children are different with different capabilities, which is certainly the case for children with EAL especially if they are new arrivals.

Bowlby

The British psychologist Bowlby was the original founder of attachment theory, he believed that children are already biologically pre-programmed when they are born and that they tend to remain close to attachment figures. This is evident in terms of young children being attached to their mothers or other primary care givers, like members of a family who make them feel safe and secure. The key focus of his theory is how separation from care givers has an impact on children's development, which in turn seems to imply that the beliefs of other key figures can be seen to be unimportant if young children are not able or willing to separate from their care givers for learning to take place.

One of the key criticisms of Bowlby's view regarding attachment has been posed by Harris (1989), who suggests that sometimes the primary care givers of a child may not be the most appropriate individuals to shape a child if they are not the best role models themselves. Furthermore, young children could also form very close attachments to those in Early Years settings especially if they spend more time with practitioners at the setting (with wraparound care) than they do with family members at home. Therefore positive relationships with all family members (not just the mother) or those who bring the child to the setting are crucial to aid transition and well-being (DfE, 2017).

Bruner

Similar to Dewey, the American psychologist Bruner was influential in the field of cognitive development and suggested that the best way in which young children learn is through discovery learning whereby children construct knowledge themselves. His theory focuses on different models of thinking and how these affect children's development through scaffolding learning in small steps through repetition of skills or knowledge like the spiral curriculum (Bruner, 1996). The emphasis here is not on repetition for consolidation of learning, but rather revising skills and concepts at a higher level each time to help build children's thinking to enable progress. However, a criticism here is if children are constructing learning for themselves then misconceptions could occur which could influence future learning, especially for children with EAL, therefore the role of the adult becomes crucial in detecting misconceptions and intervening appropriately.

Moll

Linked to Vygotsky's sociocultural theory is the notion of funds of knowledge proposed by Moll, who is a key figure in relation to education for Hispanic children in South America. His key belief is that children come into settings (including Early Years) with a range of knowledge and understanding already, which is framed by their social interactions within their culture and community (Moll, 1992). The implication here is that practitioners need to have a better understanding of children's funds of knowledge to better tailor provision, which is crucial for children with EAL. However, a criticism is that if children do not speak English fluently then there is a danger that practitioners may not recognise that they already have knowledge within them and they could be given a narrow view of conceptual understanding.

Task 3.2 – Early Years theory and practice

- How do the theorists in the table influence your current practice?
- How can you support the Early Years team you work with to have a better understanding of the impact of theorists on practice?

This task is to illustrate that even though we work with young children on a daily basis, sometimes there can be an unclear or limited understanding as to how young children learn, especially if practitioners are new or inexperienced. These theorists aim to give us a framework based on their ideology about how children develop, think and learn which in turn helps with our understanding, helping to guide our provision and practice to better meet the needs of children.

To summarise this section, it is important to be aware of how some of the ideals of philosophers have been furthered in the field of Early Years education. What is perhaps more evident is some of the similarities that exist between philosophers' and theorists beliefs on how children learn, which is discussed next.

Impact of theorists' beliefs on children with EAL

Although Froebel's ideas are useful in understanding one approach to the way in which children learn, there can be a lack of consideration for some academic skills (such as phonics and early number) for those children who might be ready for a greater challenge. For children with EAL, a focus on early number maybe more appropriate as the symbolic nature of learning is less confusing than the focus on English language word skills (Bruner, 1996). Vygotsky's ideology is relevant in Early Years especially with the social nature of learning that takes place through opportunities provided. This is crucial for children with EAL as they need to observe other children in social situations to help their understanding of what is expected of them in the setting, especially if social etiquettes in their individual cultures or contexts are different to that of the setting. For example, if children are encouraged to be quiet and allow adults to talk first in the home environment, then it can be confusing for them to come to a setting where they are encouraged to talk, give an opinion and be heard and to have their contribution valued. In addition, Vygotsky's sociocultural theory is essential when working with children who have EAL because practitioners need to be aware that these children come into settings with a range of knowledge and understanding framed by their culture and social interactions within their family and community. However, differences in culture and cultural expectations can cause cultural disorientation and confusion in children with EAL, especially if their cultural background is very different to that of the majority of the children and practitioners in the setting. This disorientation can also cause anxiety and discomfort in young children, which in turn has an impact on their willingness and ability to learn.

Piaget's stages of cognitive development can be a concern for children with EAL who may not fit into his sequence of stages or may not progress through his stages in sequence as a result of the English language barrier. Donaldson (1978) criticises Piaget's stages of cognitive development by noting his stages can imply a limit on children's thinking, so the focus should be on finding out children's starting points and what children can do. She suggests we need to look at things from different perspectives, for example, when working with children with EAL, practitioners should try to view learning from their perspective so they can better understand how to help them. This de-centred thinking is where practitioners move away from the centre of their thinking and focus on the centre of children's thinking so their children have a better opportunity of achieving success.

Bowlby's beliefs also need consideration for children with EAL because some children are part of extended families and therefore there may be issues with attachment with more than one or two key people in the family. Close relationships with family members need to be recognised as they shape children's early identity as well. Here, a potential issue can be that if family members are not proficient in the use of English then this may limit children's ability to practice English outside the setting environment. Dewey's notion of experimental learning can cause problems for children with EAL, especially if they are not familiar with the resources used or expectations in play and non-structured learning. Additionally, in discovery learning children with EAL may be heard in private speech in their home language because children tend to think in their home language first, which can cause confusion for practitioners trying to ascertain what children already know. There can also be issues associated with Bruner's notion of scaffolding for children with EAL, especially if scaffolding does not happen in play or other forms of learning where misconceptions could be taken for being true. Practitioners need to model play and learning so that misconceptions are avoided but more importantly, observations need to be carried out regularly in a range of contexts to pick up on new misconceptions and knowledge, which is challenging with limited time in settings. Similar to Vygotsky, Moll also implies it is the role of the practitioner to give children opportunities to demonstrate their funds of knowledge. The issue here is first, if practitioners do not have time to create opportunities for children with EAL to demonstrate what they already know, and second, if practitioners do not believe that these children are more knowledgable especially in terms of their home language and culture.. Furthermore, Moll emphasises that the only way to meet the needs of children with EAL is to move away from the role of the practitioner and to embrace the role of the learner to learn and understand about the position of children in their setting, especially those with EAL, which is similar to Donaldson's (1978) de-centred thinking.

By nature, theorists provide an individual framework of how they feel children learn in an abstract way through a specific model or through stages with associated key terms, though that is not to say that one perspective is better than another or more important than another. It is important to remember that theories can change as conditions in society change and new information comes to light. For example, although attachment theory originated with Bowlby, it has been furthered by Ainsworth in terms of how attachment between child and care giver varies according to the behaviour of the care giver towards the child.

Pioneers associated with shaping Early Years practice

This section looks at the main messages from a range of key pioneers in the field of Early Years because they have some impact on Early Years curriculum theory and practice alongside some associated criticisms. That is not to say that the views of philosophers and theorists are irrelevant, but rather pioneers have a more contemporary approach to the roots of how children learn which influences the changing nature of Early Years.

Pestalozzi

We start this section with the Swiss pioneer Pestalozzi, who is often referred to as the father of contemporary education today. During his time, Pestalozzi observed intense poverty in society, therefore he aimed to help reform society by providing some kind of school for the poorest children of the time. He was strongly influenced by the ideals of Rousseau in that all children deserved the right to an education regardless of their background, which can be perceived to be one of the foundations for the inclusion agenda today. In particular, his work talks about educating the whole child. In other words, a holistic approach to learning which is about learning through sensory experiences and through a hands-on approach. As suggested by Hopkins (2013), a unique feature of Pestalozzi was his view that freedom of movement to exercise the body (like physical education) is important, but this was against the regime of the time when children were seated in rows for most of the day and absorbed in a traditional form of learning. Additionally, he was against the harsh treatment of children of that time, which in his view inhibited children's natural development. Again, this went against the way in which children were treated at that time in education where corporal punishment was evident. Instead, he suggested that practitioners need to build positive relationships and trust with the children to enable full development, a view that is echoed in the current EYFS (DfE, 2017). Pestalozzi's insistence to help the poorest children was criticised by his family and friends because he became poor himself in the process of helping others.

Owen

One of the earliest nursery schools in Britain was established by the industrialist Owen in 1816 for the children of cotton mill workers through promoting 'character formation and social training' (Wearmouth *et al.*, 2017: 3). Owen's main ethos of early education was that a young person's character is influenced by their 'environment and the community' in which they live (ibid., 2017: 6). Like Pestalozzi, his humanitarian approach aimed to address social reform through education. Later establishments continued to include a focus on childrens' growth and well-being and learning through play as the best way of learning in Early Years. However, Owen was criticised by some business associates in society because he wanted to lead change (like bettering the condition of houses and sanitation) for the betterment of society on a non-profit basis. Furthermore, he was also criticised for seeing education as a means to better society through moving away from the control of the church which offered a particular view of education at that time.

Montessori

Montessori is perhaps one of the most well-known pioneers in the field of Early Years education today. Her key perspective in relation to how young children learn best is through children learning by doing in all areas of learning, which challenged the way in which education was taking place at that point in time. Like Pestalozzi, her belief was that education needs to take a holistic approach for young children in order to help them make connections in their learning to help them make sense of the world around them. Some of her key features of play include having didactic equipment (meaning child sized resources) within a carefully planned indoor and outdoor environment, with appropriate practitioner intervention (Bruce, 2001). Like other pioneers, Montessori is not without criticism. Sometimes too much freedom in learning through play may not benefit those children who require a little more structure. However, this is where the role of the practitioner becomes crucial. We argue that not all resources in an Early Years environment should be child sized. For example, child sized buttons, fastening and threading beads would not help young children's fine motor skills. Instead, children are given larger beads and buttons and thicker pencil crayons (like hand huggers) to help their hand eye coordination and fine motor skills which in turn contests Montessori's general principle of child sized equipment for manipulation. Today, there is the notion that Montessori type schools are for the children of the elite in society which contradicts Montessori's original work with the poorer children of society.

McMillan

The pioneer Margaret McMillan worked with her sister Rachel McMillan in an attempt to socially reform society by trying to improve the conditions for the poorest children in society. Together they founded clinics to help with children's health and also founded outdoor camps that later evolved into an outdoor nursery model, which partly frames the thinking behind outdoor learning today. Their thinking behind the nursery school model was influenced by the ideology of philosophers like Plato and Rousseau and theorists such as Froebel regarding the importance of active learning and first hand experiences in the outdoor environment. One of the aims of their model was to not only provide a form of Early Years education, but also the early identification of health problems in young children. In a way, this resonates with the now disbanded Every Child Matters agenda of 2003 that aimed to bring together the areas of education, health and social care (HMSO, 2003). In terms of social reform their model of a nursery school was very different to the education of the time which caused some anxiety in society.

Isaacs

Isaacs is a pioneer well-known for having a deep knowledge of child development though conducting detailed child observations in which play is fundamental to learning (Isaacs, 2013). Her focus was on how young children make sense of everything though play, and that Early Years settings, in particular nurseries, should mirror the family home in terms of warmth, love and nurture. The role of the learning environment, including the role of practitioners within it, was important in that 'none of the equipment was chosen haphazardly, for it was all intended to stimulate the child's powers of inquiry and curiosity, and thus they would learn' (Smith, 1985: 64). Today, Isaacs' vision of nursery education has become a reality. However, with limited practitioners in some Early Years settings, it is challenging to mirror the ideal family because practitioners have a greater number of children to be responsible for in terms of their development and learning. The introduction of the key worker within the EYFS framework has gone some way in nurturing and caring for a group of children in pre-schools and nurseries, however, this is not as evident in reception classes, unless there are children identified as having particular special needs issues.

Donaldson

As mentioned earlier, the pioneer Donaldson (1978) suggested that one way in which children learn best is through her notion of decentred thinking. Her perspective is partially influenced by Vygotsky and Bruner, and regards how concepts of embedded and dis-embedded thinking inform learning, which is important for all children but more so for those children with EAL because they need something familiar to connect their thinking to in order to help them make sense of a world that can be unfamiliar to them. However, Donaldson criticises Piaget's perspective on how children learn developmentally because he did not consider the extent of language or how context can influence children's thinking, which we argue are key factors in today's multilingual and multicultural society.

Impact of pioneers' beliefs on children with EAL

Pestalozzi's ideals can be viewed as the basis for the inclusion agenda we have today as he believed that all children have the right to access education regardless of their background. This is crucial for children with EAL because they still have the right to access the same education as their monolingual peers, which requires extra time and effort by practitioners. We agree with Owen's belief that education is the key in reforming society. This is because today, with the multitude of differences in children in Early Years settings resulting from their backgrounds, education is the only way to better understand these differences and to begin to develop characteristics of respect and tolerance which are part of today's British values (Young Citizen, 2018). Although we agree with Montessori's concept of learning through play and manipulation of resources, we would argue that for children with EAL there needs to be an element of modelling. This is because some children with EAL may not be familiar with expectations associated with setting resources or what is appropriate in play especially if they are from a very different culture whereby play is not common practice.

The McMillan sisters tried to emphasise social reform, and for children with EAL play is crucial to this process. As play is gender free and inclusive, it means children with EAL must have the chance to observe other children in play before joining in themselves. As play has no set criteria to be followed, it makes it easier for children with EAL to show their own interpretations and understandings. One part of Isaacs' ideology was the importance of the environment. Today many Early Years setting have a range of displays or resources to help children with EAL feel that they belong to a particular class of children. We argue that although making the learning environment inclusive is a good start, practitioners need to go further to mind map how current resources in use can be adapted for children with EAL rather than the notion that there are specific resources for children with EAL only. It is also about making the children with EAL and their families feel that they are valued within the setting environment. Donaldson illustrates her concept further by suggesting children make errors during tasks because they are trying to understand what is asked of them as well as trying to understand the task itself. This is important for children with EAL because at times they can appear not to understand the task or what is expected of them leading to them being labelled (discussed in Chapter 5) and having incorrect assumptions made about their ability (Mistry and Sood, 2010). Hence Donaldson's notion of decentred thinking is a must for practitioners of children with EAL otherwise, their progress could be hampered.

Bringing it together – how children learn in Early Years

The philosophies and ideologies of key founders are an important foundation in our thinking about how children learn and grow and furthermore, how individual childrens' development can be charted as they develop individually and socially. Having an understanding of their development and the factors that influence it also means that certain types of behaviour can be better understood. For example, if a child with EAL demonstrates frustration or anger at not being able to do a task, it may not be because they have no understanding. Rather, it is about not having the English language terminology to clarify their understanding and expectations. A key aspect of all theories is how they influence the way in which we adapt and shape practice for children. Knowing the range of these adaptations is necessary to help meet the individual needs of young children, but more importantly, how the needs of children with EAL can be better met when the English language can be a barrier in learning. Each key founder's main principles can be applied to children with EAL in different ways, which we hope we have demonstrated briefly through this chapter. There will be more in-depth discussions in the rest of the chapters of how selected philosophical and theoretical perspectives can be applied in different ways to help meet the needs of children with EAL.

Critical debate between key founders and performance

Although it has clearly been mentioned that philosophical and theoretical perspectives are important in helping us to meet young children's needs, there is a debate between what these keys founders say about learning and the current focus on child performance. All key founders have their own ideals in terms of how they feel young children learn best. However, most key founders are from the Western world which poses a challenge in terms of really understanding children with EAL from a range of different countries, especially with the very different types of languages and cultures. With the exception of Vygotsky and his concept of socio-cultural learning and Moll in relation to his funds of knowledge, the key founders have offered only a general view of learning without really considering how different children's needs can be met, like those children with EAL. This can contradict current practice today which aims to personalise learning for children in Early Years in order to help them make progress.

A key critical debate is that the perspectives of key founders in terms of the way in which they feel children learn best goes against the current performative culture we have in Early Years. Currently, children in Early Years are expected to achieve the Early Learning Goals by the end of the reception year alongside the huge emphasis on early reading and number, which directly contradicts the philosophy of Rousseau. Although the EYFS framework (DfE, 2017) clearly shows elements of key founders perspectives like learning through play (Froebel) and by doing (Dewey) and developmental stages (Piaget) through the way the guidance is set out, we argue that this can be overlooked as a result of the results orientated culture we currently have in Early Years and primary education.

Currently, the performance of young children is charted more and more as we are in an evidence and accountability based educational culture. The importance of learning key skills early seems to have taken over the understanding of the foundations of how children learn. In today's society many children are taught key skills without any connections to real life learning which the philosopher Plato suggested was a waste of time. This is further illustrated when children in education are taught to pass tests after which there is no remembrance or bearing on the skills learned. As a result, we seem to have a generation of young adults that lack the most basic skills in many aspects of literacy as well as a lack of understanding regarding mathematical concepts. We argue, how can this be possible if children in England start compulsory schooling much earlier than our European colleagues? The suggestion is that perhaps there is a disregard of what our young children need in terms of their learning, as the assumption is that learning key skills is more important for future life. We suggest that there needs to be a balance in terms of what key founders are saying in terms of how children learn and how to raise standards in key skills, knowledge and understanding. Maybe for some children, like those with EAL there needs to be a greater emphasis on the social and cultural nature of learning including a change of mind set in practitioners regarding the way key skills are taught.

Key reflection points

- Key founders were revolutionary thinkers of their time.
- They have helped to shape Early Years practice in a number of ways.
- Their ideology can be applied to children with EAL to help support current practice in a diverse population.

In summary

The nature and place of young children has changed from being viewed historically as silent miniature adults to being in an important age phase where the foundations for more complex learning are built. The beliefs and ideologies of key founders are an important foundation for basing current Early Years practice on, however tensions do exist between these revolutionary thinkers and the current expectations of childrens' progress. This is particularly important for children with EAL who do not match the given guidance or who fall outside of set criteria norms. We have tried to clear some of the differences between philosophers, theorists and pioneers and to illustrate what the main messages from these key founders are in relation to Early Years education. Finally, we have tried to show how some of these messages can be applied and adapted to meet the needs of children with EAL.

References

Bowers, H. (2013) *John Comenius's philosophy of education*. Available at: https://coffeeshopthinking.wordpress.com/2013/10/04/john-comenius-philosophy-of-education/ (Accessed February 2019).

Brickhouse, T. and Smith, N. (1995) *Plato (427–347 BCE)*. Available (online) at: www.iep.utm.edu/plato/ (Accessed March 2019).

Bruner, J. (1996) *The culture of education*. Cambridge, MA: Harvard University Press.

Bruce, T. (2001) *Learning through play: Babies toddlers and the foundation years*. London: Hodder Headline.

Chaiklin, S. (2003*) The zone of proximal development in Vygotsky's theory of learning and school instruction*. 39–64. Retrieved from www.cles.mlc.edu.tw/~cerntcu/099-curriculum/Edu_Psy/Chaiklin_2003.pdf (Accessed March 2019).

Department for Education (DfE) (2014) *The national curriculum: Handbook for primary teachers in England*. London: DfE/QCA.

Department for Education (DfE) (2017) *Statutory framework for the early years foundation stage: Setting the standards for learning, development and care for children from birth to five*. London: DfE.

Donaldson, M. (1978) *Children's minds*. UK: Harper Collins.

Harris, M. (1989) *Our kind: Who we are, where we came from, where we are going*. New York: Harper & Row.

Her Majesty's Stationery Office (HMSO) (1989) *Education Act 1988*. London: HMSO.

Her Majesty's Stationery Office (HMSO) (2003) *Every child matters*. London: Crown Copywrite.

Hirsch, D. (2013) *The cost of a child in 2013*. London: Child Poverty Action Group.

Hopkins, L. (2013) *The educational theory of Johann Heinrich Pestalozzi*. Available at: www.newfoundations.com/GALLERY/Pestalozzi.html#ft11 (Accessed February 2019).

Isaacs, S. (2013) *The educational value of the nursery school*. Available at: www.early-education.org.uk/sites/default/files/Anniversary%2090th%20Book_ONLINE.pdf (Assessed March 2019).

Mistry, M. and Sood, K. (2010) English as an additional language: Challenges and assumptions. *Management in Education*, 24 (3), July (1–4).

Moll, L. (1992) Bilingual classroom studies and community analysis: some recent trends. In *Educational Researcher*, 21 (2): 20–24.

Perrin, C. (2015) *Plato and play*. Available at: http://insideclassicaled.com/plato-and-play/ (Accessed January 2019).

Programme for International Student Assessment (PISA) (2018) *Education counts: PISA key facts*. Available at: www.educationcounts.govt.nz/topics/research/pisa/pisa-2018 (Accessed February 2019).

Schuh, K. L. and Barab, S. A. (2007) Philosophical perspectives. In J. M. Spector, M. D. Merrill, J. Van Merrienboer and M. P. Driscoll (eds), *Handbook of research on educational communications and technology* (3rd edn, pp. 67–82). New York, NY: Routledge/Taylor & Francis Group.

Smith, Lydia A. H. (1985) *To understand and to help: The life and work of Susan Isaacs (1885–1948)*. Cranbury, NJ: Associated University Press.

Vygotsky, L. (1978) *Interaction between learning and development*. (Trans. Cole, M.) Cambridge, MA: Harvard University Press.

Wearmouth, J., Davydaitis, S., Gosling, A. and Beams, J. (2017) *Understanding special educational needs and disability in early years education*. London: Routledge.

Woodhead, M. (2006) Changing perspectives on early childhood: theory, research and policy. *International Journal of Equity and Innovation in Early Childhood*, 4 (2): 1–43.

Young Citizens, (2018) *What are British values?* Available at: www.doingsmsc.org.uk/british-values/ (Accessed March 2019).

Education for children with EAL

- better understand the perceptions of children with EAL that have existed over time
- be aware of how the perceptions of children with EAL have changed over time
- have an understanding of how policies and approaches have tried to meet the needs of children with EAL

Chapter outline

We begin this chapter by briefly conceptualising what Early Years education has meant and currently means for children with EAL, including the emphasis on Standard English, as this sets the context for how provision and practice has changed over time. Following this, there is an overview of the educational responses towards immigrant children in England that have taken place over the last fifty years as this helps to explain the context of the position of children in Early Years. Next is an exploration of various policies and approaches that have been implemented to contextualise the interpretations of children with EAL through policy changes in England, as these frame the assumptions of politicians and educators which in turn influence provision and practice. The discussion then moves onto critiquing these approaches, followed by what the current EYFS framework (DfE, 2017) means for children with EAL. We argue that the perceptions of practitioners are powerful tools in developing children's own attitudes and for children with EAL because this can mean that they may have negative attitudes towards their own linguistic and cultural background a view supported by Conteh and Brock (2011). Therefore, it is vital for children with EAL not to feel that there is something wrong with them for having a different home language or a different home culture, which is why inclusion through social justice is the next focus. Finally, we conclude with a range of strategies in Early Years to help make the educational learning environment more inclusive for children with EAL.

Key words: perceptions, assimilation, withdrawal, inclusion, environment

Introduction

To understand the landscape for children with EAL it is important to be aware of discourses and practices that are 'procedures for accomplishing goals' constructed mainly outside the setting and influencing current practice as new concepts are being embedded into older agendas (Cohen, 2008: 12). Hence discourses 'provide a rationale' for the way in which practice is conducted (ibid.: 12). Therefore, education for children with EAL must be understood against the political context of the time. This is because the government and politicians have a huge influence on how children with EAL are perceived, which informs the way in which provision and practice is tailored to meet their needs. Perceptions from politicians and educators towards children with EAL have changed over time. Although today children with EAL are able, creative and full of potential like their peers from the majority culture, this has not always been the case. It is important to understand the roots of perceptions because these perceptions have influenced practitioner thinking and what they see as the right educational provision for their children with EAL, and this has changed over time. This chapter focuses on how children with EAL have been perceived as being a problem by society in the past and therefore, how educational approaches have worked toward this notion of a problem. We would like to make it clear that we are not trying to focus on a negative view of children with EAL, we are simply trying to chart the historical perceptions that have been associated in the past towards children with EAL. This is because in the past, educational practice has tried to help children with EAL become 'normal' through the approaches highlighted to help them become like their monolingual peers in terms of English language acquisition, proficiency and learning (Costley, 2013).

Conceptualising Early Years education for children with EAL

In England, 'developmental truths matter because governments use them to inform their policies' (Costley, 2013: 29). This means perceptions in society matter because policies and practices align themselves to the socio-political conditions in which they are formed and interpreted which, in the context of this book, is how young children with EAL are conceptualised and educated. Conceptual understanding regarding education for children with EAL needs to be considered against what the English language means as a subject in the curriculum (Communication and Language and Literacy within the EYFS), as well as 'English as a language and national identity' (ibid.: 276). This is because English as a subject and as a language have very different meanings and link very differently to national identity. Here, Stokes (2017) has suggested that the ability to speak the native language (English) proficiently is an important indication of being a member of the host nation (England).

Tensions exist between and within policy, provision and practice as educational perspectives differ (discussed in more detail later). There is some resonance to the work of the French philosopher Foucault when he talks about the 'branding and exile of the leper' and in some respects this could be applied to children with EAL because of their separation (withdrawal sessions) for language learning to help 'normalise' them into Standard British habits and behaviour as has happened in the past (1979: 198). To some extent this can still be perceived today as huge attempts are made to enable children with EAL to learn the English language and become proficient in its use in order to access learning. So, conceptually, in Early Years this means that every effort is made through creative learning and play to help children with EAL learn and apply the English language.

Emphasis on Standard English

Historically views, albeit positive or negative, of diverse children have been influenced by social and political changes of the time. From the British colonial perspective during the nineteenth century, there was a sense that dominance of the English language (Brook, 1980) was being diluted by the influx of immigrants speaking different languages from different cultures. Increasing immigration to England after World War II led to the emergence of discourses about different languages in British society being deemed to be inferior in comparison to Standard English. This suggests that the dominance of the English language may be viewed as discriminatory because the 'ability to read and write in standard English is regarded as a crucial measure of educational performance and therefore … can … serve as discrimination in the labour market' (Martin-Jones *et al.*, 1984: 426). Therefore, Standard English can be perceived as the correct or formal way of using English, taking into consideration the forms and functions of Spelling, Punctuation and Grammar (SPAG). Both the EYFS and the National Curriculum (NC) in England make it clear that all children should be taught to use Standard English as this informs reading, writing and communication (DfE, 2017 and DfE, 2014). The importance of the use of Standard English stemmed from the Newbold Report of 1921 that claimed to unite England after World War I through a similar use of language. This report emphasises that the inability to use this dialect could be perceived as 'handicap' (Newbolt, 1921: 67). This implies that children's ability to speak, read or write in languages other than English is irrelevant in comparison to English and this has huge consequences for children with EAL.

Focus on the use of Standard English for children with EAL implies that any other language skills these children may have are not important and therefore useless in terms of learning, because learning instruction in England is only accepted in Standard English. Any other way in which English is used is deemed improper (including accent and dialect at times) and therefore not of value regardless of the fact that other languages are still a form of communication. Halle (1968) suggested that some issues associated with the use and perception of Standard English stem from the ideology of the linguist Chomsky. Chomsky's (1965) theory of universal grammar associated with learning English was based on how children acquire language through the mental tools that they already have. However, this is not always the case as Vygotsky's (1978) sociocultural theory emphasises that children learn language in a social context and through experience not just through the mental tools they already have. In addition, for children with EAL, Chomsky's theory does not take into consideration the importance of culture (a key facet of Vygotsky's theory) and other factors that influence how English language is learned.

Educational responses towards children with EAL

During the 1950s and 1960s there was a general view in society that if children did not speak English, then they should not be put in mainstream settings. The implication being, children should be excluded from their peers until they had enough proficiency in the English language to communicate with others in the mainstream sector. Following rapid and rising immigration into the UK after World War II several approaches towards children with EAL became dominant in settings to address the language needs of these immigrant children. These approaches ranged from: assimilationist, to withdrawal for intensive English language input, to additional grants for provision to enable equity in curriculum access. More recently, we see a return to an assimilation approach which is influenced by the regime of a one size model fits all approach to assessment, and comparisons between children and schools in the current market-orientated education system. This means the current Early Years education system in England implies all children must achieve the same outcomes through the same framework and similar assessment approaches, because comparisons between settings in terms of children's outcomes seem to indicate a settings level of performance (discussed in Chapter 9). Regardless of differences between children with EAL and their monolingual peers in terms of their language needs, the emphasis on an assimilation approach means they all must work through the same framework towards the same outcomes.

Social inequality exists in every society, and increasingly through the middle of the twentieth and into the twenty-first century a few measures related to welfare reform have been developed to reduce social inequality. For example, only privileged children from wealthy families were likely to have access to schooling until compulsory Education Acts came into force due to the nature of society at that time. Furthermore, generalisations have always been made about groups of people in society (NALDIC, 2015), and diverse children like those with EAL are no exception to this, implying practice can inadvertently be discriminatory based on personal generalisations which may be influenced by dominant discourses in society. This means that personal beliefs of practitioners can influence the effort made towards putting provision (or not) in place for children with EAL.

Policies and approaches to meet the needs of children with EAL

In order to understand the changing contexts for children with EAL in England, it is important to have an overview of events that led to approaches being adopted, as illustrated by Table 4.1. Therefore, this section will begin by

TABLE 4.1 Overview of changing approaches for meeting the language needs for children with EAL

Key historical events	Approach adopted	Discourse
1960s – Increasing migration	Assimilation	Children with EAL are seen to be a problem.
1966 – Education Act 1967 – The Plowden Report	Withdrawal	Separate provision needs to be in place to help children with EAL learn English as quickly as possible.
1975 – The Bullock Report	Assimilation and withdrawal	Home language and culture should not be disregarded at the setting gate, but children with EAL still need to learn English quickly.
1985 – The Swann Report	Criticism of withdrawal	Segregation of children with EAL led to exclusion and issues of racism.
1999 onwards – Ethnic Minority Achievement Grant (EMAG) funding	Reaction to the criticism of withdrawal	Funding put in place to support the language needs of children with EAL.
2000 – Introduction of the Curriculum Guidance for the Foundation Stage (CGFS) for children aged three to five showing the beginning of regulation in Early Years	Assimilation	The inclusion agenda means that all children including those with EAL need to be integrated.
2008 – Introduction of the Early Years Foundation Stage (EYFS) framework for children aged 0–5 showing continued regulation	Assimilation	The inclusion agenda continues, and all children aged 0–5 have a standard framework to follow.
2012 – The revision of the Early Years Foundation Stage (EYFS) framework for all children aged 0–5	Assimilation	Although the inclusion agenda continues, greater emphasis is given to language through the three prime areas in the revised framework.

unpicking key historical reports and what they mean for children with EAL. This is followed by a discussion and critique of discourses associated with the approaches adopted.

The 1966 Education Act

The 1966 Education Act was the first piece of legislation to specifically deal with the provision of education and also led to the establishment of special local authorities to support children with additional needs in settings (HMSO, 1966). However, the discourse of rising immigration during the 1960s meant that children with EAL were perceived to be a problem because of their lack of English language skills. Furthermore, these children were also seen to have a type of special needs as their language needs were different in comparison to their monolingual peers. It is also important to be mindful that the educational culture at that point in time was not as inclusive as it is today therefore, there was no law in place to suggest that all children's learning needs should be met. This means, children with EAL were just assimilated into the same learning as their peers without any different provision for them.

Plowden Report

A key feature of the Plowden Report (1967) was the importance of child centred education by emphasising that 'at the heart of the educational process lies the child' (Gillard, 2004). But in contradiction to this, underpinning the Plowden Report (HMSO, 1967) there seemed to be a very negative view of immigrant children regarding their lack of competence and fluency in the English language. So, it became 'essential to overcome the language barrier' because the lack of English language proficiency was 'the worst problem of all' indicating the use of different languages is problematic (DES, 1967: 71). For children with EAL, this meant that they were withdrawn within settings from their peers for separate language provision, which in some respect could be perceived as exclusion. More critically, what this policy indicated in line with the approach adopted, were contradictions which could lead to confusion in provision and practice.

Bullock Report

This negative view of the language needs of children with EAL was seen to be problematic and further continued until 1975 when the Bullock Report tried to address this through 'a need for more and sustained tuition in English' and furthermore, that the 'language and culture of children should not be disregarded' at the setting boundary (DES, 1975: 284). This report aimed to reconceptualise what teaching English within the curriculum means in terms of how it should be taught and the content that should be covered which started in the Early Years. The discourse adopted here is that children with EAL should be assimilated into English language learning, but they were withdrawn for specialist English language input because of their lack of proficiency. Critically, although the aim of the Bullock Report was to integrate children with EAL into the setting as fully as possible, their different language needs resulted in their exclusion from their monolingual peers in terms of specialist English language input, therefore contradictions in what policy intended and the actual practice that took place. In addition, it can also be asserted that the claim for social justice in this approach was never realised as indicated by the Swann Report of 1985.

Swann Report

The Swann Report of 1985 emphasised a new approach to education by highlighting the importance of education for all (DES, 1985). This report criticised the discourse of withdrawal that took place during the Plowden Report years and aimed to better integrate all children, especially those from diverse backgrounds such as those with EAL. The ideology of this report was that the segregation of children with EAL that had taken place led to issues of racism and exclusion. Therefore, education now needed to better reflect the multicultural nature of society which was more evident by addressing some of the discriminatory practices that may have existed. For children with EAL, this meant that they needed to be better integrated with learning as much as possible to enable them to build positive relations and friendships with their peers (DfE, 2017). So, practitioners had to work harder to make the effort to meet the range of needs of the children in their setting. In one respect, the Swann Report formed one of the foundations for the inclusion agenda we have today.

Ethnic Minority Achievement Grant (EMAG)

One way to help support the language needs of children with EAL as instigated by the Swann Report was through the EMAG initiative which was about specific funding given to settings. This funding was ring fenced and allocated by local authorities to settings on a needs basis to help underachieving children with EAL. Here, the discourse was about better and more targeted interventions for children with EAL beyond the withdrawal approach. This resulted in some settings gaining an extra adult through this funding to specifically support the language needs of children with EAL which took place through integrated group work whilst working alongside other practitioners to demonstrate a more collegial approach. More critically, this funding did not last and after 2011 this funding became part of general setting funding, so settings do not have to use it for their children with EAL if other setting priorities are more important.

Curriculum Guidance for the Foundation Stage (CGFS)

The CGFS was introduced in England in 2000 as a way of regulating Early Years education for children aged 3–5 years (DfES, 2000). This framework emphasised six areas of learning along with several Early Learning Goals (ELGs) to be assessed against. For the first time in England, the discourse of formal regulation comes into play whereby the government begins to control how Early Years education is shaped through assimilation for all. This guidance outlined what all children need to have access to, demonstrating some form of fairness and equality for all young children. Although, it can be argued that the CGFS began to bring a level of consistency between all government registered Early Years settings for children aged 3–5, we argue that because practitioners were under pressure to ensure all children achieve the ELGs, the curriculum they delivered may not have been appropriate in line with what key founders say about how young children learn. More critically, for children with EAL, the CGFS meant that they were assessed against the same norms as their monolingual peers regardless of their different starting points for learning the English language, which puts these children at an unfair disadvantage.

Early Years Foundation Stage (EYFS)

Following on from the CGFS, in 2008 the EYFS was introduced in England as a way of combining the age phase birth to three and the CGFS, and initially continued with six areas of learning alongside the associated ELGs. The idea being that Early Years education is now controlled by the government and is fully regulated between the ages of birth to five. Like the CGFS discourse, now there is a set curriculum for all children to follow regardless of their diversity. For children with EAL, the emphasis on learning the English language has now started earlier (essentially from birth), rather than from the age of three as was the case with the CGFS. More critically, the emphasis on learning Standard English through a formal curriculum may devalue children's home language(s). Although the EYFS continues the inclusion agenda, we argue that this curriculum can disadvantage children with EAL for the same reasons as discussed previously.

Revised Early Years Foundation Stage framework

The EYFS framework was revised in 2012 and changed the previous six areas of learning into seven areas of learning, divided into prime and specific areas. The prominent discourse here is that learning the English language has greater importance now within the context of Early Years as communication and language is now a prime area (DfE, 2017). The EYFS (DfE, 2017) also mentions that Early Years practitioners must meet the needs of all their children regardless of their diversity which can be viewed as one way of addressing social inequality, a challenge within itself. Critically, although Early Years educational settings have policies on equality and diversity with an expressed intention of helping to reduce barriers to learning, we argue that some leaders and practitioners can view their children with EAL as an inconvenience, reflecting the view that they are perceived to be a problem which is also supported by Costley (2013). This may be the case if most practitioners are monolingual and do not understand what diversity means, or how to meet the needs of these children. Despite this, today our diverse linguistic settings are arenas of 'complex inter-relationships, interactions, and ideologies', combined with socio-economic factors and political theory influencing structures and practice (Creese and Martin, 2003: 1). Furthermore, the current assimilationist approach implies that the 'white majority view' is still dominant in an assimilationist culture whilst attempting to address the inclusion agenda which is contradictory in nature (Baker, 2006: 61).

Discussion of discourses associated with the approaches adopted

From one perspective it seems that the education for immigrant children like children with EAL is perceived to be a problem that needs to be dealt with and therefore, addressing the English language needs of these children has occurred in different ways. Through increasing migration, the resulting varied languages coming into England from the 1960s led initially to a discourse of assimilation meaning children with EAL were seen to be a problem (Foucault, 1980) in comparison to their monolingual white peers who dominated English settings. This is because the different languages and cultures that came into England were thought to place children with EAL at a disadvantage over their monolingual peers in education because they could not all be taught the same content in the same way.

Through the 1960s there was a strong discourse that children who did not speak English should not be placed in mainstream education, instead they should be placed in language units until their English language skills were at a level deemed appropriate for coping in mainstream education (Mohan *et al.*, 2001). This concept of children with EAL being a problem was further supported by documents such as the 1966 Education Act (HMSO, 1966) and the

Plowden Report of 1967 (HMSO, 1967) that implied a withdrawal approach. The 1966 Education Act implied that there could be grants for certain expenditure associated with immigrant children through Section 11 within the Act to help meet the language needs of these children through segregation. Additionally, the Plowden Report commissioned by the education minister in 1963 attempted to review primary education as it currently stood at that time (HMSO, 1967). This report was influenced by the work of key founders such as Piaget (1962) and aimed to put the child at the heart of the learning process. In the case of children with EAL, the aim being that they need to learn the English language as quickly as possible through separate provision to enable access to learning. This meant the curriculum for children with EAL can be conceptualised through withdrawal from mainstream learning, whereby separate English language support was aimed to help them integrate (Costley, 2013) with their peers. This is an alternative solution to address the language problem of children with EAL, but this exclusion can be viewed as one way by the government to focus on 'organisation as opposed to content' (ibid.: 281), which has formed part of government policy in the past. This regime of withdrawal implies children with EAL should receive a different curriculum whilst specific requirements of needs related to curriculum content can remain overlooked. Furthermore, this approach indicates the language 'problem' for children with EAL can be solved by implying the 'position of language minorities needs to improve so children are all the same' (Baker, 2006: 386).

Here, there is a debate between the needs of the child and the need to learn the English language as quickly as possible through withdrawal because the implication is that without understanding the English language, learning cannot take place. We argue that this is incorrect as children learn in different ways and not always through English language instruction in isolation and out of context alone. Both the 1966 Education Act and the 1967 Plowden Report shaped practice at that time by implying separate provision was essential to help children with EAL overcome their English language problem. More importantly, all children are not the same and should not be adjusted or changed in order to be the same.

The political solution at that time was for children with EAL to learn English quickly by being assimilated into the educational environment to help them become normal like their monolingual white peers in terms of English language fluency, therefore practice is based on a regime of truth (Foucault, 1980). However, there is a danger in trying to 'normalise' children with EAL because this could be in direct contrast to their beliefs and values especially if their cultural background is very different to Western societies (Foucault, 1981). Furthermore, normalisation (Foucault, 1975) can also be a danger to children's individual identities which could contrast with their home values and beliefs. This approach of assimilation is one way of conceptualising children with EAL, which in some respects still exists today.

The Bullock Report emphasised that

> no child should be expected to cast off the language and culture of the home as he crosses the school threshold, nor to live and act as though school and home represent two separate and different cultures, which have to be kept firmly apart.
>
> (DES, 1975: 286)

We claim that the discourses of the Bullock report can be perceived to be contradictory in nature because on the one hand it is embracing different languages and cultures from children with EAL, but on the other it is clear in terms of the expectations associated with English language teaching that there is a key focus on enabling these children to learn English as quickly as possible. What is perhaps unclear is how language provision for children with EAL might take place, which can still take place through a withdrawal approach.

One purpose of mainstream learning for children with EAL is ensuring inequality is addressed by meeting the needs of all children consistently. The Swann Report of 1985 had three key messages in relation to children with EAL. First, linguistic and cultural disadvantage should be overcome through the teaching of English. Second, all children should respect all cultures (majority and minority). Third and most important, children should not be withdrawn or segregated in their learning (DES, 1985: 406–407). This means that the learning of children with EAL needs to be reconceptualised because the withdrawal approach has led to exclusion and racism based on differences. Children with EAL being excluded from their peers in learning means it is difficult for them to re-integrate back into class when other children are already engrossed in different learning activities. This ongoing segregation of children through withdrawal sessions has also conflicted with their civil and human rights and therefore to address this criticism, a new approach was to include these children in mainstream learning so that the 're-emergence of white supremacist discourses' are challenged and eliminated as much as possible (Mac Naughton, 2005: 177).

From 1985 a change in approach implied that children with EAL had to be integrated and taught together with other children demonstrating a regime of inclusion. This change helped shape current provision in terms of ways in which the needs of children with EAL should be met, but from the 1990s this mainstream approach has been overshadowed by curriculum and policy implying an assimilation approach.

At policy level, the Ethnic Minority and Achievement Grant (EMAG) has gone some way to address the criticism of withdrawal and the underachievement of children with EAL by generating funding to assist in removing barriers to learning that 'underpin underachievement' (Costley, 2013). But many settings have variations of practice and provision based on local context which suggests differentials from the EMAG policy existed because this funding was not protected. This meant settings were free to decide how this funding should be spent and, in some cases, it was not for meeting the needs of children with EAL. More critically, this funding no longer exists so settings must manage the needs of children with EAL without any extra help, implying an assimilation approach is still evident.

Critical issues associated with these policies and approaches

Although Early Years settings began developing approaches and resources to help address the language needs of children with EAL, provision was not consistent and often on a haphazard or random basis dependent on the number of these children in the setting. This means that if settings have a higher proportion of children with EAL then more effort is likely to be made to meet their language needs in comparison to settings with none or a few isolated children with EAL. The Swann Report of 1985 clarified that although linguistic diversity was evident, teaching and learning should only happen in English and more specifically, Standard English, in educational settings. This implies that even though there may be criticisms associated with the withdrawal approach, we still have assimilation though Standard English because it is viewed as being the only superior language in which learning should take place. Hence, other language skills children may have are not recognised as being important. An analysis of Foucault's regimes of truth (1980) reveals that there are inconsistencies between policy, practice and the needs of children with EAL as they are forced to learn Standard English quickly, which is deemed normal. Furthermore, children with EAL are currently included within a centralised and monolingual curriculum (DfE, 2017) and assessment structure in which all children are taught the same content, implying prescriptive content which can lead to prescriptive pedagogy. This can mean little freedom for settings to react to the different cultures and languages of their children with EAL because the Early Learning Goals (DfE, 2017) indicate a specific level in communication and language and literacy that must be achieved by the end of the reception year.

What the Early Years Foundation Stage framework means for children with EAL

One of the four strands of the EYFS focuses on the concept of a unique child (DfE, 2017), which implies that all children are unique, different and special regardless of their differences or additional needs. So, practitioners must see each child as an individual rather than linked to a group like those children with EAL (discussed in Chapter 5). The EYFS also clearly identifies that all children have the right to access the curriculum equally, which means settings need to provide equality of opportunity and anti-discriminatory practice (ibid.,

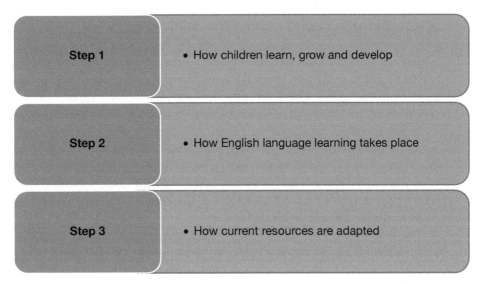

FIGURE 4.1 Three-step model for children with EAL

2017). This indicates settings must make the extra effort needed to adapt their practice and provision to ensure that children with EAL have access to the same learning as their peers (Mistry and Sood, 2014). We maintain that the fairness of opportunities for children with EAL is not just about the basics of ensuring all children have access to the same resources or learning activities, it is more than that. It is about making the effort to understand our three-step model for children with EAL.

Our model aims to illustrate how to better meet the needs of children with EAL by better understanding key aspects of learning. First, we suggest that all practitioners regardless of the age phase in which they work need to have a secure and clear understanding of how children learn, grow and develop. Without this understanding, it is very difficult to truly understand how to plan learning to meet children's different needs and abilities. Second, we suggest all practitioners would benefit from having a clearer understanding of English language learning theories for all children but more specifically how the language learning process can apply to children with EAL where language skills transfer may not be as straightforward as originally perceived (discussed more in Chapter 5). We specifically say English language learning theories because we must not assume that children with EAL have no language skills (Mistry and Sood, 2010), as it is well known these children have language skills in a different and, in some cases a more complex language than English. Third, our model is about adapting current setting resources for children with EAL, rather than having separate resources showing all children are included and integrated. Furthermore, we claim our model should be encompassed by an awareness of children's home background and culture as this also informs pedagogy and children's willingness to learn (see Chapter 7).

Inclusion through social justice for children with EAL

Changing philosophical beliefs as well as the social, cultural, economic and political nature of society has influenced the way in which education has been perceived over time. Children with EAL have been segregated (in terms of withdrawal) and categorised and grouped (see Chapter 5) and more recently included through the concept of inclusion (Salend and Duhaney, 2011). We begin this section by looking at what social justice is and what it means for children with EAL. The discussion moves on to how inclusion is a facet of social justice followed by a brief historical journey of the term inclusion. Next, we look at some key aspects of inclusion in the context of Early Years and what these mean for children with EAL.

The aim of social justice is more than securing equal opportunities, it is about equity (Lumby, 2013) and the understanding that education for opening opportunities and space for learning lies at the heart of living a life free from barriers or discrimination. A useful starting point for Early Years practitioners in meeting the needs of children with EAL is the three inter-twined elements (adapted from Chapman and West-Burnham, 2009) of social justice:

1   Equality: every human being has an absolute and equal right to common dignity, parity of esteem, and entitlement to access the benefits of society on equal terms.

2   Equity: every human being has a right to benefit from additional consideration according to need.

3   Social justice: justice requires deliberate and specific intervention to secure equality and equity.

Figure 4.2 shows social justice only exists to the extent that the principles of equality and equity are apparent. The greater the overlap of the two circles the greater the potential for social justice. Practitioners need to understand social justice requires specific interventions for children with EAL so they can access the curriculum to ensure fairness of opportunity in creating a level playing field (Wilkinson and Pickett, 2010), which is a challenge within itself.

The concept of inclusion first gained recognition in the USA and was further supported by the Salamanca statement in 1994 which called countries to promote inclusive settings at a global level (UNESCO, 1994). As a term, inclusion is related to the concepts of social justice and equity (Mistry and Sood, 2014). In essence, inclusion in education is about all children being included regardless of their different needs or abilities and although this may seem like a common feature of Early Years settings today, it has not always been the case.

Practitioners must ensure that their practice is inclusive by ensuring all children can access learning and for children with EAL this means that access to

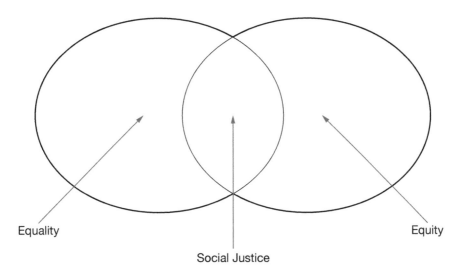

FIGURE 4.2 Equality, equity and social justice
Source: adapted from Chapman and West-Burnham (2009)

learning must be thought through and implemented in more creative ways. Essentially, inclusion is about how a setting deconstructs their systems and structures by looking at their current practice to ensure that they are responding to the diversity of their children like those with EAL by practices being grounded in social justice principles

Booth and Ainscow (2011) offer a useful summary in terms of what inclusion in education means:

- Putting inclusive values into action
- Increasing participation for children and adults in learning and teaching activities
- Reducing exclusion, discrimination and barriers to learning
- Fostering mutually-sustaining relationships between schools and surrounding communities
- Restructuring cultures, policies and practices to respond to diversity in ways that value everyone equally

For children with EAL we make a case that inclusion stems first from having positive relationships (DfE, 2017) with children to ensure that you know each child well as an individual and second, by following our 'three step how model'. There are many different day to day strategies that can be used to help make settings more inclusive (as discussed next), but we suggest the key is once you know your children well, you are better placed to meet their needs under the umbrella of social justice.

Reflecting on making the learning environment more inclusive for children with EAL

We say that as the nature of learning in Early Years is different to the rest of the educational sector, it is perhaps easier to make learning opportunities more inclusive. In reference to the EYFS, a key part of a practitioner's role is to promote learning opportunities for each 'unique child' through an 'enabling environment' (DfE, 2017). This means that practitioners must monitor the development and progress of all children through play and experiences provided. Differentiation of teaching is essential if children are not at the expected level of development as indicated within the EYFS. For children with EAL this means practitioners may need to model expectations more or provide additional learning opportunities so that these children can better understand the context to make meaning. However, before we talk about how a learning environment can be made more inclusive, it is important to remember that all children, but especially those with EAL need to feel safe, secure and valued before they become receptive to their surroundings for learning taking place. Arnerich (2018) has suggested thirteen ways in which the learning environment in Early Years can be made more inclusive for children with EAL which consist of:

1 involving children's home language
2 spending time with parents
3 prioritising listening activities
4 having friendship buddies
5 correct name pronunciation
6 basic survival language
7 non-verbal clues
8 active learning
9 understanding differences and how it can link to behaviour
10 importance of familiar activities
11 importance of song
12 other languages
13 support

Although we agree with all of these strategies, we would also like to offer some thoughts worth considering whilst trying to adapt provision. This section will focus on Arnerich's (2018) ideals of inclusion through specific discourses in Early Years like: use of the home language, working with parents, links with the home and observing through play.

Use of the home language

The use of children's home language for children with EAL is vital because we feel it is important to hear their voice in any language rather than no speech at all if forced to speak in Standard English only as demonstrated by the following case study.

Case study 4.1

Kiran was a 4-year-old boy in a reception class. His home language was Punjabi, and he was fluent in speaking Punjabi at home with his family. Although he did attend nursery for a year prior to starting reception, he was not forced by the nursery staff to speak in English. Having said this, he did pick up key words and had begun to use these words during play and with selected nursery staff. Although he could not formulate sentences in English, he would use gestures and pointing with the odd words in English to illustrate what he was trying to say. Overall, he seemed to be a happy child who was confident in his own play and shared play with others. When Kiran arrived at school the reception staff insisted that he must try to speak in English because they were aware of his ability from the nursery staff. However, rather than trying, Kiran clammed up and became withdrawn, so much so, that he did not even communicate in play if there was an adult nearby.

This case study shows that children do need time to settle in a setting. For children with EAL this may take longer initially, but this time needs to be weighed up against the progress children are likely to make if they feel secure. Kiran's mum later shared with reception staff that he felt too scared to make mistakes in his English speech and therefore refused to respond.

Working with parents

The key point from case study 4.1 is that communicating with parents through spending time with them is vital to find out what the issue could be. We say more effort is made in the Early Years to build positive relationships with parents, but this seems to taper off as children progress up the primary phase. Here, perhaps all staff need to be visible at the beginning and end of the day to briefly meet and greet parents/carers as this is particularly important for children with EAL who may have very different cultures and traditions outside the setting.

Links with home

We also highlight that although labels and notices in home languages are useful and bring some element of a child's background or home into the setting, we need to be aware of the purpose of this in terms of whether we are doing this for the parents or the child, especially if children are not familiar with reading or writing in their home language. Whilst we agree with Arnerich (2018) in terms of the importance of listening activities, we would suggest that repetitive texts with pictures and sounds (even beyond Early Years) will first help to engage children and second, help them understand contextual meaning. With pairing children together, we suggest practitioners be mindful of personalities and perhaps consider changing pairings after time so that new friendships are built.

Pronouncing a child's name correctly is crucial because if practitioners pronounce names incorrectly, then so will others and children in the setting. This is evident today when many adults from different cultures have an English alternative name to make life easier for others. In terms of basic survival language, it is beneficial for all practitioners and children in the setting to learn basic key words and greetings in the languages of their class population. This would be particularly appreciated by parents, whose life you may also be indirectly shaping through their child. It would also be useful to observe how other children use non-verbal gestures for children with EAL especially within play as this will help practitioners assess their level of understanding in specific contexts. It is already well known that the use of visual prompts is important in Early Years and for all children but perhaps some of these visual concepts need to be used outside of Early Years for children with EAL too. These good ideas should not only be restricted to young children only.

In terms of Arnerich's (2018) understanding differences and behaviour, it is useful to have an awareness of how the family culture of a child with EAL can influence their behaviour. For example, if a child with EAL is told off by a practitioner and looks at the ground, this does not mean that they are being disrespectful, rather, they are ashamed of being told off and therefore they do not make eye contact out of respect for elders.

Observing through play

The best way to understand familiar activities is to observe children with EAL in play. Here, perhaps it would be useful to have clothing in the dressing up area from a range of different cultures associated with the child population of the class as well as different items in the kitchen area such as chopsticks, rolling pins, a masala tin. Although Arnerich's (2018) information from parents is useful, we also suggest that children may also know more than what we perceive and therefore the use of talk in any language becomes essential. Singing is an inclusive way to encourage language repetition but if this is combined with visual support like a video clip then children can begin to make connections in their contextual understanding too. Finally, we would like to reiterate Arnerich's (2018) message: ask for help if you are unsure of what to do. From research by Mistry and Sood (2012), a suggestion is to build partnerships between your setting and settings with a higher proportion of children with EAL to share ideas of good practice. This is particularly important for isolated children with EAL who can sometimes be overlooked in a setting if they are the only child with EAL.

Although there are many more ways in which the learning environment can be made more inclusive for children with EAL, we argue that if practitioners favour an area of learning and development or outcome then this could influence the opportunities provided. In this case, it is important to remember Donaldson's notion of de-centred thinking (1978) to remind ourselves that we need to put ourselves in the position of the child rather than focusing on practitioner targets that need to be met.

Key reflection points

- The approaches to how children with EAL have been perceived and educated have changed over time.
- Even though children with EAL are assimilated through the current EYFS, this is through an inclusion lens.

Summary

In summary, it is important to be aware of these historical changes associated with the approaches put in place for the education of children with EAL so that you are aware of how provision used to take place. In one respect some provision is still the same as it used to be, like withdrawal or sometimes being overlooked. Children with EAL may not have time to settle and feel comfortable in a setting before they are bombarded with phonics and key words to help them assimilate into the majority language and culture as soon as possible regardless of their needs. Finally, although inclusion and social justice are key buzz words today, perhaps what we really need to think about is how inclusive are we as practitioners and how our current practice and provision for children with EAL demonstrates inclusion, especially with the current top down approach of performativity and accountability.

References

Arnerich, M. (2018) *EAL in early years: 13 ways to offer a more inclusive environment.* Available at: https://famly.co/blog/management/eal-in-early-years-inclusive-envrionment/ (Accessed March 2019).

Baker, C. (2006) *Foundations of bilingual education and bilingualism.* 4th edn. Bristol, UK: Multilingual Matters.

Booth, T. and Ainscow, M. (2011) *Index for inclusion: Developing learning and participation in schools.* Bristol, UK: Centre for Studies on Inclusive Education.

Brook, M. R. (1980) The mother tongue issue in Britain: cultural diversity or control? *British Journal of Sociology Education*, 1 (3): 237–256.

Chapman, L. and West-Burnham, J. (2009) *Education for social justice: Achieving wellbeing for all.* London: Continuum.

Chomsky, N. (1965) *Aspects of the theory of syntax.* New York: MIT Press.

Cohen, L. E. (2008) Foucault and the early childhood classroom. *Educational Studies: Journal of the American Educational Studies Association*, 44 (1): 7–21.

Conteh, J. and Brock, A. (2011) 'Safe spaces?' Sites of bilingualism for young learners in home, school and community. *International Journal of Bilingual Education and Bilingualism*, 14 (3): 347–360.

Costley, T. (2013) English as an additional language, policy and the teaching and learning of English in England. *Language and Education*, 28 (3): 276–292.

Creese, A. and Martin, P. (eds) (2003) *Multilingual classroom ecologies.* Clevedon, UK: Multilingual Matters.

Department for Education (DfE) (2014) *The national curriculum in England: Primary curriculum.* London: DfE.

Department for Education (DfE) (2017) *Statutory framework for the early years foundation stage: Setting the standards for learning, development and care for children from birth to five.* London: DfE.

Department for Education and Skills (DfES) (2000) *Curriculum guidance for the foundation stage.* London: QCA.

Department of Education and Science (DES) (1967) *Children and their primary schools* (Plowden Report). Available (online) at: www.educationengland.org.uk/documents/plowden/plowden1-06.html (Accessed March 2019).

Department of Education and Science (DES) (1975) *A language for life* (The Bullock Report), London: HMSO.

Department of Education and Science (DES) (1985) *Education for all: Report of the committee of inquiry into the education of children from ethnic minority groups* (The Swann Report). London: HMSO.

Donaldson, M. (1978) *Children's minds.* London: Harper Collins.

Foucault, M. (1975) *Discipline and Punish: The birth of the prison.* New York: Random House.

Foucault, M. (1979) *Discipline and punish: The birth of the prison.* New York: Vintage Books.

Foucault, M. (1980) *Power/Knowledge.* London: Pantheon Books.

Foucault, M. (1981) The order of discourse. In R. Young (ed.) (1981). *Untying the text: A post-structural anthology.* Boston: Routledge & Kegan Paul. pp. 48–78.

Gillard, D. (2004) *The Plowden Report.* Available at: http://infed.org/mobi/the-plowden-report/ (Accessed March 2019).

Halle, M. (1968) *The sound pattern of English*. New York: Harper and Row.

Her Majesty's Stationery Office (HMSO) (1966) *Education Act 1966*. London: HMSO.

Her Majesty's Stationery Office (HMSO) (1967) *The Plowden Report*. London: HMSO.

Lumby, J. (2013) Distributed leadership: The uses and abuses of power. *Educational Management Administration & Leadership*, 41 (5): 581–597.

Mac Naughton, G. (2005) *Doing Foucault in early childhood studies: Applying post structural ideas*. London: Routledge.

Martin-Jones, M., Mejia, A. M. and Hornberger, N. H. (eds) (1984) *Bilingualism and special education: Issues in assessment and pedagogy*. Clevedon, UK: Multilingual Matters.

Mistry, M. and Sood, K. (2010) English as an additional language: Assumptions and challenges. *Management in Education*, 24 (3), pp. 111–114.

Mistry, M. and Sood, K. (2012) Raising standards for pupils who have English as an Additional Language (EAL) through monitoring and evaluation of provision in primary schools. *Education 3–13: International Journal of Primary, Elementary and Early Years Education*. 40 (3): 281–294.

Mistry, M. and Sood, K. (2014) Permeating the social justice ideals of equality and equity within the context of Early Years: challenges for leadership in multi-cultural and mono-cultural primary schools. *Education 3–13: International Journal of Primary, Elementary and Early Years Education*. 43 (5): 548–564.

Mohan, B., Leung, C. and Davison, C. (eds). (2001) *English as a second language in the mainstream: Teaching, learning and identity*. Harlow, UK: Longman.

National Association of Language Development in the Curriculum (NALDIC) (2015) *Supporting bilingual children in the early years*. Available (online) at: www.naldic.org.uk/eal-teaching-and-learning/outline-guidance/early-years/ (Accessed March 2019).

Newbolt, H. (1921) *The teaching of English in England*. London: HMSO.

Piaget, J. (1962) The language and thought of the child. London: Routledge & Kegan Paul.

Salend, S. and Duhaney, L. (2011) Historical and philosophical changes in the education of students with exceptionalities. In Anthony F. Rotatori, Festus E. Obiakor, Jeffrey P. Bakken (eds) *History of Special Education (Advances in special education, Volume 21)*, Emerald Group Publishing Limited, pp. 1–20.

Stokes, B. (2017) *Language: The cornerstone of national identity*. Available at: www.pew-global.org/2017/02/01/language-the-cornerstone-of-national-identity/ (Accessed March 2019).

UNESCO (1994) *The Salamanca Statement and Framework for Action on Special Needs Education*. Paris: UNESCO.

Vygotsky, L. (1978) *Interaction between learning and development*. (Trans. Cole, M.) Cambridge, MA: Harvard University Press.

Wilkinson, R. and Pickett, K. (2010) *The spirit level*. London: The Equality Trust.

5

Reconceptualising the term English as Additional Language (EAL)

When you have finished reading this chapter you will

- better understand what is meant by EAL and the associated interconnected terms
- be aware of critical differences between terminology that is sometimes applied to all children with EAL
- know why the term EAL needs to be reconceptualised in relation to current educational practice in Early Years

Chapter outline

This chapter looks critically at the variety of terminology associated with and applied to children with EAL. Although these terms have different meanings, in some cases a lack of knowledge has meant that they are often used as an alternative to EAL. It is unclear from these terms the extent and level of home language(s) and English language proficiency that children with EAL may have. This chapter begins with a deeper discussion regarding the definition of the term English as an Additional Language (EAL). Next there is a discussion of other terms associated with EAL but not entirely synonymous with it, which include: bilingualism, English as a Second Language (ESL), multilingualism and plurilingualism. This is because although these terms have different meanings, the same provision could be evident for all children with EAL regardless of the differences in English language competencies between them. We then justify our choice of using the term EAL rather than bilingualism within this book. Finally, we look at the impact of labelling children with these terms to help us to understand why the term 'EAL' needs to be reconceptualised in relation to current practice in settings today.

<u>Key words:</u> English as an Additional Language (EAL), bilingualism, multilingualism, plurilingualism

Introduction

In Early Years settings, teaching English has been varied according to the English language needs of the children. For example, a child born in England with English as their first language might be at a different level of English language proficiency in comparison to a child born in England and raised with a different home or first language. We find a range of other terms used to describe children whose first language is not English in addition to EAL and these terms have already been mentioned, including: Teaching English as a Second Language (TESL), Teaching English as a Foreign Language (TEFL). Many of English Speakers of Other Languages (ESOL). Although these terms are not used widely in classrooms today, they still have resonance in terms of some of the perceptions associated with them as discussed in Chapter 4. Many of the terms mentioned can be used to describe children with EAL, but they do not define the level of language proficiency and language understanding leading to confusion between definitions. Perhaps some differences in language and English language proficiencies between these children cannot be fully understood if practitioners are monolingual themselves. There has to be clarity about what these terms mean and how they are conceptualised for children with EAL, otherwise this can be confusing for both practitioners and the children themselves in terms of how they are being labelled. It is therefore important to understand the impact of labelling children, especially for those children with EAL in terms of their language needs because these influence children's identity as discussed in Chapter 7.

Defining 'EAL'

In this book, EAL is defined as pupils 'who already speak another language or languages and are learning English in addition to this' (Mistry and Sood, 2015: 10). It is important to clarify that children with EAL could already be speaking more than one language which is not English, therefore how the term EAL is applied to these children needs careful thought. EAL is the most commonly used term in English Early Years settings and primary schools and is applied to all children who speak a language(s) other than English. At the Nursery World Show in 2017, Drury said EAL can be seen as the English language learned later at school (Cahill, 2017). However, we argue that this is not always the case and practitioners need to be aware of this as English could be learned as an additional language at home before formal school is started. Therefore, perhaps the term EAL could be used as an overall umbrella term to describe all those who

TABLE 5.1 Terminology associated with children who have EAL

Terminology	What does it mean?	Link to the term EAL
Monolingual	Children who can only understand one language.	In the context of English settings English would not be the additional language as English is the main language of instruction.
Bilingual	Children who have the capacity to communicate in two languages (not necessarily at the same level).	English is the additional language to the primary language used at home.
Multilingual	Children who can speak more than two languages (again not at the same level of proficiency between them).	English is the additional language to those already used.
Pluralingual	Children who have the capacity to communicate and switch in a range of languages.	English is the additional language being learned and can be switched alongside other languages.

are bilingual, multilingual and pluralingual *if* English is the *additional* language to children's repertoire of language (s) as illustrated by Table 5.1.

Table 5.1 shows that different terms associated with EAL have different meanings (as discussed later) and therefore this can suggest different implications on practice. Although in some settings the term EAL and bilingualism can be used interchangeably, it must be remembered that these two terms are different with different meanings – hence provision can be different too. There needs to be clarity in understanding these terms as children with EAL could be fluent in one, two, or more languages and English is the additional language especially if children speak in different languages to their parents and grandparents at home as illustrated by the following case study.

Case study 5.1

Natan was a new arrival in a reception class half way through the autumn term. Natan's mum was Polish and his dad was Italian, they moved to England with their son in search of a better life and both parents got employment quickly. Although Natan did not speak English he seemed happy to be in school and showed particular interest in learning outside. What is interesting is that both parents were able to speak enough English to get by however, when dad picked Natan up from school, they would speak in fluent Italian to each other. When mum picked Natan up from school they would speak in fluent Polish to each other. Mum and dad understood enough Italian and Polish to use both languages in the home and this meant Natan was able to switch between both languages easily. Furthermore, Natan's paternal grandparents owned a villa in Spain where Natan tended to go most school holidays therefore he was also picking up Spanish whilst conversing with his grandparents in

Italian. By the end of the reception year, Natan was multilingual and had picked up enough English language words to be able to make himself understood easily.

This case study shows that even though Natan is multilingual, English is the additional language he is currently learning both at home and school. Natan's parents were very happy that he seemed to have a love for languages and enjoyed speaking in different languages to different family members. But his dad did share with the class teacher that he finds languages easy because there are similarities between them especially in terms of the way some words sound.

What is bilingualism?

Although bilingualism is about the capacity to use two languages in which proficiency can be from minimal to advanced, defining bilingualism is challenging because of variations in bilingual ability. For example, one child could converse in two languages whereas another child could converse and be fluent in reading in two languages, meaning, they are also bi-literate. For bilingual children, variations in second language acquisition such as whether this is from birth, or whether another language was introduced later on needs consideration as this will determine the level of bilingualism. Attention to current language competence offers a challenge especially between linguistic aspects (spelling and grammar), regarding language for conversation and language for academia (Baker, 2011). Despite these variations and associated challenges in meeting the learning needs of these children, the term bilingual is used for all children speaking another language other than English. Here, it is important to recognise differences between individual children and their learning needs. In this case, NALDIC (2011) suggests pluralingual might be a better definition of children's language competence if more than two languages are spoken rather than bilingual.

Factors determining bilingualism

Other than language alone, other factors need consideration as to whether a child can be termed bilingual or not, for example, whether the focus is just on language proficiency, or language understanding, or on frequency of language use (Baker 2006). With the growing number of children who are bilingual and the increasing variety of literature associated with bilingualism, there is no one definitive definition of bilingualism accepted by all, or how it should be measured (Bhatia, 2006), or how the language needs of individual children should be met.

An inaccurate understanding of what the term bilingual means in practice will prevent practitioners ensuring provision is appropriate and effective which is also supported by Duncan (1989). In addition, Duncan (1989) goes on to say that bilingual children tend to create two communities, one is the community in which their home language is spoken and the second, where their second language is spoken – which tends to be the setting. Although the Bullock report of 1975 aimed at bringing these two communities together, there is no evidence to prove this has happened. Bilingual children can still tend to see the setting and home environments as two separate environments as demonstrated by the following case study.

Case study 5.2

Roshni was a 4-year-old girl in a reception class. Her home language was Punjabi which was used by both her parents and her older siblings. Her extended family also spoke in Urdu so Roshni was familiar with hearing this language too. At school Roshni was able to communicate through key words in English but she lacked the knowledge and confidence to structure her sentences correctly. Roshni tried very hard to explain things in English to the setting practitioners but then used to withdraw if she was unable to do this. Her mum tried to explain to her class teacher that Roshni would not share any of her home language or customs with her friends because she felt very different to her peers. During play activities Roshni would be observed talking to the toys quietly in Punjabi only if she thought no one was listening, otherwise she would just listen to the others with a few key words in English.

Key point

- Practitioners need to be aware that children with EAL may withdraw if they do not feel comfortable so it is important to observe them discreetly so their knowledge and ability can be understood.

This case study shows that even though practitioners can have many strategies in place to build bridges between home and settings, sometimes children will see these as separate learning environments, for example, Roshni only spoke in Punjabi quietly when she assumed no one could hear. This illustrates that Roshni did not feel comfortable speaking her home language in front of others in the setting. One reason for this could be because children with EAL could view themselves as being different to the majority children and they may not wish to perceive as being different by others. In the case study of Roshni, the setting focused on differences through foods from around the world followed by differences between the children and practitioners in terms of favourite foods, favourite colour, hair style, eye colour, shoe size and favourite toys, aiming to show that there are differences between us in many ways beyond the obvious regarding the way we look and how we speak. From this, the setting encouraged many different pairings and groupings of children to ensure that all children mixed together in play and explorative learning as much as possible to help illustrate the similarities between them and also to help them understand a sense of belonging.

One of the authors of this book was bilingual from the age of four, she also saw the home as a separate place from school because customs, food and traditions were very different to her monolingual practitioners and peers in school. This is because de-centred thinking (as discussed in Chapter 3) did not take place from the practitioners to try and better understand her (Donaldson, 1978).

Measuring bilingualism

How do you measure the level of language awareness, exposure and proficiency in order to be termed bilingual? In today's diverse society this is crucial as different parents may speak in different languages to their children especially if the parents themselves are of mixed heritage. Although Drury (cited in Cahill, 2017), argues that it is important for practitioners to find out as much as possible about the use of the home language, we maintain that unless practitioners have the time to do several home visits it is difficult to glean this information from one observation of a child during a home visit or through a fleeting conversation with parents. We suggest that a more creative way of seeing the home language used naturally could be through parents uploading brief video clips of language being used at home to a separate section to their child's learning platform or setting portal to help practitioners to understand the context of the language being used too. If practitioners do not have the knowledge to understand how to meet the needs of these children, then immersion in the English language could result in children not using or refusing to use their home language as it is not deemed as important as English (discussed in Chapter 6). We also note that there can be confusion between the terms bilingual and multilingual because in one respect, both terms refer to children who can speak more than one language fluently. This means these terms can be used together to describe the same child yet, both have different meanings which means different provisions and associated practice needs to be better understood. Bhatia (2017) suggests that the term bilingualism is not just about acquiring and using two languages, which we interpret to mean that understanding bilingualism is not just about being aware of the two languages a child can speak, but it is about how knowledge of these languages has helped children to form their identities (discussed in Chapter 7).

English as a Second Language (ESL)

A simple definition of English as a Second Language (ESL) is where English is the second language being learned in addition to the home language. Sometimes English as a Foreign Language (EFL) is also used alongside ESL, however these terms imply different meanings which again, need to be better understood. One concern about the term ESL is that English may not be the second language being learned, it could be the third or even fourth. An example is when a child who speaks Bengali at home could be learning English at school, but could also be learning Arabic at the same time which means that English may not be the second language being learned. More recently, the term ESL has been replaced with English for Speakers of Other Languages (ESOL), which we would agree is perhaps a more fitting description.

Growing use of the English language around the world has been illustrated by Kachru (1986) through his three concentric circles of English. In his model, the inner circle is where English is spoken as the primary language, the outer circle is where English is spoken as a second language and the expanding circle is where English is spoken as a foreign language (Kachru, 1986). However, we have adapted this model in line with increasing migration that has taken place in England since the introduction of this model as illustrated next.

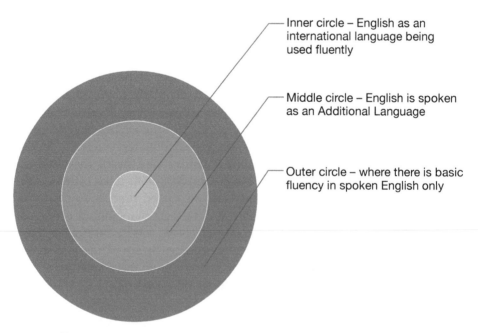

Inner circle – English as an international language being used fluently

Middle circle – English is spoken as an Additional Language

Outer circle – where there is basic fluency in spoken English only

FIGURE 5.1 Three concentric circles of English
Source: adapted from Kachru (1986)

We have started off with the inner circle whereby English is an international language because it is commonly used globally to a greater or lesser extent more so than any other language in the world at the moment. We say 'at the moment' because the use of other languages like Mandarin, spoken by a greater population may catch up to English in the future so that it could also be deemed an international language. The reason we have not said that English is the main language is because for some children with EAL it may not be their main language as they may only speak English in the setting and therefore is not the primary language for these children. Another reason is that for some children with EAL, they could be very fluent in spoken English as well as other languages, which does not mean to say that one language is prioritised over another, but rather English is recognised as a common language in their setting and wider community. Furthermore, by saying English is an international language our model could also be applied within an international context. Next, we have changed Kachru's (1986) outer circle layer to the middle circle because we believe that the word middle implies a bridge between English being used fluently, to English being used for basic communication. We believe this middle circle is particularly relevant to children with EAL as they could already be speaking several other languages other than English therefore, in this case English would be the additional language and not necessarily the second language. Finally, we have changed the expanding circle to the outer circle whereby children have basic understanding in English to understand a few key words and instructions. The reason for changing the expanding circle to the outer circle implies that other factors outside of the outer circle may need consideration in relation to language learning such as the learning context and the impact of family or other additional needs.

Multilingualism

The main difference between bilingualism and multilingualism is that there are more complex and diverse factors involved with learning and using more than two languages (Herdina and Jessner, 2002). This includes factors such as when and where languages are used out of the setting, in what context are different languages outside the setting used and what languages are deemed important in the family. Herdina and Jessner (2002) go on to suggest that those who are multilingual have greater linguistic repertoires and a better awareness of the choice of language to be used in different contexts. With increasing globalisation, it is not surprising that multilingualism has increased, so to avoid confusion with bilingualism, we would suggest that the definition should be clarified for multilingualism. So, here we say, children are multilingual if they can communicate in three or more languages.

However, there is also confusion associated with the term multilingualism. It is difficult to know the extent of languages being used outside the setting such as which language is more dominant with grandparents or cousins or other members of the family. More critically, if known languages are not used or listened to regularly, then there is a danger that they can be forgotten. The type of languages used by multilingual children also needs consideration because a child who is able to speak in Polish, Italian and English (as in case study 5.1) has a different understanding in terms of the choice of language to be used, to a child who speaks Arabic, Bengali and English because the conventions of these languages are so different to English.

Most research studies indicate that a multilingual child has linguistic advantages in comparison to their monolingual peers but, how this is utilised in settings varies (Auer and Wei, 2009) according to the type of languages being used. According to Paradis (2009) the benefits of being multilingual varies because this depends on the type of language being used in the setting as well as outside the setting. Kenner's (2000) research on a small sample of 3- and 4-year-old multilingual children from a particular cultural background indicated that it could be a great advantage for settings to use materials written in the children's various home languages however, we argue that this would need to be purposeful based on a deeper knowledge of children and their home environment. Seeing children's home languages around the setting could be a waste of time if children are of second or third generation and are not used to seeing print in their home language(s) at home. Many multilingual children especially in the Early Years are only familiar with the spoken element of language especially if parents do not read or write in these different languages themselves. Perhaps what would be more effective is for a multilingual child to be able to feel comfortable enough to use all their languages to support learning in Early Years especially through play to understand meaning. But with the focus on English language learning in settings, Tazi and Wasmuth have suggested, 'elevating the status of one language over others, or strictly controlling the use and purpose of a language, runs counter to the nature of multilingualism and creates subtractive conditions where children are at risk for language loss' (2015: 2).

Plurilingualism

The key difference between multilingualism and plurilingualism is that multilingualism is about using languages separately, whereas plurilingualism is about using the knowledge of languages to switch between them and code mix. In this respect, plurilingualism is about having the ability to communicate in more than three languages (like multilingualism) but also being able to switch between these languages depending on the context. Therefore, being plurilingual is also about having the capacity and competence to be able to learn or pick up languages easily as illustrated by the following examples which are taken from the work of Kivinen (2011).

Example 5.1: Isabelle from Brussels, 1996

The heart is Spanish (because I feel Spanish). The brain is French (but it doesn't mean that I think in French), I just have to use a lot of French to live in Belgium. The feet are Belgian, because I live in Belgium. The hands are English, because English language is important to communicate with people (really often).

Example 5.2: Jose from Brussels, 1996

Jose, Bruxelles, 1996

- The floor represents the country where I live: Belgium
- The house, it's Spain, because at home I speak Spanish.
- The tree is France, because outside, in the street and the everyday life I speak French.
- The big building it's England, because the English language is important to work and communicated with the others.

Example 5.3: Elsa from Luxembourg, 1998

Elsa speaks Finnish at home. She plays with her German and English speaking friends. She hears LëKebuergesch (which is another word for Luxembourgish, a language mainly spoken in Luxembourg), French, Italian and Portuguese at playground. Elsa's parents speak often English with their guests, whose children speak only Swedish, Danish, Dutch, etc. The TV channels are French, English, German and LëKebuergesch. In the shops people speak LëKebuergesch, German and French.

These examples show that plurilingual children have different representations and understandings of language dependent on which language is used with whom and in what context. But from a European perspective it is clear to see the importance of the English language which has been illustrated by all the children.

From a global perspective plurilingualism is about children having language skills, implying they have more of an advantage to fit into multicultural societies both locally and internationally. However, this repertoire of languages is usually associated with languages that are similar in nature such as a child who has one parent who prefers using Punjabi, another parent who prefers using Gujerati and at times both using Hindi (which is the main language used and understood in India).

Justifying the usage of the term 'EAL' over bilingualism

EAL is the term used throughout this book because the Office of Standards in Education (Ofsted, 2001) has categorised bilingual children into groups and they say that the term EAL 'is the most commonly used term to refer to bilingual children in official documentation since 2001' (ibid.: 4). The British Council (2014), has also categorised children with EAL into beginner learner, intermediate learners and advanced learners with an obvious implication for the need of differentiated pedagogy. Children with EAL form a 'heterogeneous group and can include new arrivals, those who are new to English, as well as advanced bilingual learners' who come from different social, cultural, and linguistic backgrounds (Mistry and Sood, 2015: 8). Today many settings use the term EAL over the term bilingualism because they recognise that English is the additional language regardless of whether young children are exposed to one or more languages in their family. This is also further supported by the National Association for Language Development in the Curriculum (NALDIC) in that although they talk about bilingual learners, the majority of the information they provide for practitioner support is related to the term EAL.

Davis (2012) talks about EAL pedagogy rather than bilingual pedagogy in that 'EAL pedagogy is the set of systematic teaching approaches which have evolved from classroom-based practices in conjunction with the development of knowledge through theoretical and research perspectives' (no page number). This implies that these approaches can better meet both the language and learning needs of children with EAL in a variety of learning contexts. In this way we believe that the term EAL is a broader choice of vocabulary in which there are several different categories rather than bilingualism which applies to specific children only. With the emphasis on languages in Europe and the world outside of England, bilingual children can also learn other languages as they grow older or family dynamics change, which means that they would no longer be termed bilingual only.

Critical debate associated with the term EAL

In this book we have chosen to focus on the term EAL for diverse children with language needs but we recognise that there are disputes associated with the use of this term. Although the 'term EAL is commonly used in English settings', meaning these children are also known as bilinguals, the inter use of these terms implies differences between terminology that is not recognised or understood (Wardman, 2012: 3). A lack of understanding associated with terminology can also lead to all children with English language needs being termed children with needs rather than children that have a different language ability to the practitioners in the setting.

Both Murphy (2018) and Costley (2013) suggest that usage of the term EAL implies that these children are seen to be a problem because additional effort needs to be made to support their language needs (discussed in Chapter 4). We believe that practice is changing slowly in that children with EAL are being perceived more as children with different linguistic capabilities for languages other than English, which is a clear advantage. However, if children's home language is not valued and encouraged then this may lead to a refusal to speak the home language both in the setting and at home. This is yet another matter in that children with EAL think in their home language in the early stages of learning English, but if there are several home languages in use then it can be challenging to identify which home language forms the basis of their thinking initially.

Leedham (2015) has suggested that because the term EAL does not consider children's language proficiency, some practitioners in settings may label any child with EAL just because they do not speak English well enough or just because they are new arrivals to the country. Although we partially agree with Leedham (2015), we add that in the Early Years many children may also not speak English properly because this can be dependent on the speech of their role models or family. The reason for this is because we are in a culture where street talk and shortcuts in language (like text speech on mobile phones) seem to be the norm so the conventions of standard English perhaps need to be applied to the majority of children in our settings, not just those with EAL.

Another issue with the term EAL is that community or home languages of different groups in society can be viewed as less important than English implying hierarchies and inequality exist compared to discourses associated with English language (Anderson, 2008). Hence, misconceptions in children's' English language competencies can lead to stereotypes that may stem from perceptions and labelling which focus on children's potential to underachieve rather than their current knowledge base (Gardner, 2001).

Impact of labelling children with EAL

The term EAL can be a label leading to unfortunate pejorative assumptions which are negative views associated towards children with EAL. These labels can influence practitioner expectations, as discussed in the seminal research of Rosenthal and Jacobson (1968), meaning provision could limit children's progress. This is because labels tend to identify individuals or groups of individuals in a particular way regardless of whether this identification is accurate or not. For children with EAL this means that they could be perceived in a negative way regardless of their linguistic ability and understanding. According to Rosenthal and Jacobson's (1968) research through their Pygmalion Effect, they hypothesised that practitioners' expectations of their children have an impact on the attainment they achieve. This means if practitioners have negative or low expectations of their children with EAL, it could be likely that these children will make less progress in comparison to their monolingual peers through self-fulfilling prophecy. Although we are not suggesting this exists in current settings, we emphasise that if all children including those with EAL are thought of in a positive way, then progress is likely to be more evident through positive relationships (DfE, 2017). Additionally, practitioners also need to be mindful of children's funds of knowledge (Moll, 1992) before labels of any sort are applied to them.

Currently, with increasing migration in England, Salford and Drury suggest 'large numbers of bilingual children entering mainstream education are pre-labelled as underachievers' meaning provision and support could be limited before knowing what these pupils are capable of (2012: 73). The impact of being pre-labelled is although children with EAL fall into different groups and sub groups, provision can often be the same for all these children, so different pupil competencies and language proficiency may not be recognised (NALDIC, 2015). One reason for this labelling is because practitioners may have a limited idea of where children are at other than what they look like and what their basic background is especially if they are new arrivals. Hargreaves (1975) has suggested that practitioners tend to classify children in three ways:

1   Speculation
2   Elaboration
3   Stabilisation

In this first stage perceptions are made by practitioners based on children's appearance, relationships with others in the setting and whether they engage with others and learning, but Hargreaves goes onto emphasise that within the speculation stage practitioner views are short term and can change. In the elaboration stage practitioners' classifications of children are either 'confirmed or contradicted' (1975). The third stage is where practitioners can say that they know their children and their learning needs well. We feel that these stages of classification are particularly relevant for children with EAL and more so for those who are new arrivals as it is human nature to begin to position children in setting systems from the very first time they enter.

However, it is important to be aware of a number of criticisms associated with children being labelled. First, there is no evidence to prove that children are being labelled in any way other than children with EAL's individual ability associated with language and other understanding. According to Fuller (1984), in some cases labelling children can have a reversal effect in that if children with EAL are labelled as underachievers then there is a possibility that they could prove this label wrong and eventually become high achievers. Therefore, we agree with Chen (2007) in that positive attitudes demonstrated by practitioners are key in ensuring a supportive learning environment for children with EAL. Also, if initial labels are applied to children in relation to their ability, then these must change as children make progress.

Reconceptualising the term 'EAL' in Early Years

The variety of terminology associated in relation to children with EAL is varied and therefore 'its use and misuse can underline negative attitudes' and also influence positive attitudes (Cunningham, 2017: 20). This means it is imperative that these terms are understood clearly alongside the impact they have on provision through being reconceptualised. Cunningham (2017) also suggests that some practitioners tend to use the terms they feel more familiar with in association to children with EAL without actually being clear about what these terms mean or how they overlap with other terms, which is also supported by Mallows (2012). Like Costley (2013), Murphy (2018) also reinforces that the term 'EAL is problematic' and one reason for this is the term EAL encompasses a range of different needs for children with EAL, making the term vague and general rather than specific. In our view, we do agree with Murphy in that the term EAL covers a range of children at different levels of English language acquisition and proficiency, but perhaps there needs to be some clear sub groups within the term EAL especially for new arrivals. We suggest having a five-stage model for children with EAL when they start settings to help clarify the support these children need as illustrated by Figure 5.2.

Figure 5.2 shows potential stages of EAL arrivals which in turn would make it easier for practitioners to tailor their provision for children rather than categorising all children with EAL into one group regardless of their differentials. Our ladder of stages model is different to the English proficiency scale model for children with EAL which was introduced by the Department for Education (DfE) in 2016 and later scrapped by them from January 2019 (Henshaw, 2018). The English proficiency scale model has been adapted for use by different settings and looks in particular at English language proficiency in different stages

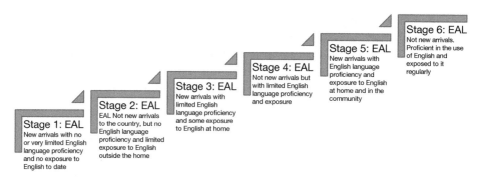

FIGURE 5.2 Ladder of different stages of children with EAL on arrival to a setting

across all literacy (reading, writing, speaking and listening). We agree with Strand (cited in Henshaw 2018) in that more research needed to be carried out in the field with EAL before a decision like this was made. Furthermore, we claim that many practitioners in Early Years and Primary struggle with positioning and assessing children with EAL, so any form of guidance is useful especially if this comes from the DfE.

We hope that through observations in play and communication with the family we can have a better idea of English language competencies for these children, which in turn will help us with planning the next stages of opportunities. Therefore, our ladder of different stages for children with EAL is to help position those children who are new arrivals to a setting (not just new arrivals to England) and furthermore, we have suggested a range of strategies that could be used to support children in each stage of the ladder.

Another reason we feel that the term EAL needs to be reconceptualised is because there is a lack of clarity of how code mixing takes place with the use of different terms. This is where children use their knowledge from more than one language to explain or express themselves especially if they lack knowledge required in the dominant language (in this case English) (Bhatia, 2017). This is particularly the case when there are no direct translations for specific words or phrases from other languages to English (discussed in Chapter 6). We are not suggesting that children with EAL should be labelled at a specific stage in the early stages of being in a setting, we are simply offering a ladder of different stages of EAL to help plan provision and practice in a setting initially. We are also mindful in that children with EAL do not and should not remain on the same stage, this is where practice needs to be reflective and observations are crucial in understanding where children are at, what funds of knowledge (Moll, 1992) they have and the progress they are making in their cognitive development, not just language development.

TABLE 5.2 Suggestions for each step of the ladder

Stage of ladder	Suggestion of activities
Stage 1 Settling stage	• Help these children to feel safe and valued • Range of play activities • Allow children the time to observe others in play • Observe children use of resources in play to see if they are familiar with what they are • Observe which children interact with the children who have EAL – and maybe use this information to build some friendship groups • Use friendship pairs/groups to help children with EAL be familiar with setting routines
Stage 2 Use of key words	• Allow children time to settle in • Use some key words in their home language • Allow the use of the home language in the setting • Use picture and word cues in English and translate into home language if possible • Use actions and gestures to enable very basic instructions to be understood • Observe how language of the home language can be translated through play
Stage 3 Finding common ground between home language used and English	• Find a friend to help the child settle in • Find out from family how English is used in the home • Build relationships with the family to find out any common ground between home culture and setting culture • Use visual clues to help with understanding • Model English language correctly and demonstrate what words mean through play and ICT
Stage 4 Finding out the reason for limited English language expose in the home	• Helping the child to feel safe and valued • Find out what if there is any reason for limited expose to the English language at home • Find out the family circumstances (for example if grandparents are helping to look after the child) • Observe awareness of the English language through play • Identify recognition of key words • Use of pictorial clues to help with understanding • Observe any child that the child with EAL gravitates towards and use this knowledge to encourage pairings
Stage 5 Exposure to English	• Observe children in play • Encourage a range of different friendship groups to build cross setting relationships • Observe how children with EAL use English in the setting • Identify and clarify misconceptions in understanding • Check comprehension of English regularly through high order questioning
Stage 6 Code mixing evident	• Observe children in play • Allow children to code mix • Ask children what words in their home language mean • Make children feel special in that they know more than you do in terms of their home language • Encourage linguistic diversity in the setting so it feels normal to hear different languages

Key reflection points

- It is important to realise that the term EAL is an umbrella term for children who have a range of different language competencies.

- Children with EAL may not necessarily be bilingual. They could be multi-lingual or plurilingual so it is important that the terminology used to describe them is not mixed up.

In summary

In summary there are numerous cross overs with terms used to describe children with EAL. Here, we argue that perhaps a clearer understanding of these terms would help practitioners meet the needs of their EAL children more strategically. Furthermore, we argue that attitudes towards children with EAL need to change (from Chapter 4) from being perceived as a problem, to individuals with a greater linguistic awareness and skills that could benefit them in their adult life if they are guided and led to believe that they have natural skills that sometimes cannot be taught. We further argue that the term EAL would benefit from being reconceptualised in terms of exactly what it does mean other than English being the additional language to a child's repertoire.

References

Anderson, N. J. (2008) *The practical English language teaching: Reading*. New York: McGraw-Hill.

Arnot, M., Schneider, C., Evans, M., Liu, Y., Welply, O. and Davies-Tutt, D. (2014) *School approaches to the education of EAL students*. Available (online) at: www.educ.cam.ac.uk/research/projects/ealead/Execsummary.pdf (Accessed March 2019).

Auer, P. and L. Wei (eds) (2009) *Handbook of multilingualism and multilingual communication*. Berlin: Mouton de Guyter.

Baker, C. (2006) *Foundations of bilingual education and bilingualism*. 4th edn. Bristol, UK: Multilingual Matters.

Baker, C. (2011) *Foundations of bilingual education and bilingualism*. 5th edn. Bristol, UK: Multilingual Matters.

Bhatia, T. (2006) Bilingualism and second language learning. In *Encyclopaedia of language and linguistics*. 2nd edn. Oxford: Elsevier. pp. 16–22.

Bhatia, T. (2017) Bilingualism and multilingualism from a socio-psychological perspective. *Oxford research encyclopaedia of linguistics*. http://dx.doi.org/10.1093/acrefore/9780199384655.013.82.

British Council (2014) *Language levels of EAL learners*. Available (online) at: https://eal.britishcouncil.org/teachers/language-levels-eal-learners (Accessed November 2017).

Cahill, K. (2017) Working with multilingual children in the Early Years. Rose Drury speaking at The Nursery World Show – February 2017. Available at: https://eyfs.

info/articles.html/teaching-and-learning/%E2%80%9Cworking-with-multilingual-children-in-the-early-years%E2%80%9D-dr-rose-drury-speaking-at-the-nursery-world-show-%E2%80%93-february-2017-r218/ (Accessed April 2019).

Chen, Y. (2007). Equality and inequality of opportunity in education: Chinese emergent bilingual children in the English mainstream classroom. *Language, Culture and Curriculum*, 20 (1): 36–51.

Cornwell, H. (2015) *English as an Additional Language (EAL) and educational achievement in England*. London: Educational Endowment Fund.

Costley, T. (2013) English as an additional language, policy and the teaching and learning of English in England. *Language and Education*, 28 (3): 276–292.

Cunningham, C. (2017) *Saying more than you realise about 'EAL': Discourses of educators about children who speak languages beyond English*. University of York. Retrieved from http://ethos.bl.uk/OrderDetails.do?uin=uk.bl.ethos.727366 (Accessed April 2019).

Davis, N. (2012) *The distinctiveness of EAL pedagogy*. Available at: www.naldic.org.uk/eal-teaching-and-learning/outline-guidance/pedagogy/ (Accessed April 2019).

Department of Education and Science (DES) (1975) *A language for life* (The Bullock Report), London, HMSO.

Department for Education (DfE) (2017) *Statutory framework for the early years foundation stage: Setting the standards for learning, development and care for children from birth to five*. London: DfE.

Donaldson, M. (1978) *Children's minds*. London: Harper Collins.

Duncan, D. M. (1989) Issues in Bilingualism Research. In: Duncan D. M. (eds) *Working with bilingual language disability. Therapy in practice*. Boston: Springer.

Fuller, M. (1984) 'Black Girls' in a London Comprehensive School. In, Hammersley, H., Woods, P. (eds) *Life in school, the sociology of pupil culture*. Milton Keynes, UK: Open University Press.

Gardner, P. (2001) *Teaching and learning in multicultural classrooms*. London: David Fulton Publishers.

Hargreaves, D. (1975) *Deviance in classrooms*, London: Routledge.

Henshaw, P. (2018) DfE urged to reconsider decision to withdraw EAL proficiency measure. Available at: www.sec-ed.co.uk/news/dfe-urged-to-reconsider-decision-to-withdraw-eal-proficiency-measure/ (Accessed April 2019).

Herdina, P. and Jessner, U. (2002) *A dynamic model of multilingualism. Perspectives of change in psycholinguistics*. Clevedon, UK: Multilingual Matters.

Kachru, B. (1986) *The power and politics of English*. Available at: https://onlinelibrary.wiley.com/doi/abs/10.1111/j.1467-971X.1986.tb00720.x (Accessed April 2019).

Kenner, C. (2000) *Home pages. Literacy links for bilingual children*. London: Trentham Books.

Kivinen, K. (2011) Bilingualism, multilingualism, pluralingualism at home and at school – a practical approach. Available at: https://kivinen.files.wordpress.com/2012/04/plurilingualism-2011-translation-forum.pdf (Accessed April, 2019).

Leedham, D. (2015) *The challenges of English as an additional language*. London: The Key

Mallows, D. (2012) *Innovations in English language teaching for migrants and refugees*. (D. Mallows, ed.). London: British Council.

Mistry, M. and Sood, K. (2015) *English as an additional language in the early years: Linking theory to practice*. London: Routledge.

Moll, L. (1992) Bilingual classroom studies and community analysis: some recent trends. *Educational Researcher*, 21 (2): 20–24.

Murphy, V. (2018) *Podagogy – Season 3, Episode 3 – EAL with professor Victoria Murphy*. Available at: https://tesnews.podbean.com/e/why-using-the-term-eal-can-be-%E2%80%9Creckless%E2%80%9D-professor-victoria-murphy-on-tes-podagogy/ (Accessed April 2019).

National Association of Language Development in the Curriculum (NALDIC) (2011) The distinctiveness of EAL pedagogy. Available (online) at: www.naldic.org.uk/eal-teaching-and-learning/outline-guidance/pedagogy/ (Accessed April 2019).

National Association of Language Development in the Curriculum (NALDIC) (2015) *Supporting bilingual children in the early years*. Available (online) at: www.naldic.org.uk/eal-teaching-and-learning/outline-guidance/early-years/ (Accessed March 2019).

Office for Standards in Education (Ofsted) (2001) *Managing support for the attainment of pupils from minority ethnic groups*, London: Ofsted.

Paradis, J. (2009) *Oral language development in French and English and the role of home input factors*. Edmonton, Canada: Conseil Scholarie Centre-Nord.

Rosenthal, R. and Jacobson, L. (1968) *Pygmalion in the classroom: Teacher expectation and pupils' intellectual development*. New York: Holt, Rinehart and Winston.

Salford, K. and Drury, R. (2012) The 'problem' of bilingual children in educational settings: policy and research in England. *Journal of Language and Education*, 27 (1): 70–81.

Tazi, Z. and Wasmuth, H. (2015) Cultural and linguistic challenges in early childhood education and care. *Global Education Review*, 2 (1): 1–4.

Wardman, C. (2012) *Pulling the threads together: Current theories and current practice affecting UK primary school children who have English as an additional language*. London: British Council.

6

Language learning for children with EAL

When you have finished reading this chapter you will

- have a critical awareness of language learning theories and language acquisition
- understand language proficiency and the impact of this on children with EAL
- understand the impact of labelling languages from positioning of Standard English
- be better informed on the critical debate regarding language learning for children with EAL

Chapter outline

This chapter begins by looking at the bigger picture with a brief discussion on the foundations of language acquisition and how this links to some of the ideals from philosophers. Then we look at how language proficiency can be linked to children with EAL alongside some of the associated issues. Next, we explore why different language learning theories such as those proposed by Chomsky (2010) and Cummins (1979, 1981, 2000) are important and the possible impact of their views on children with EAL, including links to a sociocultural approach by Vygotsky (1986). Following this, there is discussion regarding language acquisition and what this means for children with EAL. Then, there is a critique of language learning theories followed by what is meant by the positioning of Standard English. The discussion progresses briefly onto the impact of labelling languages and the debate associated with language learning for children with EAL because they are familiar with languages other than English. Finally, we bring this chapter together by summarising why understanding linguistics is important in relation to the foundations of language learning for children with EAL.

Key words: linguistics, language learning, language theories, Standard English

Introduction

Language is essential for communication and creates an instant connection whether this is social, or for learning, or for business. We have not emphasised which language should be used for communication, but in the context of this book, the reader will appreciate that the importance of English as the additional language is being emphasised. This is because learning in England takes place in English, therefore English is the additional language being learned for some children. This suggests that although all languages are generally deemed to be equal, there is a hidden hierarchy within languages whereby Standard English is deemed to be superior in comparison to other languages. This position of Standard English poses an issue for our children with EAL because learning in English can imply that these children are inadvertently placed at a disadvantage. This disadvantage can also lead to barriers in terms of curriculum access. This is currently paramount with the importance placed on early reading and phonics in Early Years and primary education. In addition, we also need to be clear about the impact of learning another language (in this case English) for our diverse children because this impacts on their outcomes. So, in this chapter, we suggest that it is vital for all those who work with children to be clear about what language learning means especially in the context of Early Years education.

Foundations of language acquisition

Language connects people together because it signifies how we think and communicate as language represents the reality constructed. As far as Plato, many Western philosophers looked at his contribution to linguistic discourse – the debate about nature versus nurture. Later, the workings of Descartes, the French philosopher, made further contributions about the distinctiveness of language reflecting the general wisdom of people. He advanced the notion of Cartesian linguistics, noting that universal principles lay behind every language, which is similar to Chomsky (discussed later). In practice, such philosophers have given us ideas about language learning, linguistics and notions about language development.

We turn to the origin of Locke's philosophy conceptualising tabula rasa, or the blank slate. He suggested that all knowledge is externally acquired of our body through sensory experience rather than through innate knowledge that we have from birth (as discussed in Chapter 3). This developed into language theory with Locke rejecting the idea that there was an innate logic behind language. Such a notion applied to practice for children with EAL would suggest offering maximum stimuli for them to engage and enjoy learning through language, hence the need to personalise language learning. The concept of sensory input was later developed in the twentieth century by Skinner, to develop the theory of behaviourism. The difference between Skinner and Locke was that Skinner perceived that all behaviour is a response to external stimuli and has no function with innate programming within a human being to learn a language at birth. He coined the term operant conditioning, where language learning grows out of a process of reinforcement and punishment, therefore a person is conditioned to say the right thing or conditioned to learn aspects of language development regardless of the connections to other learning as demonstrated by the following case study.

Case study 6.1

Megha was a 4-year-old girl in a nursery. Her home language was Urdu which she understood and spoke with her parents, even though parts of it were grammatically incorrect. By nature, Megha was shy and quiet, but she was happy to socialise with other children in play and generally copied the other children when they followed the instructions of the practitioners. Megha had observed one of the practitioners getting cross with children when the children had to do their phonics work as they did not pronounce the taught sound properly (which they had already had input on during a previous session), so she made sure she tried her best to learn the sounds she was taught. Her teacher was impressed with the sounds Megha was learning and told her mum and aunty one day during home time. Megha's aunty told the teacher, Megha has not got a clue what the practitioner is talking about, but she knows that if she does not learn the sound then the practitioner will be cross with her like she is with other children.

Key point

- We must not assume that if children with EAL seem to know sounds and key words, that they understand what it means.

This case study shows that the children were a little frightened of a practitioner in the nursery, so they felt that they had to learn what was being taught to avoid being told off. Hence, they were conditioned to learn sounds for fear of being punished, which is linked to Skinner's behaviour approach.

The Department for Education (DfE) defines the first language as 'the language to which a child has initially been exposed to during early development and which is still used in the home environment' (2013: 7). Language acquisition is the process by which children acquire and use language. However, for children with EAL, although the process of language acquisition is similar, differences can also exist because of differences between languages (NALDIC,

2011). Knowledge of language acquisition is important because it enables practitioners to tailor contexts and opportunities that promote communication and language acquisition especially through play in Early Years.

Language proficiency for children with EAL

Language proficiency is linked to an ability to speak or perform in a learned language. The term proficiency also refers to children's competency in another language to be used in the classroom and beyond. There are different levels of language proficiency as in beginner – having a novice understanding and experience; intermediate – a phase between a beginner and an expert, and an expert – with a highly developed skill level. NALDIC (2018) offer the following descriptions for a study they undertook on the language attainment profile of children with EAL in local primary and secondary schools in relation to language proficiency: Stage A (New to English), Stage B (Early Acquisition), Stage C (Developing Competence), Stage D (Competent), and Stage E (Fluent) because 49 per cent of pupils in primary schools at that time were classed as having EAL. Their data showed that there is a greater proportion of children with EAL with low levels of English language proficiency in Key Stage 1 in comparison to later key stages. Their report concludes that the national scale for English proficiency for children with EAL is useful as a diagnostic tool to inform teaching focuses, tracking progress, and providing baseline information for statistical purposes at the national and local levels. However, Early Years practitioners are already heavily burdened with supporting the language acquisition and proficiency of children with EAL from their own data set analysis, therefore offering another tool to use needs a better justification.

More critically, we need to be mindful in that there is danger of using language proficiency as vague terminology as it could misrepresent how skilled a child really is in a language. This is because a child with limited or no English language proficiency may not be the same in their own home language(s). In fact, children with EAL could be very skilled in their home language(s) and in some cases, these children can switch and code mix between languages if more than one language is used in the home. Children with EAL may not have the same proficiency in both languages at the same time because each language has its own code and conventions requiring navigation as shown by García, who suggested children with EAL need to 'be given the opportunity to show their proficiency in both languages' (2009: 377). Furthermore, a comparison of language proficiency by emergent or fluent children with EAL to monolingual children is an unfair comparison, implying the current regime of assessing language is unequal with a one size fits all approach.

Another consideration is where you have monolingual Early Years practitioners with very little awareness of other languages trying to differentiate and allocate children with EAL into artificial categories or levels especially when some children with EAL may understand many aspects of their home language but refuse to speak it. We question whether this is fair practice and what criteria of selection might they use for language and English language proficiency? Here, perhaps space could be made for these practitioners to debate the level of language proficiency of each child through a language audit and then develop an action plan that is cognisant of home languages.

Why are language learning theories important?

Having knowledge and understanding of how children learn language in different ways is essential for all practitioners because this knowledge helps practitioners plan provision more effectively to meet the language needs of their children. This is particularly relevant for children with EAL whereby practitioners need to be able to offer a range of different strategies to help their children improve their English language proficiency. Perhaps one of the issues is a lack of theoretical knowledge in practitioners leading to greater creativity in promoting different language strategies to better meet the needs of their children with EAL.

A Chomskian perspective

In one respect, Chomsky can be perceived as the father of linguistics because his contribution to the field of linguistics has changed our thinking about how we capture and use ideas which is very much centred on a philosophical notion. In the context of this chapter we are focusing on Chomsky's influence on linguistics and his influence on transformational grammar. During the 1950s Chomsky suggested that children have what is known as a Language Acquisition Device (LAD) which is essentially a hypothetical concept that assumes a child's brain has the function to rapidly learn and acquire language (Diamond, 2018), and later this thinking led to his theory about universal grammar. This is where Chomsky proposed that children are born with an understanding of the rules of language, and they just need to acquire the vocabulary needed to be able to use language (ibid., 2018). With his theory about universal grammar he believed that language is a basic instinct for all children and that they have the functions within them through the LAD to learn any language.

Essentially, Chomsky's perception is about how some structures of every language are universal to all but critically, this is where difficulties arise for practitioners in Early Years when they support a child with EAL, whose interpretation of the rules of universal grammar may not be the same as a monolingual English-speaking child. For example, the sentence 'The bus is arriving', is grammatical but 'arrives the bus', 'here bus' and 'arrives' are not; here subject matter is required for every sentence and it cannot be inverted with the verb. In the context of Early Years, we argue that young children are unaware of the rules of grammar used initially, so how would they know that a sentence is grammatical or not? Furthermore, research on how children with EAL learn another language remains complex and contested, but the clear message is to ensure that Early Years practitioners continue to encourage strategies that promote effective skills in reading, writing and oral communications, and where necessary, offer supportive corrections.

Cummins and language learning

Cummins (1979, 1981) is well known for his conceptualisations of second language learning, as he distinguished between two key terms – Basic Interpersonal Communication Skills (BICS) and Cognitive Academic Language Proficiency (CALP) in his theory. In simple terms, BICS can include gestures, visual cues, key vocabulary and essentially encourages natural communication in social contexts, but we need to be careful that the use of language in social situations does not mask fluency or proficiency in that language. CALP on the other hand builds on BICS and can include higher order thinking skills and moving from the concrete to the abstract (Krashen and Brown, 2007; Cummins, 1979). This is more linked to the demonstration of language proficiency in the academic sense but again, we need to be mindful that academic skills gained are not just restricted to one context as children can apply the skills learned to different situations. Academic proficiency is about knowledge in academic language like syntax and academic vocabulary, whereas academic content focuses on knowledge about the actual subject area like history. Both these elements can be taught directly because the academic and social language are intertwined and therefore, it may take the child with EAL longer to close the proficiency gap than an indigenous monolingual child. Cummins' iceberg model shown below depicts the BICS/CALP relationship.

Figure 6.1 shows that BICS refers to conversational fluency in a language whilst CALP refers to childrens' ability to understand and express, in both oral and written modes, concepts and ideas that are relevant to success in a setting. We note here that both BICS and CALP are more complex than a binary distinction implies and some parts of BICS are developed late and some aspects of CALP are acquired early whereas phonemic awareness (sensitivity to sounds in spoken words) are related to the development of both BICS and CALP (e.g. in helping readers to access difficult academic words) (Scarcella, 2003: 6). For children with EAL, their social language (BICS) can develop much quicker than the academic language used in learning (CALP) (Cummins, 2000), meaning these pupils need specific interventions to ensure they have opportunities to develop language skills through modelling and scaffolding, as emphasised initially by Bruner (cited in Wood *et al.*, 1976).

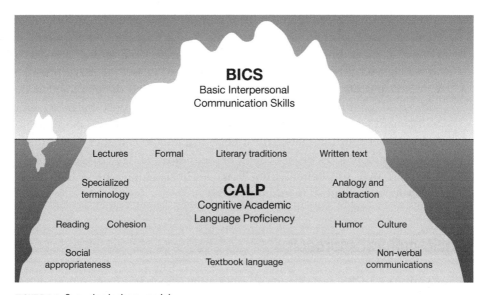

FIGURE 6.1 Cummins iceberg model

Source: Cummins, J. (1989) *Empowering Minority Students*. California Association for Bilingual Education, Sacramento, CA

Within his theory, Cummins went on to suggest that cognitive approaches to learning language are more beneficial than a behaviourist approach because he believed that those learning an additional language already have language skills within them to base the necessary foundation for the new language to be learned. However, we emphasise that this is dependent on the similarities between languages, obviously if languages are very different in nature then there may not be a necessary foundation in terms of similarities.

Cummins (1981) also suggested the theory of common underlying proficiency, implying that once the fundamentals of language are learned and understood, then the foundation for subsequent learning is formed. The ideology here seems to be that demanding cognitive tasks, such as abstract thinking and problem solving, are similar across all languages – meaning, if a concept is learned in one language it does not need to be learned in another language. But the regime of truth for children with EAL suggests this may not be true, as differences in language means the same concepts could be understood very differently in different languages and sometimes even in the same language, especially if English is becoming more dominant than the home language.

With threshold theory Cummins (1976) notes, children with EAL need to achieve a threshold level to benefit from cognitive rewards, suggesting a relationship between the level of language proficiency and cognitive ability. The premise here is children's success in their second language is dependent on their level of mastery in their first language and that cognitive benefits take place when both languages are well developed. Within this model Cummins offered two levels, 'the attainment of the first threshold would be enough to avoid cognitive retardation but the attainment of a second, higher level of bilingual competence might be necessary to lead to accelerated cognitive growth' (1976: 24). Each threshold is progressive in nature from limited bilingual ability to a balanced bilingual. However, one limitation is that it is difficult to categorise concepts such as bilingualism and cognitive development if they are viewed as continuous variables. Second, assuming only balanced bilinguals will benefit from the cognitive advantages of this model can be unfair to other bilinguals or multilinguals. This theory also fails to consider that children with EAL are taught curriculum content in their additional language (English) therefore they may not benefit from language instruction unless they have some competency in English (Cummins, 1984).

Socio-cultural approach

Vygotsky (1978) was the most influential theorist associated with a socio-cultural perspective because he recognised the importance of child variation by differences in culture, language, customs and traditions. Like Dewey (1934), Vygotsky highlighted that children need to interact with others to help understand meaning and make sense of the world by implying that children construct meaning through language depending on their experiences, which is vital for children with EAL because of cultural and language differences.

Social groups during social activities may have different interests and commonalities that bind them together, which can be one reason why some children with EAL group themselves together. The glue that holds all communities together is the ability to converse, hence Dewey emphasises the importance of language for learning which is social in nature (like Vygotsky), implying learning should involve socialisation to enable pupils to become confident conversationalists. For children with EAL, this is vital as it helps them to connect with their peers through similarities and helps clarify misconceptions in language especially if the same words are used for different meanings in different communities (even within the same culture). Lately, Smith (2016) suggests five principles of a sociocultural perspective that are useful in understanding learning which we feel are important considerations for the foundation of literacy activities:

1   Social interaction
2   Learning drives development
3   Interpersonal relationships
4   Importance of culture
5   Construction in cultural context

First, there should be an understanding that all learning and development begins with social interaction (Vygotsky) consisting 'of the internalisation of social processes' (Smith, 2016: 51). But for children with EAL, understanding of social processes could be different at home to that in a setting because of differences in beliefs and values. Second, the implication that learning drives development rather than the reverse argument can be a challenge if learning is not taking place according to need or ability. Some children with EAL can give the impression that they are not learning anything and therefore less effort can be made by practitioners, whereas it is important to keep in mind that they could be absorbing the learning around them differently because of their different cultural understanding. Third, if children with EAL do not feel safe and secure then learning is not likely to take place at an optimum level therefore, 'close interpersonal relationships' are crucial for learning to take place (ibid.: 51). These relationships are important for children with EAL, so they do not feel that they are being judged for being different. Finally, having knowledge of children's culture informs their development path rather than isolated activities promoting development. This is essential for children with EAL as they may have knowledge of concepts in different language(s) which may only be noticed through discussions or play which is crucial in helping these children to make connections whilst constructing learning. Therefore, understanding and promoting the cultural context allows for appropriate construction of learning strategies and outcomes for children.

From a sociocultural perspective, language is the main tool of thought and therefore 'language precedes development' (Lavendenz, 2011: 20). This perspective also focuses on action being mediated and therefore cannot be separated from the social context in which it is carried out. For children with EAL, the social context in which actions are carried out with more knowledgeable others or in groups can help language understanding more than traditional language learning, like instruction from practitioner to child with no context or application. From Vygotsky's sociocultural theory, Rogoff (1990) suggested the term 'guided participation', showing how childrens' learning can be supported by bridging what they already know (their starting point) to what they can achieve (goals of development), which is like Donaldson (1978). Guided participation can happen in many ways but modelling and reflecting on key teaching points using visual clues is particularly useful for children with EAL as cultural variations can influence development. Furthermore, Rogoff recommends development for children should be viewed as a cultural process, not just a biological process alone as children also develop as part of a community given many may have close extended families. Currently, with the increase in mixed heritage families and therefore cultural variations within the same household, account needs to be taken regarding how best to provide education for them.

Furthermore, Vygotsky proposed that language facilitates higher order thinking skills, meaning language is essential in knowledge construction. But higher order thinking skills supporting cognitive development are dependent on the type and availability of support (including how support staff are used) as children at different cognitive stages of development require different levels of support (Mistry and Sood, 2010). This is where a clear understanding of the individuality of children with EAL is essential as one type of language provision for all children with EAL is not appropriate since they do not form one homogeneous group (Mistry and Sood, 2015).

Language acquisition for children with EAL

Foucault (1980) perceives language as powerful because it shapes experiences. Meaning is made by how we explain things to ourselves and others. Furthermore, Foucault suggests our thoughts and actions informed by language are 'regulated and sometimes controlled by different discourses' (Danaher *et al.*, 2006: 31). This is particularly important in relation to children with EAL as the same words in a language can have different meanings, therefore some words cannot be translated directly from other languages into English. In addition, for children with EAL language learning is also influenced by theories of learning as well as linguistics (Lavadenz, 2011). Furthermore, sociocultural perspectives also have an influence on language acquisition because of the importance of social interactions and more knowledgeable others. We have chosen to focus more heavily on the work of Cummins (1981, 1976, and 1979) in relation to language learning because he focuses on second language learning which lends itself more clearly to a sociocultural perspective. We believe that by familiarising ourselves with some of Cummins' work on language acquisition, we recognised some similarity to our own early experiences of learning English. Cummins discusses language being a variable as it develops in and out of a setting, therefore it is not always under the control of the practitioner. Although Cummins talks about levels of language acquisition, he also discusses the importance of the home language and culture which is key to language development for children with EAL.

We acquire language and develop literacy by understanding messages in various forms: reading, listening, watching and conversing. In Early Years, children are making sense of the world around them, and slowly gaining larger vocabularies as they start to handle complex grammatical information presented through practitioners using different teaching strategies related to age and stage of the child's development. For example, the narrow reading strategy of using images, pictures and easier reading matter supposedly helps to ensure comprehension and later, with more complex texts, leads them to repetition of vocabulary and grammar (Krashen, 2004). Narrow reading, however, does not mean that a reader will stay narrow forever or that all children will acquire language learning strategies at the same rate. A child with EAL given some reading matter in English may not be appropriate as they cannot easily access the written code or they may remain in the reading zone (because of lack of interest/connection with the image), so it is wiser to offer him/her subject matter information in the first language first, which makes subsequent instruction and reading in the second language more comprehensible. There is an assumption here that this child has fluency in first language.

As Early Years practitioners here are some ideas for working with children with EAL:

- enhanced opportunities for speaking and listening;
- effective models of spoken and written language;
- a welcoming environment in which children with EAL feel confident to contribute;
- a recognition that the use of the first language will enhance understanding and support the development of English;
- teaching that assists children with EAL to internalise and apply new subject-specific language;
- teaching that recognises that more advanced learners of English need continuing support;
- grouping strategies that recognise children's learning and language development needs;
- clear targets in language and learning are identified and met; and
- the selection of visual aids is culturally relevant and of good quality.

These ideas need to be embedded in different contexts to help children make connections in their understanding of the world (DfE, 2017).

Critique of language learning for children with EAL

Although language learning theories are useful in suggesting how to help children learn, there are several critiques that require consideration. In relation to propositions by Chomsky, it is not clear exactly what his theory in relation to language learning is other than the structure of grammar. This is because there is no clear evidence or discussion on how this learning process actually takes place. We already know that language acquisition is the growth of the mental organ of language triggered by certain language experiences (Cook, 1985). So to acquire language, a child needs not only universal grammar (grammatical competence – the child's knowledge of the language), but also a cognitive maturity of English to know how to resolve the parameters for the order of subject – verb – object. What remains uncertain in terms of development is whether a child starts with all the principles of universal grammar available, or whether they gradually unfold as part of maturation. In addition, we question whether children with EAL mature cognitively – linguistically speaking – in different ways, in comparison to the majority of indigenous English white children.

We learn through making mistakes but in language development, several theorists suggest that where a child makes a mistake in sentence construction in his/her speech, say at 3 years of age, we should step in to frequently correct it. In addition, with the current emphasis on neuroscience, there is no evidence to say that there is part of the brain that supports the LAD. Furthermore, Chomsky's universal grammar theory was the opposite of Skinner's ideas. This is because Chomsky thought learning was an inborn means for language acquisition and that language was based on the idea that universal elements structured all languages (i.e. grammar for all languages which is already inside your head) and has nothing to do with conditioning. One criticism of Chomsky's work is that it may explain how we learn first language but remains silent on additional language learning.

Aukerman (2007) noted that BICS and CALP are arbitrarily defined and therefore, Cummins' work did not go far enough in critiquing these concepts as they were dependent on culture and context. Arguably, context is always salient for the practitioner and for the child, therefore one cannot use context-free language whilst being mindful of needs of children with EAL. The following example illustrates this:

> When his kindergarten teacher asked the class for the 'first sound' in the word made, Joaquín seemed to know what he was doing. He independently segmented the word aloud ('/m/, /a/, /d/') with no problem. But then he gave his answer: '/d/'. Joaquín, a second language learner of Mexican heritage, knew how to segment sounds, but he did not understand what his teacher meant by 'the first sound', and so he got it wrong.
>
> (Aukerman, 2007: 3)

This quote shows how children like Joaquín can understand conversational English (BICS) more easily than struggling to complete academic tasks (CALP) (Cummins, 1979). According to Cummins then, if children with EAL lack CALP in either their native language or the English language then this puts them at an academic disadvantage. In Joaquín's teacher's view, his lack of familiarity with important concepts in either English or Spanish made kindergarten especially hard for him: 'Joaquín is sort of caught in this trap of, he doesn't have enough Spanish nor English, so that he's just going to be, yicch, sort of limited bilingual unless his Spanish gets promoted to a strong language' (Aukerman, 2007: 3). The BICS/CALP framework offers practitioners ideas of the importance of developing the native language which may cause children with EAL some pedagogical difficulties. So, in the above example, when CALP gets developed in the native language, it is more easily transferred to a second language, but again this depends on the languages in question. In our example with Joaquín, if he understood the concept of 'first sound in a word' in Spanish, he would have comprehended what was being asked of him when faced with a similar task in English.

Furthermore, Ackerman (2007) has turned CALP on its head and argues that language must be reinforced in a social context where children for example understand what each other is saying when they are playing and use suitable language to communicate. By doing so, he argues, 'children must draw upon the linguistic resources that they already know – even ones that are not "academic" – and re-contextualise and transform them in new contexts' (p. 19), thus, … 'each child continually recreates her/his own unique *context-embedded academic language*' (ibid., italic and bold print as in original text). Thus, for example, when a practitioner asks a question of a child with EAL that s/he does not understand, the practitioner then needs to make a connection to the child's context to aid re-contextualisation.

Disruption of first language learning when second language acquisition has begun has not been considered by Cummins' theories. From personal experience of one of this book's authors, the home language of Gujerati was discarded when English learning began as it was deemed unimportant because 'institutionally … truths govern and regulate us which informs the way we talk and how we talk' (Mac Naughton, 2005: 29). As children with EAL can be playing catch up in their additional language, assessments in English are not a true reflection of their ability. Emphasis on English language learning without considering factors such as the social nature of learning, culture and identity can be a challenge if home language, prior experiences and culture are dismissed or ignored, as this puts these children at a disadvantage because it implies their funds of knowledge have no relevance (Moll, 1992).

Foucault (1980) argues against theories of language in general as they have a structured approach to learning which may not benefit children with EAL in social discourse, because language and social roles are linked together suggesting unequal relationships in which power can be hidden. Whilst all languages are deemed to be equal in terms of their structure, the actual vocabulary can change and grow with time depending on context. But the superior position of the English language means all languages in England are not valued equally therefore the different languages of children with EAL are viewed to 'disrupt dominant discourse in western childhood research', … because only the voice and participation of … 'listening to predominantly monolingual … voices' are promoted (Salford and Drury, 2012: 78). Here, language equality does not translate to social or cultural equality.

Positioning of Standard English

Globalisation has both its advantages and disadvantages in educational terms. Namely, it has brought greater inter- and intra-communication and with it, the use of English as a predominantly recognised global language. This is of course a stereotypical assertion, as the local, indigenous non-English speakers are perceived to be disadvantaged by not having the privilege and power status of

English language speakers. Indeed, there exist discrete varieties of English (Snell, 2013). Historically, this is a paradox, as English is made up of many different words and grammar 'borrowed' and 'tweaked' to develop into English as we know it today, thus paying little homage to the origin of English from international non-native speakers, which seems to deny the part 'others' played. Stubbs (2008) defines Standard English as 'a variety of language which can be defined only by reference to its role in the education system' (p. 83). He goes on to suggest that there is much confusion about terms such as 'standard', 'correct', 'proper', 'good', 'grammatical' or 'academic' English, and such terms need careful analysis, but cannot be discussed further given the limited space.

Language is linked to identity as well as a means of communication, so denying 'others' languages' seems rather precocious. We believe that if we examine closely what is Standard English, we will see that the role of language perpetuates perceptions of Standard English as 'linguistically neutral regardless of personal or field-wide views about linguistic equality and the value of linguistic diversity' (Davila, 2016: 127). Good practice in Early Years indicates that where there is diversity of staff with different skills and abilities linguistically and culturally, then there is good potential for supporting children with EAL in appropriate ways. With appropriate use of English language in the context of the setting, there is avoidance of misunderstandings by the child or the practitioner because of poor accent, dialect or pronunciation, leading to fewer barriers regarding communication.

Stubbs (2008) found that children who have difficulty in using Standard English in the education system do not talk and write as they do in their own language (p. 83). This was also concluded by Snell (2013) on studies in two primary schools with children aged 9–10, living in lower-class areas of Teesside, north-east England. He found that children used a blend of ideas in communicating in English – the 'combination of Standard English, non-standard forms, local vocabulary, musical influences and stock phrases, together with indexical meanings – reflects how speakers actually use language' (2013: 127). We need to celebrate diversity of languages spoken through taking a language audit of children and staff and working closely with parents. By denying the home language used by non-native speaker of English in the Early Years setting we may problematise non-standard voices and risk marginalising the group and their parents if we persist with prejudicial and 'deficit views of non-Standard English' (Snell, 2013: 110).

We also need to understand that children with EAL often acquire conversational fluency in English within about two years, but it requires considerably longer (5–10 years) to catch up academically in English (Collier, 1987; Cummins, 1984).

According to Ofsted (2019):

> It takes five–seven years to become fully competent in a second language, although individuals will vary in the speed with which to acquire this

competence. Fluency in spoken English is usually achieved within two years, but the ability to read and understand more com texts containing unfamiliar cultural references and write the academic English needed for success in examinations takes much longer.

(p. 27)

Furthermore, we maintain that in today's educational settings what is deemed to be Standard English varies from some monolingual white English practitioners in terms of the way in which they model spoken English. From the authors' wide range of experiences in carrying out observational assessment visits in a range of Early Years and primary settings, very often class teachers are saying that the teacher trainee students need to work on clarity of their speech and pronunciation especially when words like 'fink' and 'akse' (instead of ask), and phrases like 'children … now we gonna …' are used as part of speech modelled in the classroom. In addition, we argue that with street language and text language, what is deemed to be Standard English only seems to reflect a small percentage of the white English majority therefore, maybe the perception of Standard English could be diluted out in the future especially if fewer people are using it.

Impact of labelling languages

The primary form of languages is interpersonal. In the context of language learning, labelling is about how we phrase language learning – in this case English language learning. This is because the way we view and understand our surroundings is dependent upon the words we choose to describe, explain, or label them. Each word has its own symbolic meaning. Language transforms the objective world into our subjective realities. As the theory of Linguistic Relativism (Whorf, cited in Carroll et al., 2012) suggests, differing vocabulary and grammatical structures influence the way people perceive the world, whether it is within the same language or between separate ones. This means that a child with EAL will have their cultural background influencing how they think, speak and act. Here, the implication is that cultural influence plays an important part in the way a child will experience the world from his/her own viewpoint. Hence, language will impact some aspects of thinking and vice versa. Different minority ethnic groups will have different linguistic capability and a differing bank of vocabulary and grammar to draw upon as the way they make sense of the world, so it is palpable that there will be different consequences in cognition and behaviour, a point that sometimes needs to be appreciated more by Early Years practitioners when working with children with EAL. This does not mean for example, that a Hungarian child's knowledge is limited to their heritage/mother tongue, they will draw on a reservoir of other language vocabulary given the opportunity. Early Years practitioners need to open spaces for these children to experience new languages as appropriate. Accordingly, different cultural concepts will affect cognition in different ways, which is the basis of the theory of linguistic relativity, as language empowers us. The following case study illustrates how in a multicultural reception class there are differences in CALP skills to access learning.

Case study 6.2

Midori, a 4-year-old Japanese girl is a happy child who had a range of experiences prior to starting school which developed her cognitive abilities very well to comprehend English. This made settling into the English setting easy for her because her Japanese matched the English language, having enough CALP in the language of instruction. Whereas Kwanze, a 4-year-old girl from Ghana, had severe limitations of understanding English language with limited oral ability and very poor reading and writing skills, making learning and settling difficult for her.

Key point

- We need to critique how the BICS/CALP framework offers an appropriate conceptual schema for making academic judgement on these two children

This case study illustrates the potential danger of labelling children with EAL as having English language deficiency because a practitioner may perceive the child's abilities as limited, their instruction is thus tailored to that perception. If Kwanze is 'tested' on her use of English on concepts she has limited understanding of in both English and her own home language, then she will fail on both. The child will struggle, not due to a lack of CALP, but rather because the classroom context and tasks set have no relevance for Kwanze. Her cognitive abilities may not be socio-culturally shaped. It may be a case of re-contextualising-re-orienteering (i.e. creatively reinterpreting) Early Years pedagogy to better match childrens' linguistic strengths (rather than expecting the children to simply adapt to the existing language of the setting).

As content is taught in English, there is a danger that the home languages of children with EAL are devalued in comparison to English by the children themselves. Imagine a Bengali child having to suppress his/her own home language to learn another, dominant language like English in our English schools. This is likely to influence their self-esteem when they can demonstrate that they are bilingual, even, multilingual, speaking fluently at home and within their communities. If these children are in a classroom which is not diverse, has mainly monolingual population, then they are more likely to be immersed in the dominant English language, the monolingual habitus (Gogolin, 1997 cited in Cunningham, 2018: 2). The power and dominance of English language is all that these children will experience. In a multicultural, multi-linguistic society, this cannot be fair. Consequently, practitioners need to use appropriate strategies to overcome these potential difficulties for the child who is EAL, starting from the child him/herself to co-learn the language that opens spaces for dialogue with all. We suggest that practitioners also need to be aware that some parents could be worried about their home language(s) being 'surpassed' by English and therefore may insist on their child only speaking in their home language at home in order to preserve their heritage. Hence, we need to be aware of the impact of labelling languages.

Critical debate regarding language learning for children with EAL

From Cummins' (1978) work, language learning for children with EAL is about how knowledge of the first language can be used to help the development and understanding of the second language (English in the context of this book). But differences in language understanding and comprehension need consideration when planning provision for children with EAL because linguistic transfer does not happen in the same way for both (or more) languages in all aspects (reading, writing, speaking and listening). One assumption that might be made and can be incorrect, is that children with EAL will 'pick up English naturally and quickly', hence changes are not made to provision meaning they have to cope with current provision (NALDIC, 2015). From experience, a lack of adjustment in provision can lead to the silent period as it can be easier for children with EAL to cope if they are overlooked. Another debate is that for some children with EAL, learning to use English in day to day contexts where words can have different meanings from those in formal curriculum contexts (NALDIC, 2006) can be confusing, resulting in a lack of language understanding which is challenging for practitioners. Consequently, children are more likely to pick up daily language and its contextual meaning through modelling and play (DfE, 2017). There is also no clarity on exactly how the language needs of children with EAL should be met, especially when there is confusion regarding what type of data needs to be collected, assessed and monitored. The debate focuses around the issue of different practitioners having different values, consequently, different ways of meeting the language needs of children with EAL.

Importance of understanding linguistics

Understanding how linguistics works is a complex concept and this chapter has briefly previewed what it means in simple terms. However, for a deeper understanding we suggest it would be useful to the reader to further delve into Chomsky's work like 'Language and mind'. It is important to understand what linguistic means because it covers areas like semantics, grammar, syntax, phonology and so forth and each of us will likely to have different levels of linguistic proficiency which is to do with the ability of an individual to speak or perform in a language. So, for example, if a child is immersed in the English language, over time and with repetition of its use with their peers or at home, they will become adept at it. In the same way as a child who speaks Swahili at home all the time will become skilled at it. This does not mean either child is good or bad at each other's language – it just means they just have not been exposed to that language in their context. This, put simply, leads us to understand Systemic Functional Linguistics (SFL), which is a theory of language and how it works in the context in which it is used.

Therefore, we can visualise that the importance of language learning needs to be organised before meaning-making, which in the context of Early Years is vital as young children need to attach language to meaning in order to have a better understanding of the world (DfE, 2017). Halliday (1985: 10) says context is important whenever language is being used, noting relevance of three meta-functions (modes of meaning): the ideational (related to referring to categories of experience), the interpersonal, and a third that draws the first two together, the textual. It appears that SFL is founded on the idea that 'context is crucial and that our understandings of what we mean and intend to say are co-constructed' (Cunningham, 2017: 65), very much like Bruner's (1974) scaffolding talk related to cognitive development.

This poses an interesting conundrum for practitioners teaching children with EAL, in that if the main language of communication is English and the child has little comprehension of it, how do they co-construct meaning? As we know, different strategies are used to enhance the child's metacognition using Vygotsky's notion of zone of proximal development and Bruner's concept of scaffolding as discussed in Chapter 3. But the child may not be ready to make conscious and unconscious linguistic choices given their limited cognitive understanding, development and vocabulary necessitating the adult to partition the language as described by Halliday (1985). Explained from the Vygotskyian (1986) point of view, when a child uses words. Wellington and Osborne (2001), explain that 'language development and conceptual development are inextricably linked … thought requires language, language requires thought' (p. 5). Thus, the child's socio-cultural background and linguistic tools available to him/her play a significant role in concept development (Sapra, 2011: 503).

Adopting any analytical framework about linguistics requires engaging with the underlying assumptions and beliefs inherent in different models. There are a range of theoretical frameworks open to readers in the development of this field – Critical Discourse Analysis (CDA) is rooted in Critical Theory and the rise of post-structuralism and critical linguistics, as is the work of Foucault (1972, 1982), and Bourdieu's (1977) theory of practice and language and symbolic power (1991), which will enhance your awareness of this complex and fascinating topic in more depth.

Key reflection points

- As Early Years practitioners we need to be aware of not only language learning theories, but those which are tailored more to children with EAL.
- We also need to challenge misconceptions that just because children can speak one language, they can learn another language easily through skill transference – because this is dependent on the language in question.
- Children with EAL have many language skills such as being able to converse in very different languages with little similarity between them.

Summary

This chapter has looked at some thinking in relation to language learning. Although we have used Chomsky as a starting point, our focus has been the work of Cummins as we feel this is more relevant to the focus of this book. The process of learning language varies for children and these factors require consideration in terms of language acquisition. Most importantly we are aware that experienced Early Years practitioners will know when it is the appropriate time to introduce English reading or other forms of cognitively challenging content instruction (introducing children to use higher-order thinking abilities rather than the low-level memorisation and application skills) in English, increased in a coherent way throughout the Early Years setting and beyond. Although English is still perceived to be the most prominent language in the world, we question the positioning of Standard English given the differences in English dialect and uses that exist today within the monolingual English community. Furthermore, research on how children with EAL learn another language remains complex and contested, even though there is much good practice in Early Years that continues to encourage strategies that promote effective skills in reading, writing and oral communications, and where necessary, offer supportive corrections. Finally, we strongly believe that understanding and promoting the cultural context allows for appropriate construction of learning strategies and outcomes for *all* children.

References

Aukerman, M. (2007) A culpable CALP: Rethinking the conversational/academic language proficiency distinction in early literacy instruction. *The reading teacher*, 60 (7): 626–635. April 2007. DOI: 10.1598/RT.60.7.3 (Accessed July 2019).

Bourdieu, P. (1977) *Outline of a theory of practice*. Cambridge: Cambridge University Press.

Bourdieu, P. (1991) *Language and symbolic power*. (J. Thomason. (ed.)) Harvard: Harvard University Press.

Bruner, J. S. (1966) *Towards a theory of instruction*. Cambridge: Harvard University Press.

Bruner, J. S. (1974) *The relevance of education*. Harmondsworth: Penguin.

Carroll, J. B., Levinson, S. C. and Lee, P. (eds) (2012) *Language, thought, and reality: Selected writing of B. L. Whorf*. 2nd edn. Cambridge, MA: MIT Press.

Chomsky, N. (2010) *Language and mind*. 3rd edn. Cambridge: Cambridge University Press.

Collier, V. P. (1987) Age and rate of acquisition of second language for academic purposes. *TESOL Quarterly*, 21: 617–641.

Cook, V. (1985) *Chomsky's universal grammar and second language learning*. www.vivian cook.uk/Writings/Papers/AL85.htm (Accessed July 2019).

Cummins J. (1976) The influence of bilingualism on cognitive growth: a synthesis of research findings and explanatory hypotheses. *Working Papers on Bilingualism*, 9: 1–43.

Cummins, J. (1979) Cognitive/academic language proficiency, linguistic interdependence, the optimum age question and some other matters. *Working Papers on Bilingualism*, No. 19: 121–129.

Cummins, J. (1981) The role of primary language development in promoting educational success for language minority students. In California State Department of Education (ed.), *Schooling and language minority students: A theoretical framework*. Los Angeles: Evaluation, Dissemination and Assessment Center California State University.

Cummins, J. (2000) *Language, power, and pedagogy: Bilingual children in the crossfire*. Tonawanda, NY: Multilingual Matters Ltd.

Cunningham, C. (2018) Terminological tussles: taking issue with 'EAL' and 'languages other than English'. *Power and Education*, 11 (1): 121–128.

Cunningham, C. M. (2017) *Saying more than you realise about 'EAL': Discourses of educators about children who speak languages beyond English*. PhD, York: University of York.

Danaher, J., Schirato, T. and Webb, J. (2006) *Understanding Foucault*. London: Sage.

Davila, B. (2016) The inevitability of 'standard' English: Discursive constructions of standard language ideologies. *Research Article*, 33 (2): 127–148. April 2016. https://doi.org/10.1177/0741088316632186 (Accessed July 2019).

Department for Education (DfE) (2013) *Schools, pupils, and their characteristics*. London: DfE.

Department for Education (DfE) (2017) *Statutory framework for the early years foundation stage: Setting the standards for learning, development and care for children from birth to five*. London: DfE.

Dewey, J. (1934) *Education and the social order*. New York: League for Industrial Democracy.

Diamond, A. (2018) Chomsky's language acquisition device: Definition and explanation. Available at: https://study.com/academy/lesson/chomskys-language-acquisition-device-definition-lesson-quiz.html (Accessed July 2019).

Donaldson, M. (1978) *Children's minds*. London: Harper Collins.

Foucault, M. (1972) *The archaeology of knowledge*. Bristol: Tavistock.

Foucault, M. (1980) *Power/Knowledge*. London: Pantheon Books.

Foucault, M. (1982) The subject and power. *Critical Inquiry*, 8 (4): 777–795.

García, O. (2009) Emergent bilinguals and TESOL: What's in a name? *TESOL Quarterly*, 43 (2): 322–326. June 2009.

Gogolin, I. (1997) The 'Monolingual Habitus' as the common feature in teaching in the language of the majority in different countries. *Per Linguam*, 13 (2): 38–49.

Halliday, M. A. K. (1985). *An introduction to functional grammar* (1st edn). London: Edward Arnold.

Krashen, S. (2004) The case for narrow reading. *Language Magazine*, 3 (5): 17–19.

Krashen, S. and Brown, C. L. (2007) What is academic language proficiency? Singapore Tertiary English Teachers Society (STETS) *Language & Communication Review*, 6 (1), 2007.

Lavendenz, M. (2011) From theory to practice for teachers of English learners. *CATESOL Journal*, 22 (1): 18–47.

Mac Naughton, G. (2005) *Doing Foucault in early childhood studies: Applying post structural ideas*. London: Routledge.

Mistry, M. and Sood, K. (2010) English as an Additional Language: Assumptions and challenges, *Management in Education*, 24 (3), July 2010. 111–114.

Mistry, M. and Sood, K. (2015) *English as an Additional Language in the Early Years: Linking theory to practice*. London: Routledge.

Moll, L. (1992) Bilingual classroom studies and community analysis: some recent trends, *Educational Researcher*, 21 (2): 20–24.

National Association of Language Development in the Curriculum (NALDIC) (2006) *Response to the Rose review of the teaching of reading and the NLS*. Watford: The National Association for Language Development in the Curriculum.

National Association of Language Development in the Curriculum (NALDIC) (2011) *The distinctiveness of EAL pedagogy*. Available (online) at: www.naldic.org.uk/eal-teaching-and-learning/outline-guidance/pedagogy/ (Accessed Dec 2011).

National Association of Language Development in the Curriculum (NALDIC) (2015) *Supporting bilingual children in the early years*. Available (online) at: www.naldic.org.uk/eal-teaching-and-learning/outline-guidance/early-years/ (Accessed September 2017).

National Association of Language Development in the Curriculum (NALDIC) (2018) *Attainment: What does the national EAL assessment data tell us?* https://naldic.org.uk/https-ealjournal-org-2018-01-29-eal-english-proficiency-and-attainment-what-does-the-national-eal-assessment-data-tell-us/ (Accessed July 2019).

Ofsted (2019) Inspecting subjects 3–11: Guidance for inspectors and schools, p. 27, in Schools inspection handbook, January 2019). https://assets.publishing.service.gov.uk/government/uploads/system/uploads/attachment_data/file/801615/Schools_draft_handbook_180119_archived.pdf) (Accessed July 2019).

Rogoff, B. (1990) *Apprenticeship in thinking: Cognitive development in social context*. New York: Oxford University Press.

Salford, K. and Drury, R. (2012) The 'problem' of bilingual children in educational settings: policy and research in England. *Journal of Language and Education*, 27 (1): 70–81.

Sapra, R. (2011) Concept formation: A linguistic construct. *International Journal for Cross-Disciplinary Subjects in Education (IJCDSE)*, 2 (4), December 2011, pp. 502–509.

Scarcella, R. (2003) *Academic English: A conceptual framework*. Santa Barbara: The University of California Linguistic Minority Research Institute Technical Report 2003–1.

Smith, A. B. (2016) *Children's rights: Towards social justice*. New York: Momentum Press, LLC.

Vygotsky, L. (1978) *Interaction between learning and development.* (Trans. Cole, M.) Cambridge, MA: Harvard University Press.

Vygotsky, L. S. (1986) *Thought and language.* Massachusetts: MIT Press.

Wellington, J. and Osborne, J. (2001) *Language and literacy in science education.* Milton Keynes: Open University Press.

Wood, D., Bruner, J. and Ross, G. (1976) The role of tutoring in problem solving. *Journal of Child Psychology and Child Psychiatry,* 17: 89–100.

7

Developing Culturally Appropriate Pedagogy (CAP) in Early Years

When you have finished reading this chapter you will

- understand the importance of culturally appropriate pedagogy
- know the philosophical and theoretical foundations of culturally appropriate pedagogy
- be aware of how a culturally appropriate pedagogy model has the potential to increase equity
- be better informed on how culturally appropriate pedagogy can help to adapt learning for children with EAL in Early Years

Overview of chapter

The introduction sets out how the concept of culture links to Early Years education and why it is important in relation to planning and teaching. The chapter then looks at what is meant by the notion of cultural identity and why this concept is important in education in terms of meeting the needs of children like those with EAL. It focuses on the work of key theorists like Vygotsky (1978) among others as a theoretical foundation to help understand why we need to go beyond just acknowledging culture and cultural identity in our settings. Next, the notion of cultural identity is explored before the chapter debates what is perceived as Cultural Appropriate Pedagogy (CAP) prior to presenting our CAP model which, offers practitioners strategies they can deploy to ensure that curriculum and pedagogy that reflects the ideologies of inclusive education for children from diverse cultures and ethnicities like those with EAL. Finally, we emphasise the importance of CAP and how using CAP in Early Years can enrich children's experiences.

<u>Key words</u>: culture, pedagogy, inclusion, relationships, diversity, equity

Introduction

The role of education is to help raise awareness of the positive value of cultural (and linguistic) diversity, meaning the opportunities offered through the Early Years framework should promote realistic and positive ideas about inclusion. The culture of children is paramount in their learning because it gives them a frame of reference to link their understanding to, especially in the Early Years. We have a mosaic of social identities (Harro in Adams *et al.*, 2013: 27) in which there exist multiple cultures based upon the diversity of people. It is therefore important to learn about different peoples 'history, culture, language and identity' (UNESCO, 2003: 33). But we are aware that there are challenges and opportunities for Early Years practitioners in promoting the concept of culturally appropriate pedagogy. To foster a more inclusive ideology requires an ethos of mutual understanding, feeling valued and having empathy shown by practitioners towards all children in their care. This is because children may come from different homes and cultures, and for some children they may have faced difficult circumstances due to poverty, fractured home or vulnerable backgrounds and therefore have different cultural identities. Our CAP model for Early Years settings promotes the culture of inclusion where children from different backgrounds feel they are wanted, loved, valued and shown that they have huge potential to succeed. Singh (2011) reminds us of the need to share stories with children from diverse backgrounds that enrich the cultural milieu and offer us different perspectives. This demands us to offer deliberate policy development and action to ensure the inclusion of all children. Where practice is exclusionary at times, we need settings not to discriminate against any group as laid out in equality legislation, thus leading to settings recognising all children equally.

The next section looks at what cultural identity is and the factors that require consideration in forming an individual's cultural identity. Then, we discuss how Socio-Cultural Theory (SCT) forms the basis of CAP, before progressing onto the application of SCT in Early Years settings.

Cultural identity

One definition of culture is about shared ways of being, knowing and doing as suggested by Kana'iaupuni *et al.*, (2010). Their research was based on a Hawaiian setting and showed that culture-based educational strategies 'positively impacted student outcomes ... and ... by teaching and learning about children's own culture improved their social relationships' (ibid.: 1), because practitioners allied themselves more closely to the Hawaiian culture. Additionally, Ndhlovu (2007) found that the use of languages forms the 'prime markers of ethnic and national identity' (p. 131) so, settings should celebrate linguistic diversity to ensure children feel good about themselves and their own different identity. But we need to be cautious in defining cultural identity as this is a multiple concept. The dynamics of migration mean we are seeing individuals now having multifaceted identities 'encompassing occupational, class, regional, local, gender, religious, political and economic factors' (Barbour, 2000: 9). Furthermore, Barbour (2000: 9) contends that:

> The cultural coherence of an ethnic group is often partly expressed by language [in the sense that] a distinctive language may help to demarcate the ethnic group from other groups, and a common language may facilitate communication and hence coherence within an ethnic group.

This means that the language(s) children speak or hear in Early Years settings are always closely linked with their ethnic and national identities. But in a setting, you may have multiple languages present which poses interesting dilemmas and opportunities for practitioners in terms of greater creativity in their teaching and learning, planning and implementation. Early Years leaders must continue to review their policies and systems to challenge any factors that lead to oppression or inequity for any members in their settings. This calls for developing and modelling positive relationships with children, taking care as to not undermine children's self-esteem through unintentional actions such as using words or phrases inappropriately or out of context. We need to empower children to 'deal confidently and fairly with each other and with others in an unjust society' (Siraj-Blatchford and Clarke, 2001: 5).

SCT has its origins in the writings of Vygotsky (1978) and argues that our brains process external activities like children with EAL mimicking home language(s) through what they hear from family to create new thinking and behaviours. In this theory, the use of language is the main way of mediation, although other forms of mediation may be through symbolic artefacts (such as languages, literacy, numeracy) as well as material artefacts and technologies. Practically speaking, developmental processes take place through participation in cultural and linguistic settings such as family life and peer group interaction in settings and other social activities. This implies Early Years practitioners need to further encourage children's higher-order mental functions through activities like memory games, logic thought situations and participation in culturally organised activity. So, SCT highlights the role of imitation in learning and development in children. The Zone of Proximal Development (ZPD) is a useful conceptual and pedagogical tool that practitioners can use to better understand aspects of children's emerging capacities that are in the early stages of maturation. We maintain that improved understanding about social and cultural aspects of children through SCT go some way to better understanding why cultural identity is a central cogwheel in our CAP model.

The Early Years framework is grounded in promoting learning that reflects a global vision and the world as experienced by young children. For children with EAL, this means making the effort to talk with them about their daily lives, their stories and their aspirations, and using a wide variety of pedagogical strategies linked to individual child's different learning styles as illustrated by Gay (2010: 31–32), who talks about the importance of 'children to know and praise their own, and each other's cultural heritages'. We also emphasise that practitioners should continue to form links with communities from different minority ethnic groups and cultures to improve their own knowledge and understanding about cultures, faiths, customs and traditions. Furthermore, higher education institutions with teacher education programmes should adequately prepare teachers for culturally responsive pedagogy and place students into a variety of both mono- and multicultural settings so that students are better prepared to work with diverse children which we understand is challenging if geographical locations are not multicultural.

Philosophical underpinning

The notion of culture related to education in this chapter can take different hues from sociolinguistics, psychoanalysis, philosophy, the history of ideas, cultural studies and media studies – which all provide ways of looking at and understanding the field of cultural pedagogy beyond the knowledge presented in this chapter. Thinking about key individuals influencing cultural pedagogy, we can draw on philosophers like Heidegger, Derrida and Foucault. The work of Foucault (1970), the thinker most strongly associated with a far-reaching re-description of modernity, helps us to explore what he called 'regimes of truth'. Hence, truth can be interpreted in different ways by different people in different contexts. Asking a child with EAL about their culture may lead to one explanation, yet another child from the same cultural group may elicit a different view. Who is to say what is right and what is the truth? There could be multiple interpretations of truth, requiring a 'relationship between the speaker and what he says' (Foucault, 2001: 12). Furthermore, this requires the interpreter to develop a language that opens thinking by questioning everything and by looking carefully at the question of questions (Heidegger, 1962; 1968). The work of the philosopher Derrida (1973) offers us views about the deconstruction of Western metaphysics, opening deconstruction and critique of ideas, for example, an approach to understanding the relationship between text and meaning. This is like critiquing the teaching and learning policies in settings in relation to how they embed culturally appropriate pedagogy and its equality policy on cultural diversity, which in turn requires opening spaces for dialogue for action.

Theoretical perspective associated with CAP

This section will begin with what Vygotsky (1978) says about learning in that practitioners have a crucial role in helping children make meaning of their surroundings through social interaction. Vygotsky (1978) came close to making the link between activity and consciousness and showed how play determined the formation of thinking and formed a key learning activity for children. This notion is recognised by other psychologists noting that culture shapes cognitive development by influencing what and how a child learns from their surroundings. For example, a young Bengali girl learning Arabic through formal teachings by the Imam (priest) in her community in an informal context could use her new-found knowledge in telling stories through play.

In Early Years, Vygotsky's ideology translates to children needing to be exposed to many different practitioners to help children make meaning of their surroundings, of self and of others. As early as the 1930s, Vygotsky's socio-cultural theory of learning encouraged the use of cultural tools to develop learning. In Vygotskian terms, such cultural tools may be different ways of thinking as well as ways of doing like inherited language, learned behaviours or ideas developed through experience. For example, on visiting Delhi recently, one of the authors observed street children who had never gone to school selling hand-made kites to passers-by on the street and they used refined mathematics skills to carry out the bartering and cost process. It could be argued that social interactions in different cultures, languages and experiences expand childrens' depth of knowledge. The more experiences a child is exposed to, the more enriched their world will be. Vygotsky proposed three ways in which learning is passed along to an individual:

1   Imitating learning – when the child copies another child/person
2   Instructed learning – when a child recalls direction given by the practitioners and then puts it into practice in play
3   Collaborative learning – this takes place when a group of children cooperate with one another to learn and achieve a specific goal together

(adapted from Woolfolk *et al.*, 2008: 61)

We give brief examples of how these three ideas work for children with EAL next:

Example 7.1

Amelia is a 2-year-old Bengali girl who quickly learned that by mimicking what her older sister did to get a sweet for picking a toy up and putting it into a toy box, she too could get such a reward.

Example 7.2

India is 6 years old, from a mixed heritage family, and after hearing an exciting adventure story of a bear walking in the woods she soon re-told and re-enacted the story using her own toys.

Example 7.3

Kaya, an 8-year-old Malaysian girl, worked with her friends to make a pizza at home as she had learned to do this when she was part of a group of friends and given this task under adult supervision.

These examples show that such scenarios are not unique or culturally specific to children with EAL, as learning happens all around children and with guidance from an adult, their cognition is enhanced in social situations.

What is CAP?

Settings generally have an organisational culture founded on their values, beliefs, traditions, customs, mission and vision. They also have particular ways of doing things, or thinking about practice like; what expectations do practitioners have of diverse children in their setting (by gender, ethnicity etc.), how are they accountable to different stakeholders, is there a culture of collaboration between practitioners, is there a culture of organisational learning (Senge, 1990) which we call the culture of the setting. In child-centred settings it is important to consider practice that adopts an appropriate culture for different learning contexts, whether culturally diverse or not. Therefore, CAP offers an ideological approach that can be embedded in Early Years to ensure practitioners develop a more inclusive curriculum.

With increasing social problems, increasing migration and the need for settings to be even more inclusive to meet the needs of disadvantaged children, social justice calls for change in the culture of a setting. This means reviewing teaching and learning approaches, staffing, training, resources to educate for an information-based technological and competitive global economy. We believe that a culturally informed setting will address these issues in pursuit of an inclusive culture through critiquing the utility of our CAP model. But we have scepticism about practitioners' knowledge, experience or indeed the *will* to *really* reflect on their own practice to question its validity, accessibility or viability for children with EAL. A tokenistic approach to developing CAP to suit the needs of children with EAL will not suffice for modernity, therefore calling for stronger leadership that delivers justice and equality is a must. It is time for leaders and practitioners to move from rhetoric to real engagement with diversity. Each setting needs to make greater strides to attract greater diversity of staff rather than driving out diversity (Milliken and Martins, 1996), that is, people from a much wider range of backgrounds and cultures are needed in this profession. In the leadership chapter (Chapter 10), we introduc the idea about leaders having to lead *for* diversity, which means to increase the diversity of people in different roles, and *with* diversity, that is leading within a diverse group or team.

Considering these arguments, we have proposed a model that puts the concept of *culture* more centrally within planning for teaching and learning in the Early Years context. To achieve equality and social justice for inclusive education, we should find out through research how to demonstrate the appropriateness of culturally appropriate pedagogy. To help us develop a robust understanding of culturally appropriate pedagogy, we need to learn from other cultures and to be mindful of different perspectives to fill in our gaps in knowledge. Furthermore, it is important to understand that no curriculum or framework is politically neutral including the EYFS which means practitioners need to critically review the curriculum to ensure it meets the needs of diverse children. Time for feigning allegiance to hollow ideologies has passed, so now we need action to ensure that the impact of cultural understanding is clear in opportunities presented for our children with EAL.

Model of CAP

Our model of Culturally Appropriate Pedagogy (CAP), shown in Figure 7.1, has the following characteristics: equity, diversity, social justice, gender, ethnicity, customs, traditions, religion/faith, beliefs/values, collective identity and languages. All these characteristics are inter-related and informed of and by each other – philosophically and pedagogically. At the centre of the circle in Figure 7.1 is pedagogy that is culturally informed and influenced by commitment to diversity and equity principles through social justice which lies at the heart of many Early Years' practitioners working practices. The internal arrows to and from the centre connect to each outer circle in Figure 7.1. These represent connectivity where the setting develops their strategies for action. For example, connecting Culturally Appropriate Pedagogy in Early Years to the language and equity characteristic will require discussion about staffing and resources. This needs to be incorporated within a setting's action plan (which most settings have) then, allocating a key person to lead the action followed by monitoring and evaluating outcomes of this action.

This is our vision of how we envisage our CAP model (Figure 7.1) to be implemented in practice as discussed next.

Regardless of whether a setting is multicultural or mono-cultural, all children are entitled to high quality education. Mistry and Sood (2013) in their study of multicultural and mono-cultural primary settings with Early Years

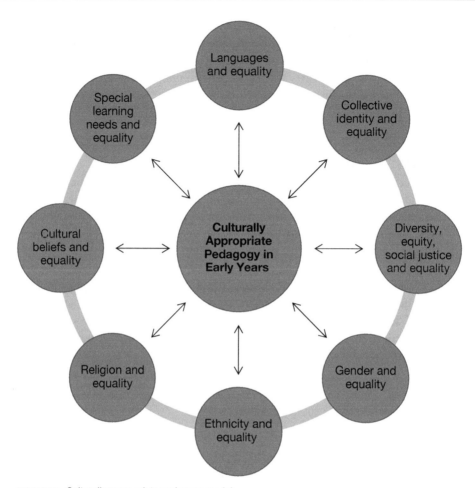

FIGURE 7.1 Culturally appropriate pedagogy model

phases explored how diversity and equity are promoted through the Early Years framework. Their findings suggested that pedagogical approaches need to make a positive difference in the lives of all children which requires innovative re-thinking of Early Years setting policy and practice on how to *ma*ke this difference. We suggest in our CAP model (Figure 7.1) that Early Years practitioners need to demonstrate and teach children how to develop empathy, build relationships with fellow peers and others, encouraging collaborative cultures leading to a commitment to the well-being of all through play and discovery learning. This is further emphasised through the DfE (2016: 1) document which states 'all schools will continue to play ... in promoting ... values of mutual respect and tolerance for all backgrounds and faiths'. According to Carroll *et al.* (2018), understanding values can be done as part of teaching and learning and is 'critical to the learning process' (p. 79). Indeed, practitioners need to continue to develop in children the values of respect and tolerance by questioning everything (Heidegger, 1962) and promoting independent thinking so they can develop empathy with others. We can never be sure practitioners hold the same values so the challenge in Early Years is how practitioners align different values in the interest of their children and educational practice. Therefore, it is important to explore each characteristic from the CAP model in Figure 7.1 as discussed next starting with languages and equality and going around clockwise.

Languages and equality

In our model (Figure 7.1), languages and equality are about all languages being valued and respected equally. Although, we do appreciate that Standard English is deemed to be superior to any other language(s), that does not mean to say that other languages should be devalued. The importance of celebrating different languages reflecting the diversity of children population in a setting is an important pre-requisite for an inclusive education. For example, if children with EAL are marginalised (Foucault, 1981) then their life chances are reduced, but if they undergo 'culturally and linguistically appropriate education', then they 'are better equipped to ... participate in wider society' and become more successful learners (Skutnabb-Kangas, 2009, xvii). The CAP model in Figure 7.1 therefore needs to incorporate the cultural knowledge and experiences (Gay, 2010) of children with EAL to help make learning more meaningful for them. The focus for children with EAL is not only on academic achievement, but also on valuing the importance of their cultural heritage and identity by embedding pedagogy and curriculum into the fabric of childrens' lives. This requires all communities of practitioners, children and families co-constructing knowledge, insight and linguistic awareness into their teaching and learning, indeed interweaving such a philosophy across all aspects of setting life, policy and practice, which can be challenging.

With language learning for children with EAL, a culturally responsive consideration (Gay, 2010) of the most commonly used language at home is required especially if unfamiliar languages are used. This is because differences in language usage influences childrens' abilities in reading, writing, speaking and listening in languages other than English, resulting in different language competencies. However, settings need to be mindful that diversity management through interventions are not exclusive to specific minority ethnic children only, whilst other minority ethnic groups are ignored. The implications for practice include: a need to widen the meaning of diversity and inclusiveness beyond the current focus on children with EAL initiatives; a need for practitioner development on the topic of minority ethnic inclusion; and a need to engage in dialogue about minority ethnic group inclusion with the school community as demonstrated by the next case study.

Case study 7.1

Dipeeka is a 2½-year-old girl coming into a nursery. After her mother had left her and gone home, she got upset by the strangeness of her new environment in that she could not talk and speak her language (Punjabi). But the teaching assistant Manpreet was Punjabi speaking and soon got Dipeeka settled. Manpreet started to talk with Dipeeka about her favourite toy, usual home routines, what food she liked/disliked. This built up over the term and Dipeeka soon settled and became a confident user of English and readily formed friends in the setting. Both Dipeeka and Manpreet shared story time with the class where Dipeeka was able to use her home language which was celebrated by all.

Key point

• It is important to allow and encourage children with EAL to use their home language so that they become confident speakers.

This case study shows that the promotion and celebration of child's home language cannot be emphasised enough as this helps children to feel settled, to be accepted and form friendship to learn through co-operation. Such activities help children to develop successful relationships with practitioners (Siraj-Blatchford and Clarke, 2001) and their peers.

Collective identity and equality

This section is about being aware of childrens' identity individually and how this can change when part of a group. Each child's identity is important to them and is influenced by their family and social context like friendship and schooling amongst other factors. Difference, in terms of identity is a source of richness, a resource to be welcomed but contrary to such rhetoric, difference is often experienced as difficult and discomforting, providing the grounds for division and exclusion (Reynolds and Trehan, 2003: 163). To theorise the term collective identity in any depth in this chapter is not possible as it requires profounder analyses of sociocultural issues, critically reflecting on beliefs, knowledge, biography and values. However, what might work in Early Years settings is to develop better critical consciousness in practitioners and encourage them to appreciate possibilities of multiple perspectives about collective identity, diversity and justice, and then engage in actions to enhance equality.

Arguably, one can take on multiple identities known as intersectionality of identity (Ecklund, 2012) which refers to the way in which an individual symbolises within the self various identities formed by their cultural, ethnic, geographical and group backgrounds. Intersectionality offers an opportunity for people to understand the numerous influences of the diverse cultural group values, norms and expectations that contribute to the complex individual identity. For example, a child with EAL may hold multiple intersecting cultural identities because a child's family member could each signify 'intersectionality of identity within the family unit' (Hawkins, 2014: 121). Therefore, practitioners need to demonstrate knowledge of intersectionality of identity and skill in working with multiple cultural identities in children and families they serve. But this can pose a challenge for settings where the diversity of staff does not reflect the diversity of its community or indeed if they have not had the opportunity for wider staff development in terms of gaining experience in different communities of young children.

For reflection and discussion

• Why is it important to embrace an individual child's identity?

Each child is unique as emphasised in the EYFS (DfE, 2017), so a practitioner will do everything possible to embrace a commitment to equality. By knowing an individual child well their needs can be assessed to give them every opportunity to have equal access to reach their potential. An individual's identity, to coin an analogy, is reflected in the clothes they wear, their personality and character, the colour of the skin they show off and the language they speak, which needs nurturing and celebrating.

Diversity, equity, social justice and equality

We are in no doubt that the foundations of learning, good habits and being aware of self and others starts in the Early Years and has an impact on future outcomes. Children are also developing their moral compass by learning and mimicking the attitudes and values of their family, friends, culture and society (Vygotsky, 1978). It is the right time in Early Years for children to begin learning about ethnicity and language differences and forming positive attitudes towards difference and diversity. Practitioners too can enhance their own cultural awareness by learning few words in the language of a child with EAL and by being aware of their customs, their beliefs and their interests through daily teaching and pedagogy. Here, children are empowered as co-constructors of knowledge alongside practitioners (Piaget, 1952).

When we use the term diversity in common usage it denotes a range of differences. But it is not as simple as this because the term diversity has so far been used un-problematically, but it is, of course, highly problematic. The concept of difference points to notably observable difference, such as ethnicity and gender, and non-observable difference, such as educational background. Milliken and Martins (1996) noted that the emotional response is likely to be stronger and prejudice more likely to follow when difference is visible and that some differences matter more than others to some people. The inescapable deduction is that diversity is a social and political construct by the majority group and, as such, likely to serve their ends (Lumby *et al.*, 2005).

Consequently, practitioners have a moral duty of guiding children towards a more positive attitude towards what it means to be different under the guise of equity and justice. Equity is an approach to try to address some of the inequalities through fairness that exist in society as every human being has a right to benefit from additional consideration according to need. One example is how to help children with EAL access the curriculum to ensure fairness of opportunity. This can only happen if practitioners have a positive attitude and a better understanding of fairness and what it means to enable them to respond to discriminatory behaviour that could lead to oppressive action to those oppressed.

Social justice requires deliberate and specific interventions to secure equality and equity. Early Years practitioners need to understand that social justice requires specific interventions for children with EAL so they can access the curriculum through discourses of fairness, which is a challenge within itself. We say this because the impact of stereotyping, prejudice, discrimination and racism towards minority ethnic groups remains an area of potential inequality in the education sector. Part of Locke's philosophy implied that leaders and practitioners need to act to help level society which is crucial for children with EAL to help them have access to the same opportunities as their monolingual peers. This also means they need to look at the curriculum to ensure that 'whiteness is not the norm against which everything else is measured' (Lumby and Coleman, 2016: 117). Hawkins (2014) however, declared that 'teachers may struggle to find suitable pedagogical strategies that work to support and promote teaching for social justice and inclusion' (p. 121). We do not accept this view as there are many resources available nowadays to enrich the Early Years phase from key texts to web sources (such as NALDIC), to observing good practice in a range of different multicultural settings and building partnerships with a range of different settings to share experience and practice ideas. Our CAP model encapsulates the ideologies of diversity, equity, social justice and equality as inter-related factors which should underpin the Early Years pedagogy and the part practitioners play is vital to bring the rhetoric into reality for action.

For reflection and discussion

- Evaluate your setting's policy context in relation to children with EAL. How is this policy different for these children who have additional support needs?

This discussion point allows the reader to critically look at their own policy documents for children with EAL and then drill down to see if any updates need to be added considering recent evidence and national directives. This reflection shows understanding the interplay between learning additional language(s), curriculum access and additional support needs, like language support for children with EAL is vital.

Gender and equality

Gender issues affect men, women and children as all are subject to gender stereotyping, and worse, are subject to sexual exploitation, bullying, sexual harassment leading for some to self-harm and having an impact on emotional well-being. We see subtle discrimination that disadvantages girls or issues relating to sexual identity (Lumby and Coleman, 2016; Ringrose *et al.*, 2013). There are concerns of the academic achievement of boys or assumptions about the stereotypical ways of performing 'male' laddish behaviour reflecting macho images (but not all boys conform to this image) or girls stereotypical image of compliant children (Lumby and Coleman, 2016: 80).We need to be careful not to assume that boys and girls display the same characteristics as 'gender intersects with ethnicity, class and religion' (ibid.: 80).

The gender imbalance in Early Years settings is glaring with the workforce being mostly females at approximately '99% despite policy shifts in favour of men working in this setting' (Roberts-Holmes and Brownhill 2011: 119). The debate that females are more caring, sensitive and creative (Browne, 2008) than men, has moved on but society still views men in Early Years settings as suspicious, deterring some men from entering the profession. This culture is slowly changing as shown by research carried out by Mistry and Sood (2015) in that we are seeing more men applying to teacher training courses, but the figure remains low in comparison with those of women, despite many positive initiatives by HEIs promoting such career pathways such as taster courses for men into primary schools. The gender imbalance may also be a result of the low status of the profession. So, we need a better understanding of gender stereotyping and how to make the Early Years sector more attractive to both men and women practitioners (Carrington *et al.*, 2008). Research with head teachers showed that practitioners were not always aware of the impact of gender (Fuller, 2013). Furthermore, the issue of gender and children with EAL in education appears to alert in people signs of 'silence, blindness and fear' (Rusch 2004: 19). So, we need strong leadership that promotes a culture of inclusion for practitioners, children and their families. It is only through dialogue with each other and the community that fears can be allayed.

The EYFS (DfE, 2017) makes it clear the need to understand that every child is a unique child and that children learn to be independent through positive relationships. The characteristics shown in the CAP model in Figure 7.1 have close connectivity to these two out of the four EYFS principles. In promoting cultural diversity in Early Years settings prominence on developing childrens' language and identities is necessary (Issa and Hatt, 2013). A recent study by Civitillo *et al.*, (2019) with German teachers in a secondary school setting found that more culturally responsive teachers promoted ethical values of care and compassion for all learners.

For reflection and discussion

- When observing boys and girls working in small groups, find an opportunity to record conversations between boys and girls regarding choice of toys. Are stereotypical gender choices evident?

Early Years settings use many successful strategies to counter gender stereotyping. But it is easy to disregard the subtlety of gender issues – who dominates the conversation in selecting the toy, who is showing leadership, who is not as assertive, who is portraying authority or submissive type behaviour in the above scenario? Fuller (2013) has noted that practitioners are not always aware of the impact of gender stereotyping in the learning of girls and boys. This suggests that it might be timely to revisit a settings gender equality policy to monitor how subtle discrimination that could disadvantage both girls and boys.

Ethnicity and equality

Ethnicity in sociological terms refers to a shared culture and a way of life. This can be reflected in language, religion, material culture such as clothing and cuisine, and cultural products such as music and art. In this section we emphasise that ethnicity is often a major source of social cohesion as well as social conflict. Whereas 'race' refers to physical differences that groups and cultures consider socially significant, whilst 'ethnicity' refers to shared culture, such as language, ancestry, practices and beliefs. Jenkins (2008) considers it is important to rethink the term ethnicity and how it works. Lumby and Coleman (2016: 108) refer to ethnicity in terms of culture and skin colour. Regardless of whether children are from a Black and Minority Ethnic (BME) background or not, all children should be able to 'learn and be respectful of difference' (McAllister, 2013: 1). In England, the EYFS statutory framework makes it clear that the legal requirement is to ensure:

> Providers *must* promote equality of opportunity and anti-discriminatory practice and must ensure that every child is included and not disadvantaged because of ethnicity, culture or religion, home language, family background, learning difficulties or disabilities, gender or ability.
>
> (DfE, 2017: 25)

Early Years settings need to (re)emphasise a commitment to equality of opportunity as a fundamental value. This term embraces related, often tricky words, terms like equity, social justice, inclusion, fairness, diversity and human rights. But we are mindful that the impact of racism on the educational outcomes of children with EAL and the aspirations of black minority ethnic practitioners has been the subject of much debate because racist practices and policies can lead to potential inequality for all groups but more so for minority ethnic groups (Miller, 2016; Troyna and Hatcher, 2018). Crucially, settings need to have the commitment of leaders, practitioners and governors that will provide justice and fairness for all. This requires dialogue with each other and the communities the settings serve to interrogate what these terms mean, consider how the language is used, and together move forward to look at theory to underpin good practice. Where there are marginalised groups, like children with EAL, it is appropriate to take a cultural approach, as developed in the CAP model (Figure 7.1), so that such groups are more strongly accepted and supported. In summary, this suggests a focus on the curriculum, relationships with parents and the local community and promoting a positive, inclusive overall setting ethos.

For reflection and discussion

- A nursery is set in a predominately multicultural, multi-ethnic, multi-faith and multilingual urban city. The head teacher says they do not just tolerate children because they are Sikh, Muslim, Hindu, Black or White but rather, they accept each as a unique individual.

This statement regarding tolerance certainly offers useful and challenging concept for reflection. Different views will arise in this debate and what is important perhaps is not the difference of views about specific words or concepts but the use of language to achieve shared understandings that underpin the ethos of inclusion.

Religion and equality

Researching and writing this section of the chapter proved to be quite challenging. This is because religion and faith constitute some of the most contested and difficult concepts to define because some see an overlap and some see meaning to be interchangeable in their meaning (Harris *et al.*, 2018). Religion is an organised collection of beliefs and world views that gives a code to lead our lives by. Over time these ethical codes, sacred texts and rituals may develop into cultural traditions. Faith is a personal journey one takes for spirituality and might be a key component in the lives of children and their families, and education could bring into arena yet more disagreement (Torevell *et al.*, 2013). The debate that continues centres on adopting the majority religion of the country that underpins religious education versus consideration of more inclusive approach informed of ethical and humanist values.

We are seeing more faith settings in UK and Ireland (Hammad and Shah, 2018). But whatever the denomination of schools, religious equality should lead to social cohesion, safety for minority ethnic groups and tolerant society (King, 2010). According to Lumby and MacRuairc (2018), we need an educational process that 'focuses on an explicitly inclusive approach to difference and diversity' (p. 4). For children of different faiths/religions, wearing a turban or niqab or specific jewellery may render faith visible, thus denote difference, provoke a reaction, and consequent discrimination. This will deeply affect their setting's experience. Goffman (2009) explores the notion of a stigmatised identity, requiring action by practitioners if such behaviour is noticed. Religion and equality may be contested terms but, Early Years settings need to continue to develop global citizens who share a set of values, across faiths and develop in children use of critical skills and confidence.

In terms of religion and equality, practitioners need to know how to interpret British values such as the rule of law and to *tolerance* of different faiths, showing *respect* for different faiths (Ofsted, 2015: 37), and being aware of similarities and differences amongst diverse children populations, whether in a mono- or multicultural/multilingual settings. The act of carrying out religious activities is not confined in settings alone, this is because we are seeing religious practices at home and across generations; religious education classes and places of worship and bridging home, settings and community.

In promoting intercultural/multicultural education, there is greater opportunity to develop in children an understanding about the psychology of how we respond to difference and an understanding of how world faiths have developed. Such approaches can be rare in Early Years settings, thus suggesting that many settings are not fulfilling their role in supporting religious equality, which forms both a challenge and an opportunity to make real the CAP model indicated in Figure 7.1. For practitioners, developing a more in-depth understanding of types and ideologies of religions within the settings is important to avoid offence and seeing diverse groups as distinct groups such as Christian, or Jewish or Muslims.

For reflection and discussion

- A quote in Lumby and MacRuairc gives an example of religious education lesson for very young children. Through a fantasy story about a letter covered in glitter from an angel led practitioner to ask children to think and talk about 'what did angels mean to them … within their own belief system' (2018: 27).

Using stories to develop the wonder of awe, discovery and imagination in children is a well-tried strategy in Early Years. So, perhaps this kind of example could be extended into the primary phase, because through story telling a practitioner can guide children into deeper understanding of what angels mean for Christians, and to look at stories from other religions such as where else are angels talked about. Of course, there may be children who do not believe in God and this offers a chance to reflect on that using imagination.

Cultural beliefs and equality

Under this umbrella we have included the terms values/customs/traditions in the CAP model in Figure 7.1. In a plural society, there are likely to be several customs and traditions carried out. A loose definition of a custom (also called a tradition) is a common way of doing things – an approach to behaviour of a group of people (Woolfolk *et al.*, 2008). You can have customs/traditions handed down from the past and during their journey they get modified, changed and moulded according to the country, culture or religion. We can see an example of a custom in the Islamic faith of giving time as a volunteer or money. A normal tradition/custom for a Hindu festival is Diwali which celebrates the festival of lights and brings with it the ritual of visiting families, taking and exchanging gifts/food with each other alongside some customary fireworks. An older Hindu-Gujerati custom often practiced is to give sweets like jalebis when a girl is born and penda for when a boy is born and offering sweets (mithai) to people at any religious ceremony or when celebrating the Hindu New Year. These are normative traditions and with changing times, the plural community in England for example may adapt such traditions to their own means. There are no longer hard and fast rules and it will be hard to moderate beliefs, attitudes and behaviour formed over many generations.

An ethos of a setting is informed of its stakeholders and together, they develop the culture embodying values such as inclusion, tolerance and empathy. Space needs to made in the Early Years framework and beyond to celebrate other cultures, learn about different traditions and customs through stories around the world, here, using children with EAL to share their experiences, including in their own language if they choose to do so. The nature of the curriculum and pedagogy must be assessed against the values of the setting and choices made of what is acceptable and what needs challenging. This leads to increasing equality where different cultural approaches are recognised to better support marginalised groups. We also believe that by giving children a voice, leads to participatory justice, thus equipping them to form social relationships. We need to further improve the notion of distributive justice – allocating resources to 'level the playing field' (Pickett and Wilkinson, 2010: 3). We recognise that not all practitioners recognise what culturally appropriate pedagogy looks like for children with EAL for example, so professional development is needed through knowledge and skills acquisition to translate commitment into action.

Boon and Lewthwaite (2015) offered a different perspective compared to our CAP model on how to develop culturally appropriate pedagogy, implying practitioner's need to:

- promote their ethics of care (like values of respect);
- endorse cultural values (like valuing children's cultural identity);
- plan their curriculum through culturally informed pedagogy (like literacy, developing independent learners, variety of teaching methods);
- create a climate that promotes good behaviour (like setting classroom expectations and encouragement of co-operative behaviours).

Such comparative approaches are worthy of further debate by leaders and practitioners in Early Years settings.

Special learning needs and equality for children with EAL

Finally, when discussing special learning needs within the concept of equality, we also include reference to disability, as these pose a challenge for leadership and practitioners in their application. To provide equitable provision requires adopting appropriate measures to support the learning of children with special needs, as implied in the CAP model in Figure 7.1. Here we have chosen to make a brief link to children with EAL who may also have an additional special need. For some, a child with EAL poses a 'problem' in the same way they attribute such a label for child with special needs. The concept of special educational needs came from the Warnock Report (DES, 1978) and defined as those who have a learning difficulty that calls for special educational provision to be made (Education Act 1996, Section 312, Online: legislation.gov.uk). Giving labels in this way only exacerbates issues of teachers and ITE students (Richards and Armstrong, 2016), and they go on to say that it is better to focus on individual children and how they learn rather than any labels attached to them. Mistry and Sood (2010) found in their study that some schools wrongly labelled children with EAL within the SEN category, thinking their language requirement constitute special needs. According to the NALDIC (2011), lack of fluency in English for children with EAL should not be thought of as a special educational need in cognition and learning.

Although all parents want the best possible outcomes for their child, it is perhaps worth being mindful that in some cultures, special needs of any kind can still be a taboo subject. This means that children with EAL could be labelled not only by practitioners, but also by members in their family and community for having any kind of special needs as well as having EAL as illustrated by the following case study.

Case study 7.2

A Hindu family who live in in the Midlands area in England has three boys aged 12, 6 and 4. The 12-year-old has autism so is classed as a child with aspects of EAL as well as SEN; the 6-year-old has a severe physical disability and is in a care home and the 4-year-old has no SEN or disability. When the parents go out to a social function, most of the time only the 4-year-old child accompanies them because they do not want their children to hear any negative comments like 'they are the ones who have disabled children'. Furthermore, when they have gone out to events as a family, they get stared at if the older two children call out or tap people on their arm or need help with eating. The family is caring and loving yet the societal pressures, real or perceived, haunt their everyday way of living.

This case study shows that the issue for the family is both cultural and religious as they perceive the society judges them as 'outcasts' and the subject of disability amongst some Indian families is not only a taboo subject, but for some is something to be ashamed of in terms of their children. The hidden assumption is if you do not talk about it, it will go away. Sadly, this perception is far too common in some cultures, but things are improving. From all our research carried out in Early Years settings to date in relation to children who have EAL, we have found that those parents from different cultures that have children with EAL and SEND are some of the most open minded, flexible and appreciative parents. This is because they are so grateful to practitioners and other specialist staff in helping them to help their child, because they may not get this kind of understanding and support in their extended family or communities. For Early Years practitioners this means that they need to show sensitivity and understanding goes a long way to embrace inclusion. Also, the care and support the children and the family need cannot be underestimated to ensure that children with additional needs do not grow up with negative perceptions.

Why is CAP important?

There are many reasons as to why CAP is important but, most importantly, it is about how settings can better understand and meet the needs of their children with EAL to ensure that optimal progress is made in a discreet way that also helps them to make permanent connections in their learning. CAP is also relevant for children with EAL as it maintains and develops their 'cultural competence' and develops in children a 'critical consciousness to challenge the status quo' (Woolfolk *et al.*, 2008: 715–716). Furthermore, CAP in education perpetuates and builds pride in the childrens' home culture according to Ah-Nee Benham and Cooper (2000, cited in Singh, 2011). Such a vision is likely to better succeed if the staffing reflects the cultural make up of their children to promote practice that is culturally responsive.

Too often formal education systems appear to ignore and underutilise the knowledge and experience that children with EAL bring to settings. As a result, children find it difficult to cope with the challenges that emerge from the so-called standard language of instruction (which in this case is English), which can ultimately alienate them. This needs to be addressed in the current pedagogy to reflect the cultural diversity of the children to help meet their needs as suggested by Gay (2010). For children with EAL, their cultural context frames their thinking and reasoning in sometimes very different ways and therefore this informs the way in which they communicate and use language, meaning it is vital for practitioners to construct 'culturally responsive pedagogy' (Wearmouth, 2016: 4). Here, children need to feel safe in their setting, parents need to know that there is cultural compatibility between home and setting if miscommunication and alienation is to be avoided. In addition, McAlpine and Crago (1995) argue it is best to avoid a culturally alien school, which is why successful pedagogy requires that practitioners become culturally literate as culture-based misunderstandings can create tensions between practitioners and children.

Linguistic identity

We turn next to the theme of linguistic identity as it forms a key focus of what culture is about, giving children a sense of belonging through offering them opportunities in the setting to use and practice their own language. In philosophical terms we might see an array of identities and ways of being (Lacan, 1968). We appreciate that language does not define identity, but it can help us express our identity or our perceived identity. For example, children with EAL may stick together with their peers because of commonality of culture or that they may speak the same language, thus giving them a sense of belonging to a group, for cultural security. Turning to ethnolinguistic identity theory from Giles and Johnson (1987), we find that the construct of linguistic identity is shaped by the linguistic landscape or context of the setting. Furthermore, Giles and Johnson (1987) proposed in their ethnolinguistic identity theory the importance of maintaining one's language. As we have noted previously, the language of any minority ethnic group is of value to them as this defines their identity and culture. However, talking with elders in some Asian communities has shown some children are maintaining their home language but invariably there is some erosion of such ability in children settling in England or those born here. This may be evidenced by undertaking a simple language audit amongst children with EAL in the setting. The ethnolinguistic identity theory suggests that children with EAL may use ethnolinguistic differentiation, such as code-switching, in their interethnic encounters meaning they may accentuate or attenuate their linguistic strategy like dialect which gives these children linguistic distinctiveness.

To illustrate this further, one of the authors of this book speaks fluent Gujerati with her family members and can switch to English simultaneously, without thought. The language or dialect code used is specific to those she is talking with because this varies, thus showing ethnolinguistic differentiation. Linguistic identity is about different groups of people having a common link between each other through the language they speak/write/understand. For example, a simple explanation is where Gujerati Hindus who speak Gujerati will be understood by other Gujerati speaking people. So, there is linguistic identity formed. Philosophically, there is an argument that minority ethnic languages in specific contexts are seen to characterise cohesion by encouraging positive practitioner-child relationship, and good relationships between setting and different sections of the community. This suggests settings must continue to cultivate and drive for linguistic and cultural harmony and build alliances with the community where the knowledge and understanding of particular minority ethnic groups. Such an ideological stance is likely to lead to better identity formation and offer relevant framework for understanding the marginalisation of and exclusion of certain minority ethnic groups.

However, as Anders-Baer *et al.* (2008) write:

> The dominant language medium of education prevents access to education because of the linguistic, pedagogical and psychological barriers it creates … most indigenous peoples and minorities have to accept **subtractive** education where they learn a **dominant** language at the cost of the mother tongue which is displaced, and later often replaced by the dominant language.
>
> (pp. 3–4, emphasis in original)

This means that at the core of cultural identity lies the notions of 'right *of* languages and right *to* languages' (Ndhlovu, 2007: 135). The argument is advanced by Ndhlovu in that, if the right of language is rejected then this 'affects entire linguistic communities' (ibid.: 135). This means that Early Years practitioners should not inadvertently undermine the language(s) children use or as we have witnessed when undertaking research in Early Years settings, where home language of a child with EAL is not encouraged between other children with EAL. Instead, greater credence is given to speaking English over other languages which might be appropriate in a given context, but we need to be celebrating all languages and the settings language policy should cater for valuing all languages. The right to language is more about an individual's right to one or more languages of choice. Thus, settings should celebrate the diversity of languages in their settings as language empowers an individual and promotes their self-worth and self-identity. By denying a child's right to language constitutes a form of marginalisation. This elaborate theorisation of the notions of right of languages and right to languages is therefore pertinent to this chapter.

How our model of CAP can help to support the EYFS

We propose that our CAP model in Figure 7.1 can help support and adapt aspects of the Early Years pedagogy in several ways. First, practitioners need to look for opportunities within the EYFS that can naturally embrace and embed the notions of cultural identity. Here, children with EAL can be co-constructors of knowledge (Piaget, 1952) and understanding through social interaction with others (Vygotsky, 1978) facilitated through a supportive learning environment.

Second, to ensure whether there is diversity or not amongst the setting population, practitioners need to develop a holistic approach to teaching and learning that embraces different cultures, languages and customs to ensure children feel valued, loved and safe. These approaches can be developed in the Early Years framework through four pillars stated in UNESCO (1996): learning to know, learning to do, learning to be and learning how to live together. The first pillar is about encouraging the development of intellectual curiosity and sharp critical faculties. The second pillar focuses on developing life-long learning habits that enable children to grow into adults with knowledge of work and work ethics. The third pillar develops a sense of freedom for children where they can experiment and develop independence of thought and personally develop. The fourth pillar relates to children needing to be taught tolerance, non-violence and the value of human diversity – so very much about children accepting, understanding and having empathy of other people and communities.

Third, for practitioners to ensure planning the curriculum (often planned as a Western norm) and pedagogy, is grounded in the values, norms, knowledge, beliefs, practices, experiences and language forming a diverse cultural, linguistic and minority ethnic groups. Any curriculum and pedagogy that is informed of majority ethnic group values and beliefs *alone* is likely to distance attempts at inclusive practice.

Good Early Years practice is underpinned by a philosophy that makes visible justice, equality, diversity and emancipation, for all genders and ethnicities, necessitating Early Years leaders' and practitioners' requirement for re-examining the ethics of practice – creating accessible language of engagement with children of diverse communities. We contend that Early Years practitioners and those in the primary sector need to teach children about fairness, rights and wrongs, justice, equality and human rights, many of the classical philosophical explorations of how to teach about and use the ideas of justice in pedagogy are under explored in the context of education (Rawls, 2007).

Key points

- The culture of all children is of paramount importance in supporting their learning.

- Several factors influence CAP and practitioners need to be aware of how they all interconnect with each other.
- Practitioners and leaders need to be aware of the sensitive aspects of CAP for children with EAL from being labelled to being ignored.

Summary

In this chapter we have attempted to permeate the discourse of culture in Early Years pedagogy through some philosophical debate. A CAP model is proposed to offer a mind map to Early Years practitioners to assess for themselves, in their context, strategies to help increase equality. Through opening spaces for effective communication with different stakeholders, Early Years settings need to continue developing a dialogue about some of the issue raised in this chapter like ethnicity, religion, culture, gender and diversity to promote the best outcomes for children and their families. Settings need to be braver to challenge thinking that views about children with EAL or their families as being in deficit, and instead looking at ways in which the setting's ethos and values are portrayed as a barrier to learning and access for children.

By examining the overt and hidden curriculum, settings must ensure that English Whiteness is not the norm against which everything else is measured. They cannot lump together groups of children because they have their own culture and identity that need to be recognised through staff development and through a positive mind-set of high expectations, tolerance and respect for all. In our research for this chapter, the key message that came through for us was to explicitly educate children, those with EAL, or with special needs or disability, to understand the psychology of intolerance (religion or sexuality or others) and to develop critical self-awareness and empathy. Interestingly, Furman and Shields' (2005) framework, in addition to our CAP model, can be used to critique curriculum and pedagogy and, where possible, add views of multiple perspectives against established set of values, rather than primarily one. Early Years settings must work towards a policy that embeds CAP.

References

Ah-Nee Benham, M. K. and Cooper, J. (eds) (2000) Indigenous educational methods for contemporary practice: In our mother's voice. Mahwah, NJ: Erlbaum.

Anders-Baer, L., Dunbar, R., Skutnabb-Kangas, T. and Henrik Magga, O. (2008) 46 Forms of Education of Indigenous Children as Crimes Against Humanity? Expert paper written for the United Nations Permanent Forum on Indigenous Issues (PFII), New York: PFII. In PFII system: www.un.org/esa/socdev/unpfii/documents/E_C19_2008_7.pdf (Accessed April 2019).

Barbour, S. (2000) Nationalism, language, Europe. In S. Barbour and C. Carmichael (eds) *Language and nationalism in Europe*. Oxford: Oxford University Press.

Boon, H. J. and Lewthwaite. B. (2015) Development of an instrument to measure a facet of quality teaching: Culturally responsive pedagogy. *International Journal of Educational Research*, 72: 38–58. www.sciencedirect.com/science/article/pii/S088303551 5000439#bib0105 (Accessed March 2019).

Browne, N. (2008) *Gender equality in the early years*. London: Open University Press.

Carrington, B., Tymms, P. and Merrell, C. (2008) Role model, school improvement and the 'gender gap': Do men bring out the best in boys and women the best in girls?, *British Educational Research Journal*, 34 (3): 315–327.

Carroll, J., Howard, C. and Knight, B. (2018) *Understanding British values in primary schools: policy and practice*. London: Sage.

Civitillo, S., Juang, L. P., Badra, M. and Schachner, M. K. (2019) The interplay between culturally responsive teaching, cultural diversity beliefs, and self-reflection: A multiple case study. *Teaching & Teacher Education*. Jan 2019, 77: 341–351. DOI: 10.1016/j.tate.2018.11.002.

Cummins, J. (1984) Bilingualism and special education. Clevedon: Multilingual Matters California State University, Evaluation, Dissemination and Assessment Center.

Cummins, J. (1978) Bilingualism and the development of metalinguistic awareness. *Journal of Cross-Cultural Psychology*, 9: 131–149.

Department for Education (DfE) (2016) *Educational excellence everywhere. The schools' white paper 2016*. London: DfE. Available (online) at: www.gov.uk/government/uploads/system/uploads/attachment_data/file/508447/Educational_Excellence_Everywhere.pdf (Accessed September 2018).

Department for Education (DfE) (2017) *Statutory framework for the early years foundation stage: Setting the standards for learning, development and care for children from birth to five*. London: DfE.

Department of Education and Science (DES) (1978) *Special educational needs. Report of the committee of enquiry into the education of handicapped children and young people*. London: HMSO.

Derrida, J. (1973) *Speech and phenomena and other essays on Husserl's theory of signs*, (Trans. Allison, D.) Evanston, IL: Northwestern University Press.

Ecklund, K. (2012) Intersectionality of identity in children: A case study. *Professional Psychology: Research and Practice*, June 2012, 43 (3): 256–264.

Education Act 1996, Section 312. www.legislation.gov.uk/ukpga/1996/56/section/312/2006-02-01 (Accessed April 2019).

Foucault, M. (1970) *The order of things: An archaeology of the human sciences*, (Trans. Sheridan, A. M.) New York: Pantheon.

Foucault, M. (1981) The order of discourse. In R. Young (ed.) (1981). *Untying the text: A post-structural anthology*. Boston: Routledge & Kegan Paul. pp. 48–78.

Foucault, M. (2001) *Fearless speech*. Los Angeles: Semiotext (e).

Fuller, K. (2013) *Gender, identity and educational leadership*. London: Bloomsbury.

Furman, G. and Shields, C. (2005) How can educational leaders promote and support social justice and democratic community in schools? In W. A. Firestone and C. Riehl (eds), *A new agenda for research in educational leadership*. New York: Teachers College Press. pp. 119–137.

Gay, G. (2010). *Culturally responsive teaching: Theory, research and practice.* 2nd edn. New York: Teachers College Press.

Giles, H. and Johnson, P. (1987) Ethnolinguistic identity theory: a social psychological approach to language maintenance. *International Journal of the Sociology of Language*, 1987 (68): 69–99.

Goffman, E. (2009) *Stigma: Notes on the management of spoiled identity.* New York, London, Toronto: Simon and Schuster.

Hammad, W. and Shah, S. (2018) Leading faith schools in a secular society: Challenges facing head teachers of Muslim schools in the United Kingdom. *Educational Management, Administration and Leadership*, pp. 1–17 (online).

Harris, A. H., Howell, D. S. and Spurgeon, D. W. (2018) Faith concepts in psychology: Three 30-year definitional content analyses. *Psychology of Religion and Spirituality*, 10 (1): 1–29.

Harro, B. (2013) The cycle of socialisation. In M. Adams, W. Blumenfeld, D. Catalona, K. DeJong, H. Hackman, L. Hopkins, B. Love, M. Peters, D. Shlasko and X. Zuniga. (eds) 3rd edn. *Readings for diversity and social justice.* London: Routledge.

Hawkins, K. (2014) Looking forward, looking back: Framing the future for teaching for social justice in early childhood education. *Australasian Journal of Early Childhood*, 2014, 39 (3): 121–128.

Heidegger, M. (1962) *Being and time* (Trans. Macquarie, J. and Robinson, E.) Oxford: Blackwell Publishing.

Heidegger, M. (1968) *What is called thinking?*, New York: Harper and Row.

Issa, T. and Hatt, A. (2013) *Language, culture and identity in the early years.* London: Bloomsbury.

Jenkins, R. (2008) *Rethinking ethnicity arguments and explorations.* 2nd edn. London: Sage.

Kana'iaupuni, S., Ledward, B. and Jensen. U. (2010) Culture-based education and its relationship to student outcomes. Honolulu: Kamehameha Schools, *Research and evaluation.* pp. 1–30. www.ksbe.edu/_assets/spi/pdfs/CBE_relationship_to_student_outcomes.pdf (Accessed March 2019).

King, C. (2010) Faith schools in pluralist Britain: Debate, discussion and considerations. *Journal of Contemporary Religion*, 25 (2): 281–299.

Lacan, J. (1968) *Speech and language in psychoanalysis.* Baltimore, MD: Johns Hopkins University Press.

Lumby, J. and Coleman, M. (2016) *Leading for equality-making schools fairer.* London: Sage.

Lumby, J. Harris, A. Morrison, M. Muijs, D. Sood, K. Glover, D. Wilson, M. with Briggs A. R. J. and Middlewood, D. (2005) *Leadership, development and diversity in the learning and skills sector.* London: LSDA.

Lumby, J. and MacRuairc, G. (2018) *All faiths and none: School leadership and religion in multifaith societies.* Southampton, UK: University of Southampton.

McAllister, N. (2013) BME children and young people draft action plan response. Early Years – the organisation for young children. Belfast. www.early-years.org/policy/docs/63.pdf (Accessed March 2019).

McAlpine, L. and Crago, M. (1995) The induction year experience in a cross-cultural setting. *Teaching and Teacher Education*, 11 (4): 403–415 July 1995. DOI: 10.1016/0742-051X(95)00009-9. www.researchgate.net/publication/222473065_The_induction_year_experience_in_a_cross-cultural_setting (Accessed March 2019).

Miller, P. (2016) 'White sanction', institutional, group and individual interaction in the promotion and progression of black and minority ethnic academics and teachers in England. *Power and Education*, 8 (3): 205–221 https://doi.org/10.1177/1757743816672880 (Accessed March 2019).

Milliken, F. J. and Martins, L. L. (1996) Searching for common threads: Understanding the multiple effects of diversity in organizational groups. *Academy of Management Review*, 21 (2): 402–434.

Mistry, M. and Sood, K. (2010) English as an Additional Language: Challenges and Assumptions. *Management in Education*, 24 (3) July (1–4).

Mistry, M. and Sood, K. (2013) Permeating the social justice ideals of equality and equity within the context of Early Years: Challenges for leadership in multi-cultural and mono-cultural primary schools. *Education 3–13: International Journal of Primary, Elementary and Early Years Education*, 43 (5): 548–564.

Mistry, M. and Sood, K. (2015) Why are there still so few men within Early Years in primary schools: views from male trainee teachers and male leaders? *Education 3–13: International Journal of Primary, Elementary and Early Years Education*, 43 (2): 115–127. DOI:10.1080/03004279.2012.759607.

National Association of Language Development in the Curriculum (NALDIC) (2011) Session 3 Overview of the inclusion statement Development and diversity Self-study task 3 English as an additional language and SEN www.naldic.org.uk/Resources/NALDIC/Teaching%20and%20Learning/Documents/eal-sen-trainingfile.pdf (Accessed April 2019).

Ndhlovu, F. (2007) The role of discourse in identity formation and the manufacture of ethnic minorities in Zimbabwe, *Journal of Multicultural Discourses*, 2 (2): 131–147, DOI: 10.2167/md073.0 p. 131 (Accessed March 2019).

Office of Standards in Education (Ofsted) (2015) *School inspection handbook*. Manchester: Ofsted.

Piaget, J. (1952) *The origins of intelligence in children*. New York: International Universities Press.

Pickett, K. and Wilkinson, R. (2010) *The spirit level: Why equality is better for everyone*. London: Bloomsbury Press.

Rawls, J. (2007) *A theory of justice*. Cambridge, MA: Harvard University Press.

Reynolds, M. and Trehan, K. (2003) Learning from difference. *Management Learning*, 34 (2): 163–180. https://doi.org/10.1177/1350507603034002001 (Accessed April 2019).

Richards, G. and Armstrong, F. (eds) (2016) *Teaching and learning in diverse and inclusive classrooms: Key issues for new teachers*. 2nd edn. London: Routledge.

Ringrose, J., Gill, R., Livingstone, S. and Harvey, L. (2013) Teen girls, sexual double standards and 'sexting': gendered value in digital image exchange. *Feminist Theory*, 14 (3): 305–323.

Roberts-Holmes, G. and Brownhill, S. (2011) Where are the men? A critical discussion of male absence in the Early Years. In *Professionalization, leadership and management in the Early Years*. L. Miller and C. Cable (eds), London: Sage. pp. 119–132.

Rusch, E. (2004) Gender and race in leadership preparation: A constrained discourse. *Educational Administration Quarterly*, 140 (1): 16–48.

Senge, P. M. (1990) *The fifth discipline: The art and practice of the learning organization*. New York: Doubleday.

Skutnabb-Kangas, T. (2009) MLE for global justice: issues, approaches, opportunities. In Skutnabb-Kangas, T., Phillipson, R., Mohanty, A. and Panda, M. (eds) *Social Justice through multilingual education*. Bristol, UK: Multilingual Matters.

Singh, N. K. (2011) Culturally appropriate education: Theoretical and practical implications. In J. Reyhner, W. S. Gilbert and L. Lockard (eds) *Honoring our heritage: Culturally appropriate approaches to indigenous education.* (pp. 11–42). Flagstaff, AZ: Northern Arizona University. http://jan.ucc.nau.edu/~jar/HOH/HOH-2.pdf (Accessed March 2019).

Siraj-Blatchford, I. and Clarke, P. (2001) *Supporting identity, diversity and language in the Early Years.* Buckingham, UK: Open University Press.

Snell, J. (2013). Dialect, interaction and class positioning at school: from deficit to difference to repertoire. *Language and Education* 27 (2): 110-128

Stubbs, M. (2008) What is Standard English? In Stubbs, M., 1986 *Educational linguistics,* Oxford: Blackwell, 83-97

Torevell, D., Felderhof, M. C. and Thompson, M. P. (eds) (2013) *Inspiring faith in schools: Studies in religious education.* Aldershot, UK: Ashgate.

Troyna, B. and Hatcher, R. (2018) *Racism in children's lives: A study of mainly-white primary schools.* First Published 1992, eBook Published 3 October 2018. London: Routledge.

UNESCO (1996) *Learning: The treasure within.* Hamburg: UNESCO Institute for Learning.

UNESCO. (2003) Language vitality and endangerment. UNESCO Ad Hoc Expert Group on Endangered Languages. Paris. www.unesco.org/culture/ich/doc/src/00120-EN.pdf (accessed July 2019).

Vygotsky, L. S. (1978) The role of play in development. In Cole, M., John-Steiner, V., Scribner, S. and Souberman, E. (eds) L. S. Vygotsky, *Mind in society: The development of higher psychological processes,* Cambridge, MA: Harvard University Press.

Wearmouth, J. (2016) Employing culturally responsive pedagogy to foster literacy learning in schools. *Cogent Education,* 4 (1).

Woolfolk, A., Hughes, M. and Walkup, V. (2008) *Psychology in education.* London: Pearson Longman.

8

No regulation to regulation in Early Years

When you have finished reading this chapter you will

- understand the history of Early Years education in England
- be aware of how changes in Early Years education has had an impact on practice
- understand the critical debate between the ideology of key founders and the impact of regulation in Early Years practice

Chapter outline

Historically, there has been little government intervention in Early Years education in England. This chapter will begin by briefly discussing the historical context of Early Years educational provision, followed by how Early Years education has changed in England through a series of progressive Educational Acts and Reports. This chapter extends some of the discussions started in Chapter 4 in relation to education for children with EAL namely, contested issues between key founders in terms of how young children learn best against a control approach advanced by the government in terms of curriculum and standards. Next, there is a deeper discussion of the discourses associated with the movement from no regulation in Early Years to regulation. A critical debate regarding the implications of the Early Years framework follows. The discussion then moves to what regulation in relation to the Early Years Foundation Stage (EYFS) framework means for practitioners and their practice towards children with EAL. Finally, the discussion moves to suggested ways forward in an Early Years regulated climate for children with EAL to ensure they are not disadvantaged.

Key words: no regulation, government intervention, regulation, goal orientated curriculum, standards

Introduction

From the beginning of the last century, Early Years education has undergone rapid changes. Some of these changes are a result of the industrial revolution where child labour was prominent in society through a range of Factory and Educational Acts. However, education in general and Early Years education specifically, has moved from an unregulated approach whereby education was perceived to be for the children of the wealthy in society, to the current approach of regulation. This is also supported by Lizardo (2004) who by citing Bourdieu's thesis on cultural reproduction infers an affiliation between social class status and educational attainment. Formal government intervention has increased in Early Years in an attempt to improve consistency of the quality of provision and standards across the sector. This began with the Desirable Learning Outcomes (DLOs) which was introduced in 1996 as a framework for Early Years settings (SCAA, 1996), followed by the Curriculum Guidance for the Foundation Stage (CGFS) framework in 2000 and the Early Years Foundation Stage (EYFS) framework from 2008 onwards. These curriculum frameworks are goal orientated as they indicate a number of targets to be achieved by young children within a given time frame. But the arising debate is how the new formal Early Years education is shaped, especially with the current emphasis on performativity which sits uncomfortably against the ideology of natural learning within Early Years education from key founders as discussed in Chapter 3.

Historical context of Early Years educational provision

As with other forms of state education, Early Years provision is rooted in socio-political context and regimes of truths associated with it at any one point in time. Understanding this point is important in deconstructing what lies behind change in Early Years provision and how these changes can be contested if they are detrimental to the education of children with EAL. This is because designing the curriculum fit for twenty-first century children requires practitioners to understand and critique what constitutes good Early Years learning based on values of entitlement, equality and inclusion for all.

Historically, there was little government intervention in Early Years at a time when education was not centrally funded. Hence, regimes of truth (Foucault, 1981) in relation to what young children need in educational contexts and what their education should comprise of, were dependent on the ideology of individual philanthropists, intentions and beliefs until the beginning of regulation following the 1988 Education Reform Act (HMSO, 1989), which aimed to reform education through policies being put in place to help raise standards. What we saw next was the introduction of a focused market-orientated approach to education which led to a greater degree of central regulation. This led to an on-going debate between a child-centred developmental curriculum on one hand by Rousseau (1993 from original works, 1762), Froebel (1895), Dewey (1934), Piaget (1952), and Montessori (1913) as explained in Chapters 2 and 3, and policy makers who tended to focus on settings' effectiveness through directed learning (Woodhead, 1989), measurement of progress, targets, and competition between institutions. The latter implies that addressing the learning needs of children with EAL poses a challenge to provision and practice when, for example, there is a one size fits all approach to policy and practice in education, as currently present through the EYFS framework (DfE, 2017).

How has Early Years in England changed?

This section discusses the debate between those who support an individualised child-centred approach to learning and those who support a more formal structured approach. It might be argued that although different views of children in Early Years from key founders (see Chapter 3) imply different provision and practice, at the same time regulation of provision and practice create different discourses related to the child (Foucault, 1981) as illustrated by Table 8.1.

In 1833 the Factory Act was passed to restrict the working hours of children in factories and furthermore, aimed to address the slavery nature of using

TABLE 8.1 Showing the impact and Early Years discourses related to key Acts and Reports

Key events	Impact	Discourses related to Early Years children
1833 Factory Act	An attempt to improve the working conditions of children.	Children under the age of nine were not allowed to work in factories.
1870 Education Act	Beginning of compulsory state education.	The church still played an important role in the education of young children.
1902 Balfour Act	Helped in the creation of local authorities.	Further reform in education.
1918 Fisher Act (also known as the Education Act 1918)	Raised school leaving age from twelve to fourteen.	Widening of nursery provision.
1923–1931 Hadow Reports	Distinct phases for primary and secondary education and further educational reform.	Discussion of what the primary curriculum should look like including some recognition to child development theories.
1944 Education Act	Stages in education.	
Role of local authorities		
Emergence of the curriculum	Beginning of regulation in Early Years.	

young children in industrial work (National Archives: no date). By restricting the working hours of children, the assumption was that their working conditions were improved. However, restricting working hours does not necessarily mean that working conditions were improved, rather, all it meant was that children had to endure terrible working conditions for less time per day. This meant that young children were not allowed to work in factories so the earning capacity of a family was reduced.

The 1870 Education Act led to the start of compulsory state education where the emphasis in relation to what children should learn was on reading, writing, arithmetic and religious education. The ideology here was to ensure that society had the basic skills they needed to survive making the three R's (reading writing and arithmetic) important. In addition, the church was heavily involved in education making religious education just as important as the three R's. Within discourses for children in Early Years, the church continued to play an important part in their educational provision as discussed in Chapter 2, as children attended only voluntary provision. Today we still see the emphasis on reading writing and number for all children including those in Early Years which stems from 1870, but now, there is less emphasis on religious education in both the Early Years and primary sectors as the religious nature of society has changed.

The introduction of the Balfour Act in 1902 further reformed education in that all primary schools were under the control of newly created local authorities which also had some responsibility for a general curriculum. Although there was also greater reform in secondary education with the introduction of grammar schools for specific sectors of society, the emphasis was still on how all education was being regulated in different ways. In the Early Years this meant control of education was beginning to be led by local authorities rather than the church, illustrating a change in society, with diminishing influence of the church. Today, this control of local authorities has diminished further as settings are now more responsible for their own management and finances.

The 1918 Fisher Act, also known as the Education Act of 1918, reformed education by raising the school leaving age from twelve to fourteen. This aimed to restrict children's working hours again and resulting in less money coming into the family home. Part of this Act suggested that primary education should become free so that all young children have access to educational provision implying that access to education was no longer deemed to be for the wealthy only. This Act also suggested that nursery education should be widened thus giving greater status to Early Years whilst being regulated at the same time.

One key feature of the Hadow Reports was the separation of education into primary and secondary phases, whereby primary education ended at the age of 11. Due to the inter war years this did not materialise until the 1944 Education Act, which is still evident in the two tier school system we see in parts of England today. Another feature of the Hadow Reports was what the primary curriculum should look like alongside the need to recognise the importance of child development theories. This discourse emphasises the importance of primary education whilst also beginning to regulate the type of curriculum deemed to be appropriate. Critically, the Hadow Reports were perceived as progressive in nature as they began to focus on a different way of learning in comparison to what had been the norm (traditional form of learning that was reticent of the time). However, Gillard (2006) suggests the 1931 Hadow Report say a 'good school is not a place of compulsory education', but a place where there is community of learning (1931: Introduction). Furthermore, the primary curriculum should be 'thought of in terms of activity and experience rather than knowledge to be acquired and facts to be stored' (1931: Section 75). The ideology of these reports seem to resonate with the ideals of philosophers like Plato in that learning is not a series of facts to be memorised, in contrast to the foundations of regulation.

The 1944 Education Act divided education into three sectors: primary, secondary and higher but, no formal reference was made to Early Years education implying once again the non-existent status of Early Years. The assumption here seems to be that any educational provision prior to primary school provision is perceived as a preparation stage for proper or real learning. This is because it is assumed that learning only happens in a school environment whilst children are seated at tables and chairs which contradicts the philosophy of key founders regarding how and when children learn. More responsibility was given to local authorities in managing schools and how best to meet the needs of children like those with special needs, but no reference was made to the diverse needs of children such as those with EAL. This suggests that meeting their educational needs was not perceived to be as important as meeting the needs of children with particular special needs. In addition, although the Act did not clarify the details of the curriculum, it did give schools the freedom to create their own as long as the focus on literacy and numeracy remained, so as to enable children to be successful in their eleven plus exam.

More critically, policy changes from the 1990s and into 2000 showed the government was beginning to centralise education in terms of curriculum content through the introduction of the National Curriculum in 1989 (DfEE, 1999), the Curriculum Guidance for the Foundation Stage in 2000 (DCSF, 2000) and the Early Years Foundation Stage in 2008 (DCSF, 2008). These changes suggested all children 'irrespective of ethnicity, language background, culture, gender, ability, social background, sexuality or religion' should have the opportunity to experience the same curriculum/framework (DfEE, 1999: 12). Since 2000, Early Years seems to be recognised as a distinct stage within its own right through the guidance frameworks now in place and more importantly, regulation is now evident in Early Years.

Discourses of unregulated Early Years provision

The development of Early Years provision at the beginning of the eighteenth century in England must be understood against a context in which child labour was evident during the rapid expansion of industry. Even though Factory Acts such as that of 1833 (BBC, 2014) attempted to control childrens' working hours in industry, young children still worked to support their family as discussed earlier. During the second half of the nineteenth century the 1870 Education Act, reinforced in 1880, made 'school compulsory between the ages of five and ten' to limit young children working in difficult conditions in industrial England, but the discussion being, as yet no formal educational provision was available for children under five (ibid.: 11).

One of the earliest nursery schools in Britain was established by the industrialist Robert Owen in 1816 for the children of cotton mill workers through promoting 'character formation and social training' (Wearmouth *et al.*, 2017: 3) by learning through play, a view influenced by Pestalozzi (1962). Owen's main ethos of early education was that, a young person's character is influenced by their 'environment and the community' in which they live (Wearmouth *et al.*, 2017: 6). His humanitarian approach aimed to address social reform through education. Later, establishments continued to include a focus on childrens' growth and well-being and learning through play. For example, the McMillan sisters began an outdoor nursery in 1913 to help address the health and well-being of poorer children in society, implying the discourse for younger children was that they needed separate educational provision (Nutbrown and Clough, 2013). Paradoxically, we are currently seeing an upsurge of ideas under the guise of well-being illustrating how times have changed.

The two World Wars created a fracture in society and the development of education for all children. After 1945, society, typical family life and working patterns began to change, leading eventually to a change in educational provision and practice generally. Until and somewhat beyond this point, Early Years education was not regulated and depended, as noted, on principles that its individual founders thought were important (as discussed in Chapter 3). Although the 1944 Education Act indicated nursery provision would be expanded, it was not until the Plowden Report of 1967 (HMSO, 1967) that provision began to be more prominent (see discussion in Chapter 4). The basis of nursery education stemmed from Dewey's (1902) principle of experimental learning and Montessori's principles (1913) of the importance of age appropriate materials for young children, both furthering the ideas of Pestalozzi (1962) and Froebel (1895) regarding play being crucial to childrens' learning and development. This was further supported by Isaacs who felt that young children should attend nursery as part of their 'normal social life' (1952: 31). Growth of other Early Years provision such as playgroups (indicating the continuance of the importance of play) and child minders became evident after

1960 but this was still mainly unregulated and unsupported by the government.

Critically, this movement of no regulation in Early Years education meant that education for the youngest children in society was not deemed to be important as they were not seen to be learning, but just playing – a view that is still echoed today. Here, the lack of understanding of the importance of play is influencing views such as this. Therefore, we suggest that the concept of play forms an overarching umbrella for learning in Early Years with connections made to areas of learning initially, especially for diverse children like those with EAL. Parents and families need to have information on how learning through play takes place in settings for given topics, in that way leading to change in perceptions of play.

Discourses of regulation in Early Years provision

The 1990s onwards showed significant changes regarding the quality of care and educational provision for young children and their families as highlighted by the Rumbold Report in 1990 which focused on Early Years education alone. Some attempt was made to regulate (Foucault, 1981) Early Years through the introduction of Desirable Learning Outcomes (DLOs) that aimed to improve and raise quality of Early Years provision (SCAA, 1996). However, in 2000 the Curriculum Guidance for the Foundation Stage (CGFS) (DfES, 2000) was introduced to regulate education for pupils aged 3–5 to raise standards, but emphasis here seemed to be on the concept of school readiness through target setting and children's performance (Adams et al., 2004), rather than the child-centred curriculum that many, such as Rousseau (1993 from original works, 1762), Froebel (1895), Dewey (1934), Piaget (1952), and Montessori (1913), had implied through their ideology (DfE, 2017).

In 2008, the EYFS (DCSF, 2008) framework combined phases from birth to three (which was unregulated) and three to five in an attempt to gain coherence and control (Foucault, 1981) over the range of Early Years settings. In 2012 the EYFS framework was revised from six areas of learning to seven, grouped under prime and specific areas (DfE, 2016). This division of areas into prime and specific is a clear indication of regulation and control intending to ensure all children, including those with diverse needs, learn and develop towards a prescribed template of core skills. Although some key features of the EYFS framework include learning through play with clear opportunities and experiences to explore, investigate and support challenge (as discussed in Chapter 3), the major focus is on the prime areas of learning and surveillance (Foucault, 1981) by settings on these areas, meaning Early Years practitioners are constrained in their approach to fostering learning. Rhetoric from the Department for Education (DfE), asserts the challenge for 'great teachers and leaders' is to achieve the 'vision for excellence in education' implying Early Years is a vital phase for setting the foundations of learning (2016: 11). However, whether this vision that is to be achieved through regulation and control is appropriate for all children is highly questionable.

Critical debate regarding the Early Years framework

Aspects of the EYFS framework can have some resemblance to international influences. First, the EYFS includes the importance of positive relationships (DfE, 2017) which can be linked to New Zealand's Te Whariki approach that also emphasises the importance of developing positive relationships between settings and families (Ministry of Education, 1996). Second, the EYFS identifies the interests of the child which can be linked to the Reggio Emilia approach that also emphasises the importance of leading learning from the children's interests (Edwards, Gandini and Forman, 1998). Next, the EYFS highlights the importance of outdoor learning which can be linked to the Scandinavian context with their prominence on the outdoor environment and forest schools (Maynard, 2007). However, we say that although these influences are important perspectives, the culture of the community behind each approach is different to that of England and therefore it is difficult to implant aspects of Early Years practice from around the world without thinking through the needs of diverse children. For children with EAL, these selected international perspectives maybe more useful because of their diverse cultures and differences in languages form the foundation of their Early Years approach as illustrated by the following case study.

Case study 8.1

Julie was a reception class teacher in a primary school and had been teaching in the same year group for five years. Twenty per cent of her class had EAL with the majority speaking Eastern European languages. Although Julie liked the consistency that the EYFS framework offered her Early Years team, she began to notice that the curriculum demands did not fit the needs of her EAL children especially if they were new arrivals or in the very early stages of learning English. In addition, she also felt helpless in understanding aspects of English language learning for EAL children as she was monolingual herself. Although she was familiar with some learning theories from her university days she was unsure how to implement these in practice for her EAL children.

So Julie began doing some reading on different Early Years approaches in Europe and started an inter-school dialogue with an Early Years teacher at a kindergarten in Finland that had children ranging from six months to starting school at the age of seven. Through video chat she was able to link the practice of the setting to her reading in terms of these factors:

- how the environment was set up
- how outdoor learning was central to all learning
- how social routines linked to the social aspects of the curriculum
- how communication with parents took place especially since most of the parents were at least bilingual.

Over time, Julie embedded some of the ideas from her conversations with the Finnish setting especially in terms of taking learning outside beyond general free flow. Slowly she began to notice that as she did more work in the outside setting with the children, her children with EAL began to grow in confidence and communicate their understanding. She felt that this was because her class saw outdoor learning as something that was fun in comparison to group activities based at tables inside. Therefore, she began her phonics and number learning outside through play that aimed to increase cognitive challenge. In that way she was able to use her ideas to adapt the EYFS framework to suit the learning needs of her EAL children.

Key point

- By collaborating and building up networks with other settings that have a higher proportion of different children with EAL, ideas can be shared and implemented to have a positive effect on both the practitioner and the children.

This case study shows that although the EYFS framework is useful, it is guidance which needs to be adapted to enable all children to access learning. For children with EAL, Julie's conversations with the Finnish setting were particularly useful as she was able to share the difficulties in meeting the language needs of children with EAL. In turn she was given a range of strategies to try out over time that were used in the Finnish setting for their children learning Finnish, especially as some children were used to hearing other languages in the home too. Illustrations from the study of Mistry and Sood (2010) shows how vital it is for settings who are unsure of how to meet the learning needs of their EAL children to connect and collaborate with other settings that have a higher proportion of children with EAL to share good practice.

According to Wood and Hedges (2016), curriculum theory in the context of Early Years 'remains underdeveloped' (p. 338) because Early Years education seems to be influenced by theories of development as well as how they are interpreted. As we have seen through this chapter so far, there is a debate between how much core subjects and skills should be taught to young children in comparison to play and learning creatively. The argument so far has been that learning processes are seen to be more important than learning outcomes as suggested by Wood (2014) which means that the link to curriculum theory lacks emphasis. Therefore, the EYFS (DfE, 2017) is the guidance through which the government controls the 'content and coherence' of learning (Wood and Hedges, 2016: 338). Furthermore, we are in agreement with Wood and Hedges (2016) in that there are two positions that need consideration. First, key founders ideology linked to how young children learn best. Second, the guidance given through the curriculum with a range of goals that need to be achieved are time bound. These two positions seem contradictory and controversial in nature and form the basis of this critical discussion.

From earlier on in this chapter we can see that Early Years education has moved from a laissez-faire approach towards a control-based discourse which had only been evident in relation to compulsory schooling (Wood and Hedges, 2016). At a rudimentary level, the introduction of the EYFS was aimed at gaining consistency in the sector through having structured guidance regarding areas of learning (subject content), knowledge, skills, understanding and dispositions in a progressive manner. However, we argue that the division of learning into prime and specific areas already indicates a level of hierarchy with the prime areas dominating learning, in which communication and language is a key feature. Furthermore, control of the EYFS takes place through Ofsted inspections, practitioner accountability, raising standards and measures of performance and outcome for both practitioners and children (Oates, 2010). The second position is based on the philosophy of learning (Chapter 3) and how the ideology of key founders is the essence of how young children learn best which is in direct contrast to position one.

Position one is the development theories considered in Chapter 4. Essentially the focus here is on how young children learn, grow and develop with an emphasis on their 'cognition, behaviour and competence' through explaining phenomenon such as the 'biological process, mechanisms for learning, social and emotional adaptation and explanations for individual differences' (Wood and Hedges, 2016: 389). Although the international perspectives of key founders has merit today, much of their ideology was based on a laissez-faire approach in that young children should be free to learn through play and explorative learning. However, as government intervention in Early Years began to increase as demonstrated by Table 8.1, structure and content became evident in Early Years and therefore development truths became evident in terms of what normal achievement should be. Critically, this shows a change in perspective from children learning naturally through play to evidence-based learning. This is not to say that play does not have value, rather the emphasis on learning in Early Years has changed to how curriculum content is structured and measured for childrens' progress. However, according to Roopnarine and Johnson (2013), there is extensive evidence that the learning and development of young children is promoted through play and guided by practitioners. Critically, this means that play has now become part of the discourse of control because opportunities for each area of learning can take place through play.

But despite this, there is still a debate about the role of play in Early Years pedagogy.

Part of the debate associated with play in Early Years is about allowing children the time to learn through play (as highlighted by key founders in Chapter 3) alongside the time needed for specific subject input. In addition, there is the debate as to the views of other stakeholders such as parents regarding whether they value the importance of play in learning or not because there is still the assumption that young children do not really learn anything in Early Years as all they do is play. Therefore, without an agreed understanding of the importance of play, pedagogy and learning, 'Early Years has become open to levels of control' that is evident in the EYFS framework (Wood and Hedges, 2016: 391).

Position two comes from the perspective that content, coherence and control are the central strands of the EYFS framework. Critically, the issue is how the interpretations of Early Years from the key founders in position one have been translated into position two. Evangelou *et al.* (2009) have suggested that the current EYFS emphasises three models of development which include constructivist, neuropsychological and interactionist as highlighted by Vygotsky's (1978) sociocultural theory. Therefore, there is a degree of influence from key founders but we argue that that with the multicultural society we have today, the cultural aspect of learning has been missed out from key founders in terms of cultural beliefs and values (Rogoff, 1998), with the exception of Vygotsky. Part of government control in this position is that set goals (ELGs) have to be achieved by all children through quantifiable indicators by the end of the reception year leading into school readiness (DfE, 2012). However, this implies children are not ready for learning until they achieve the targets set in Early Years, when in reality children are learning from conception. Therefore, we challenge this notion of school readiness in terms of young children being ready for learning by the time they move into a Year 1 class.

Essentially, Wood and Hedges (2016) argue that development theories proposed by key founders in terms of position one, 'speak to government policy agendas to organise frameworks with measurable outcomes' that form part of the foundation of position two (p. 400). Position two emphasises the importance of achieving outcomes to prove progression in learning, but these outcomes are quantifiable and academic in nature which are controversial for children with EAL. We suggest that both these positions need to be deconstructed for children with EAL as they may not fit these perceptions of the norm.

Impact of regulation on children's well-being

According to The Children's Society (2018), the term well-being is used in relation to the quality of childrens' lives are divided into subjective aspects (such as how children are feeling) and objective aspects (such as the condition of these feelings like health and family context). It is also about the skills children need to cope with a range of situations to boost their confidence, competence and self-development. In terms of the EYFS framework, positive relationships are one of the four key features, so feelings of well-being are essential to help young children feel secure and comfortable enough to engage with learning positively (DfE, 2017). This is further supported by The Children's Society (2018) that emphasises that children need to have the right conditions for learning and development to take place. With a highly regulated Early Years, debate continues on the standards children are required to achieve within a tight time frame against their well-being. This is illustrated in the next case study.

Case study 8.2

Melissa was an Early Years teacher in a mixed nursery and reception class. Although there was a lot of in the moment learning and planning, the Early Years team used the EYFS framework to plan learning around the children's interests. However, Melissa was also aware that the team were under pressure from Key Stage 1 teachers to ensure that the children achieved all their Early Years Outcomes, as well as exceeding expectations in the core subjects of literacy and numeracy. As the year progressed Melissa began to notice slight differences in the Early Years team in that they were working extremely hard to ensure all targets in core areas were addressed at the expense of childrens' spontaneous learning that was initially cherished in the first term of the year. Furthermore, she also noticed that childrens' attitudes and behaviours began to change as a result of being put under pressure by staff to achieve the results required.

The children began to gravitate towards outdoor learning and creative learning as much as possible to avoid doing some of the formal activities in the setting that were now taking place every session every day. Melissa also noticed that the increased formal learning seemed to have a negative impact on childrens' well-being. The parents began to complain their children were not happy about the time they had to spend on reading, writing and number work. For children with EAL in her setting, Melissa noticed that they were happy and secure when they began in September, but by February some seemed withdrawn and made very little progress in learning. Again, the parents also began to complain that some of the EAL children did not want to come to the setting.

Melissa had a staff meeting with the Early Years and the Key Stage 1 team and also asked the senior leaders of the school to attend. At this meeting Melissa declared all her concerns regarding what the children were expected to achieve and the impact of this on their well-being and enjoyment of learning. The head made a brave decision in that childrens' well-being must be a priority, otherwise they will not be in the right frame of mind to learn and make progress. The head advised the Early Years team to do all core skills and subject related learning through play and investigative activities. Over time this strategy worked, and both the children and the practitioners were happy. What was interesting in this case study was that within the final half term of the reception year, the children seemed to fly with the progress they were making beyond what was expected.

Key point

- Sometimes the pressure of meeting targets in core areas of learning can be at the cost of childrens' well-being, so perhaps there needs to be some consideration as to how this can be better balanced for a happy learning environment for all.

This case study shows common issues in relation to regulation versus childrens' well-being. For the Early Years team, it was fortunate that they were able to have an open meeting to share their concerns with other practitioners. They were also lucky in that their head teacher focused on the well-being of children more than the targets needed to be achieved at this very early stage of education. Parents also seemed to be much happier as their children were happy and enjoyed coming to the setting.

How does regulation affect children with EAL?

From Table 8.1 we can see that regulation in Early Years has become tighter with greater control being asserted, but the way curriculum content is framed varies between settings as does the degree of control. Control over learning may restrict the creativity of practitioners because they feel that they have to focus more on helping children achieve specific outcomes rather than in the moment opportunities for learning which puts children with EAL at a disadvantage. This is because the focus on acquiring key skills in literacy and numeracy can outweigh childrens' natural way of learning through play. As already discussed earlier in this book, children with EAL need time to absorb and become familiar and comfortable with a different type of learning environment and emphasis on key skills could reduce this time. Hence, the discourse of regulation does not favour children with EAL in the context of learning of core skills within a specific time period over more natural play-based learning.

An alternative perspective to this argument is that practitioners may feel that if they do not show their children are making progress in core key skills, then they could be perceived as being ineffective. Here, the results of children point to practitioner and setting effectiveness. The time children with EAL generally need to achieve basic skills in core skills implies practitioners can feel ineffective in comparison to the speed of skills gained by monolingual children because they feel they are being judged against inspection and National Curriculum criteria. This is why many practitioners want a range of strategies to help meet the learning needs of children with EAL. However, this checklist of strategies is only a short-term solution to meet the learning needs of children with EAL, as discussed in Chapter 3 – there needs to be a deeper rooted understanding of how all children learn. In addition, under this discourse of regulation the structure of the EYFS framework (DfE, 2017) may seem like a welcome and safer option for practitioners in terms of meeting the needs of children with EAL regardless of whether they make basic progress or progress to meet their potential. This is because the freedom and space to create opportunities for learning are narrow with the top down results regime from Key Stage 1.

Our discussion so far suggests it is important to remember that regulation implies one model suitable for all children. In reality, all children are different, with different strengths and areas of development which are more evident for children with EAL. Because of their language and cultural differences, how can it be assumed that children with EAL can all be encouraged to be the same as their monolingual peers by working towards exactly the same Early Years framework in exactly the same way? In this respect, we are perhaps inadvertently trying to diminish the differences between children by making them all the same, which goes against all the principles of inclusion. We are not suggesting that children with EAL need a separate Early Years framework to follow, rather, the framework should be used as guidance to be adapted and adjusted for the learning needs of all children, but especially for those children with EAL.

Way forward with regulation for children with EAL

Despite the impact of regulation on children with EAL, the EYFS framework offers consistency within the sector. It also makes it very clear that the learning needs of all diverse children should be met as well including those children with EAL. Although the EYFS framework emphasises the prime areas of learning equally, perhaps for children with EAL the focus should be more on communication and language followed by personal, social and emotional development rather than physical development (DfE, 2017). Although the focus within communication is on listening, attention and understanding, this does not necessarily have to be proven through Standard English. It is important for practitioners to be aware that children with EAL can demonstrate their listening, attention and understanding in different languages(s) and different ways – like through play and in the moment learning. Therefore, for children with EAL perhaps there needs to be a consideration of how learning is modelled in different ways for both the prime and specific areas of the EYFS framework to ensure that there are alternative ways for children to demonstrate their understanding beyond English language instruction alone.

Interestingly, Sellars (2013) suggests that rather than practitioners controlling what children must learn and when, perhaps the curriculum should emerge from children's lived experiences as this illustrates 'what matters to them and why' (Wood and Hedges, 2016: 10). We believe this would be more beneficial for children with EAL because their lived experiences could be very different to their monolingual peers and monolingual practitioners.

Key reflection points

- As Early Years has become regulated, practice has had to change to reflect this.
- There is controversy and debate in relation to the position of the EYFS framework because how children learn best from key founders, is at risk of being overlooked with the emphasis on results, standards and accountability.

Summary

In summary, we have considered in this chapter key milestones in the development of Early Years education in England and how key founders have shaped our thinking. We have seen that historically there has been little government intervention in Early Years education in England and pose the question for further debate as to the movement from no regulation in Early Years to regulation. These discourses are necessary in going forward to see how in an Early Years regulated climate this has an impact on children with EAL. Even though learning in Early Years is contextually different to the rest of the educational sector, some still have the view that children 'just play' and are not learning anything formally. Maybe this is one reason why there is greater emphasis on achieving key skills in core areas of learning like literacy. For children with EAL, regulation of Early Years means that they may lack the time needed in settling into a new environment, as well as lack time to absorb the context of the English language used especially within play. The message here is to use the EYFS framework as guidance which needs to be adapted in more creative ways for children with EAL.

References

Adams, S., Alexander, E., Drummond, M. J. and Moyles, J. (2004) *Inside the Foundation Stage: Recreating the reception year: Final report.* Association of Teachers and Lecturers.
British Broadcasting Corporation (BBC) (2014) *Six government acts on working conditions.* Available online at: www.bbc.co.uk/schools/gcsebitesize/history/shp/british society/livingworkingconditionsrev5.shtml (Accessed April 2019).

The Children's Society. (2018) Promoting positive well-being for children. Available at: www.childrenssociety.org.uk/sites/default/files/tcs/promoting_positive_well-being_for_children_final.pdf (Accessed, June 2019).

Department for Children Schools and Families (DCSF) (2008) *Statutory framework for the early years foundation stage: Setting the standards for learning, development and care for children from birth to five.* London: DCSF.

Department for Education (DfE) (2016) *Educational excellence everywhere. The schools' white paper 2016.* London: DfE. Available (online) at: www.gov.uk/government/uploads/system/uploads/attachment_data/file/508447/Educational_Excellence_Everywhere.pdf (Accessed April 2019).

Department for Education (DfE) (2017) *Statutory framework for the early years foundation stage: Setting the standards for learning, development and care for children from birth to five.* London: DfE.

Department for Education (DfE) (2012) *Statutory framework for the early years foundation stage: Setting the standards for learning, development and care for children from birth to five.* London: DfE.

Department of Education and Employment (DfEE) (1999) *The national curriculum – Handbook for primary teachers in England.* London: DfEE/QCA.

Department for Education and Skills (DfES) (2000) *Curriculum guidance for the foundation stage.* London: QCA.

Dewey, J. (1902) *The child and the curriculum.* New York: Martino Fine Books.

Dewey, J. (1934) *Education and the social order.* New York: League for Industrial Democracy.

Edwards, C., Gandini, L. and Forman, G. (1998) *The hundred languages of children: The Reggio Emilia approach to early childhood education.* Westport, CT: Ablex.

Evangelou, M., Sylva, K., Kyriacou, M., Wild, M. and Glenny, G. (2009) *Early years learning and development literature review* (Report No. DCSF-RR176). Department for Children, Schools and Families. Available at: www.dcsf.gov.uk/research (Accessed May 2019).

Foucault, M. (1981) The order of discourse. In R. Young (ed.) (1981). *Untying the text: A post-structural anthology.* Boston: Routledge and Kegan Paul. pp. 48–78.

Froebel, F. (1895) *Friedrich Froebel's pedagogics of the kindergarten: Or, his ideas concerning the play and playthings of the child.* New York: D. Appleton. pp. 244–246.

Gillard, D. (2006) *The Hadow Reports: An introduction.* Available at: www.educationengland.org.uk/articles/24hadow.html (Accessed June 2019).

Her Majesty's Stationery Office (HMSO) (1967) *The Plowden Report.* London: HMSO.

Her Majesty's Stationery Office (HMSO) (1989) *Education Act 1988.* London: HMSO.

Isaacs, S. (1952) The nature and function of phantasy. In: J. Rivière (ed.) *Developments in psycho-analysis.* London: Hogarth. pp. 62–121.

Lizardo, O. (2004) The cognitive origins of Bourdieu's *Habitus. Journal for the theory of social behaviour*, 34 (4): 375–401.

Maynard, T. (2007) Forest schools in Great Britain: An initial exploration. *Contemporary Issues in Early Childhood*, 8 (4): 320–331.

Ministry of Education (1996) *Te Whariki: Early childhood curriculum.* Wellington, New Zealand; Learning Media.

Mistry, M. and Sood, K. (2010) English as an Additional Language: Challenges and assumptions. *Management in Education*, 24 (3), July (1–4).

Montessori, M. (1913, 10 August) Montessori schools [Letter to the editor]. *New York Times*, p. 10.

National Archives (no date) *1833 Factory Act: Did it solve the problems of children in factories?* Available at: www.nationalarchives.gov.uk/education/resources/1833-factory-act/ (Accessed June 2019).

Nutbrown, C. and Clough, P. (2013) *Inclusion in the early years*. CA: Sage.

Oates, T. (2010) *Could do better: Using international comparisons to refine the national curriculum in England*. Available at: www.cambridgeassessment.org.uk/images/112281-could-do-better-using-international-comparisons-to-refine-the-national-curriculum-in-england.pdf (Accessed May 2019).

Pestalozzi, J. H. (1962) *Ausgewählte werke*. Band I–II Berlin: Volk und wissen Volkseigener Verlag.

Piaget, J. (1952) *The origins of intelligence in children*. New York: International Universities Press.

Rogoff, B. (1998) Cognition as a collaborative process. In D. Kuhn and R. Siegler (eds), *Handbook of child psychology* (5th edn). pp. 679–744). New York, NY: John Wiley.

Roopnarine, J. and Johnson, J. (eds) (2013) *Approaches to early childhood education*. (6th edn). New York, NY: Pearson.

Rousseau, J. (1993) Original work published in 1762. *Émile* (Trans. Foxley, B.). London: Everyman Publishing.

Rumbold, A. (1990) *Starting with quality*. London: HSMO.

School Curriculum Assessment Authority (SCAA) (1996) *Desirable outcomes for children's learning*. London: SCAA and Department for Education and Employment.

Sellars, M. (2013) *Young children becoming curriculum: Deleuze, Te Whāriki and curricular understandings*. London: Routledge.

Vygotsky, L. (1978) *Interaction between learning and development*. (Trans. Cole, M.). Cambridge, MA: Harvard University Press.

Wearmouth, J., Davydaitis, S., Gosling, A. and Beams, J. (2017) *Understanding special educational needs and disability in early years education*. London: Routledge.

Wood, E. (2014) The play-pedagogy interface in contemporary debates. In L. Brooker, M. Blaise, and S. Edwards (eds), *The SAGE handbook of play and learning in early childhood* (pp. 145–156). London: Sage.

Wood, E. and Hedges, H. (2016) Curriculum in early childhood education: critical questions about content, coherence, and control. *The Curriculum Journal*, 27 (3): 387–405.

Woodhead, M. (1989) School starts at five ... or four years old? The rationale for changing admission policies in England and Wales. *Journal of Education Policy*, 4 (1): 1–21.

9

Performativity in Early Years

When you have finished reading this chapter you will

- understand what the term performativity means and how this influences practice for children with EAL
- be aware of how performativity can be a contentious issue in relation to learning
- be informed of the critical debate between the link between play and performativity

Chapter outline

This chapter begins by exploring the notion of performativity and the underlying theory that informs it before looking at what it means in the context of Early Years education. Next, there is a discussion of theory underpinning the theory of performance which has been illustrated by our performativity model and how this can be translated within Early Years. Furthermore, there is a discussion of the critical debate in terms of the emphasis on performativity and what the key founders have said about the way in which young children learn. Following this, there is an exploration of the impact of performativity on children with EAL. It is well known that children learn though play, but for children with EAL this is a vital form of learning especially when English language skills are limited, so the next theme is the how the contentious issue of play is perceived against the current performative agenda. Finally, we consider how performativity can be managed to ensure that children with EAL are not disadvantaged.

Key words: performative culture, performance, practice, play

Introduction

Performativity in any field can be a contentious issue and education is no different. Education, like other fields in the business world is now subject to a range of processes which measure results, grades, levels and tests to ensure accountability. These judgements and evaluations are linked to both the performance of practitioners and children and performance indicators can include target setting, monitoring and performance management. Today, education is run like a business and is viewed as an area of 'social production and reproduction which have not escaped the influence of neo-liberal policy' (Hennessy and McNamara, 2013: 7). This means that practitioners are under pressure to ensure that they teach children to make progress in specific areas of learning, implying that the broadness of the curriculum claimed is actually in fact rather narrow. According to Hill (2007), education has become a process of 'surveillance through the imposition of tightly monitored chunks of knowledge deemed suitable enough to advance the dominant culture' (p. 207) which is particularly relevant for children with EAL as their background, culture and needs seem irrelevant in relation to the progress they have to make.

Performativity is about how young children are trained and taught to meet certain goals and targets and in the context of Early Years this is about children achieving Early Learning Goals (ELGs)/Early Years outcomes. According to Hill (2007) the culture of schooling right from Early Years has changed and education is now aligned towards performance, results and efficiency meaning that the importance placed on results and progress seems to outweigh the importance placed on the actual value of education (Ball, 2003). The notion of performativity in education can be controversial because on the one hand we claim to personalise the learning journey for children in Early Years, whilst at the same time we tailor learning to ensure that children work towards and achieve similar levels in core areas of learning like early reading and early number regardless of their individual learning needs. So, the challenge is how can effective teaching take place to meet the needs of children with EAL if teaching is being aligned to specific measurable outcomes to prove progress? In line with the current emphasis on performativity, Early Years practice needs to be reconceptualised so that it moves 'beyond the methods fetish towards a humanising pedagogy' to ensure that young children and their needs are at the heart of the learning process (Bartolomé, 2009: 408).

What is performativity?

One definition of performativity is that it is a process that is a 'culture and a mode of regulation that employs judgements, comparisons and displays as means of incentive, control, attrition and change – based on rewards and sanctions (both material and symbolic)' (Ball, 2003: 216). It also includes

> the performances (of individual subjects or organizations) that can serve as measures of productivity or output, or displays of 'quality', or 'moments' of promotion or inspection. As such they stand for, encapsulate or represent the worth, quality or value of an individual or organization within a field of judgement

which in this case is education in Early Years (ibid.: 216). Perryman (2006) further argues that performativity is 're-regulation' or a form of 'hidden regulation' because performativity is about 'increased accountability and surveillance' which seems to underpin the performance of settings and practitioners (p. 150). This means that there exists constant pressure to improve and further improve to gain higher results which seem to have become normal in classrooms today (Ball, 2013), regardless of the needs of children, which is why we sometimes have a culture of teaching to the tests rather than encouraging children to develop skills and connections in knowledge.

This means the national government has exercised their control to centralise education meaning they dominate what takes place (in terms of what should be taught by practitioners and learned by children). This is illustrated by Tan and Goldberg (2009) who talk about how performativity is linked to how schools have to take responsibility for transforming themselves … by improving themselves and competing with one another. Furthermore, the monitoring systems the government uses to assert their control for performativity includes league tables, performance management reviews of staff, observations and inspections. This means settings must respond to targets, indicators and evaluations under state regulation (Tan and Goldberg, 2009). In addition, it can be perceived that childrens' performativity is 'the mirror image of teacher performativity' meaning that childrens' progress is in direct correlation to practitioner effort (Macfarlane, 2015: 338).

However, this accountability of teacher performance is seen as an 'unwarranted assault on the profession and the autonomy' of practitioners (ibid.: 338). Thus implying practitioners are not capable of teaching young children in the way they feel works best for their children. This notion can be particularly damning for children with EAL as their learning can be overlooked in favour of meeting given targets.

Theory linked to performativity

The 1988 Education Act in England introduced competition in education to help increase standards, because funding gained was based on pupil numbers. During the 1990s additional reforms in education included the publication of setting league tables and Ofsted reports (Ball, 2013). The public scrutiny on these tables and reports can indicate a level of performance by practitioners as perceived by the outside world as illustrated by the following case study.

Case study 9.1

Mary was a reception teacher in a central London school and had been teaching for over 30 years in the primary sector. In their most recent Ofsted inspection, the primary setting went from a rating of 'Good' to a rating of 'Special Measures'. The parents and local community assumed that the practitioners and leaders were all underperforming and as a result their children were not making progress. During a whole setting staff meeting, many of the staff were very upset by the grading they received from Ofsted as they felt it was unfair. The setting had a high staff turnover not because the staff were not good in relation to teaching and learning, but because new staff could not afford to live and work locally and therefore the travel became too much for some of them especially if it involved public transport. In addition, increasing migration meant that children were coming into the setting with varied and sometimes unknown languages and also a range of additional special needs which resulted in challenges for practitioners. Although the setting had been very well respected in the community, once the Ofsted report became public, animosity against the setting and staff began.

This case study shows that the outside world may assume that if a setting that achieves special measures or inadequate in their Ofsted inspection, it means that all the staff and children are underperforming and therefore not working to and beyond their capacity. However, we argue that other factors need to be taken into consideration in relation to the performance of all. If practitioners and children are not happy, then they will not perform at their optimal levels.

Theory of performance

The relationship between performance indicators and actual performance is known as performance theory. Like all theories, performance theory can change over time dependent on the performance of those in question and their context. The Theory of Performance (ToP) advances and connects six key factors which include: perform, performer, level of performance, performers mind set, immersion, and reflective practice (Elger, nd). Surrounding these factors there are a range of other influences that need consideration in terms of how these factors work individually and together to have an impact on performativity. We have tried to visualise this theory suggested by Elger (nd) through our model as illustrated by Figure 9.1.

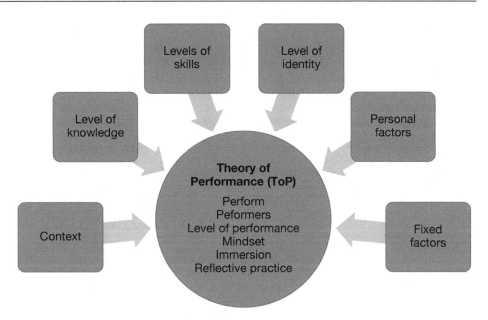

FIGURE 9.1 Model of the Theory of Performance (ToP)

Central to our model are the factors that make up the theory of performance. In this section we discuss the key factors of this theory in relation to the context of education and then critically discuss the influencing elements. The first key factor is to perform which means the actions required for results to be produced, in this case it is young children achieving the Early Years Outcomes (DfE, 2017) in ideally all seven areas of learning. However, in reality the emphasis seems to be on key skills associated with early literacy and numeracy which can disadvantage children with EAL especially in terms of their english language proficiency. The second key factor is performers which in an Early Years setting can be children, practitioners, leaders, parents and the wider community because the ideology is that all should work together to help children widen their knowledge and understanding of the world (DfE, 2017). It is important to remind ourselves that in terms of performance children can perform individually and collaboratively in terms of Vygotsky's 1978 sociocultural theory. The level of performance is the progress children (and practitioners) make in their learning journey and to what level as the academic year progresses. For example, experienced practitioners will know that much of the first part of the academic year is about introducing and reinforcing basic concepts and skills, as the year progresses and children begin to make greater and deeper connections in their learning and understanding, higher order thinking skills and investigative skills begin to emerge as illustrated by the light bulb moment. Here, we would make the link to Vygotsky's ZPD (discussed in Chapter 3) whereby the level of childrens' performance can be enhanced by more knowledgeable others. In addition, it is also important to remember that children are co-constructors of learning in collaboration with others (both practitioners and other children) as suggested by Piaget (1952). A performers mindset is about positive actions and behaviours. We believe this is particularly important for practitioners to demonstrate because the mindset of practitioners

TABLE 9.1 Showing how performance descriptors can be adapted to Early Years

Influences on performance	Description	Application in Early Years
Context	This context includes variables associated with the situation that the individual or organisation performs in.	Context can include: classroom setting, indoors/outdoors, and can also include the theme of learning taking place (including through play) along with the associated resources.
Level of knowledge	Knowledge involves facts, information, concepts, theories, or principles acquired by a person or group through experience or education.	This includes having a good secure knowledge of how young children learn, grow and develop in the context of Early Years and beyond. It is also about having pedagogic awareness of how subject learning can take place through themes and in isolation.
Levels of skill	Skills describe specific actions that are used by individuals, groups, or organisations in multiple types of performances.	Skills in this context are about people (because solid relationships need to be built with the family and a range of other Early Years practitioners) and how to create appropriate learning opportunities to help children make connections in their learning.
Level of identity	As individuals mature in a discipline, they take on the shared identity of the professional community while elevating their own uniqueness. As an organisation matures, it develops it mission, its way doing business, and its uniqueness.	Understanding the roles and responsibilities of the different practitioners that can be in an Early Years setting. Also, to understand both adults and children in terms of strengths and areas of development. But more importantly, all practitioners must know their children well – what makes each child tick!
Personal factors	This component includes variables associated with the personal situation of an individual.	This is about personal Early Years philosophy initially and how this fits in with the way the setting is run. It is also about what individuals believe what and how things should be done in Early Years alongside accountability of progress made by children.
Fixed factors	This component includes variables unique to an individual that cannot be altered.	These factors can include the physical size of the physical environment alongside fixed resources such as the location of the outdoor area, doors, windows, wet area. These are the factors that have to be planned around in terms of available space to set up opportunities.

will influence the mindset of children. For children with EAL this means that they must feel valued and included in all aspects of setting life rather than just left to follow others around with the hope that they will eventually assimilate.

In our view, immersion is about all children being included in the setting environment and the learning taking place. It is about making sure learning is adapted for children with EAL to ensure that they have the maximum opportunity to achieve just like their monolingual peers. This also means that opportunities need to be provided for all children, not just those that have the English language skills to understand tasks. Most importantly, immersion should be about making every child feel valued, respected and comfortable so that they look forward to coming into what can be an unfamiliar environment everyday. Finally, reflective practice should be a key part of learning for all, not only for practitioners in terms of in and on action (Schön, 1983), but also for all children through higher order questioning. For example, asking children questions in their learning such as, how do you know?, why do you you think that?, and can you tell me why?

Surrounding the theory of performance are a range of other influences that also require consideration because these have an impact on the performance of individuals and groups. Therefore, we have used Elger's (nd) performance descriptors and adapted them to the context of Early Years as shown by Table 9.1.

Table 9.1 shows how general performance influences can be applied to the Early Years context. Performance in education is not just about results gained by children at a primary and secondary level. With the top down approach in education currently, there is greater emphasis on practitioners in Early Years to be more accountable for their performance in relation to children progress. We argue that sometimes the influences on performance can be ignored to achieve a certain level of result. In the case of children with EAL, the focus on English language proficiency can easily overtake the performance influences, which means that it becomes all about results gained rather than understanding the context and other influences affecting children's progress.

Link to Vygotsky

Furthermore, Vygotsky's (1978) theory can also be applied to performance outcomes. One key concept associated with Vygotsky's sociocultural theory is mediation, more specifically, mediated object orientated behaviour which is about actions being adapted to gain particular benefits or work towards certain goals. In this case, how teaching and learning is adapted by practitioners to ensure that children achieve specific results required which, in the context of Early Years is about key skills in early reading and number initially. This means that activities and opportunities that promote English language and mathematical concepts have greater emphasis in the curriculum presented to children rather than an equal division of all seven areas of learning in the EYFS (DfE, 2017).

According to Eun (2008), Vygotsky's notion of mediation has three aspects that require consideration when thinking about performativity which are tools meaning resources and guidance which is external support (examples can include resources such as teaching materials, texts and online resources, and general classroom resources), signs meaning internal support (examples can include research, professional journals and academic texts) and other people (examples include advice and support from professional networks, conferences and general professional development). This is because learning is perceived to be a mediated process which is affected by tools and signs (Shabani, 2016), implying practitioner actions are mediated by the targets they have to achieve (in terms of children's progress). Shabani (2016) implies tools and signs help practitioners to extend their own ZPD and we argue that this process could help them to become more critically reflective.

How is performativity translated within Early Years practice?

Educational policies have dominated settings from the introduction of the Curriculum Guidance for the Foundation Stage in 2000 and the Early Years Foundation Stage in 2008 to assessments and inspections. Prior to this as discussed earlier, education in Early Years was laissez-faire. However, this new regime of surveillance on performance could imply that the autonomy of Early Years practice that has existed to date is now at risk of a top down approach. This is more evident as settings demonstrate their progress through their self-evaluation document, which reinforces the education system of being a self-surveillance regime (Ball, 2003). This means that in some cases practitioners in Early Years adapt their teaching and the opportunities they present to children in line with what is required to be achieved rather than the needs of children, which implies that children with EAL could be overlooked altogether. More specifically, Ball (1998) has suggested that performativity can translate into three different ways in the context of education, which we have adapted to the context of Early Years practice in Figure 9.2.

First, Ball (1998) talks about a system of judgements which is about practitioners working towards a set of targets and judgements which they are

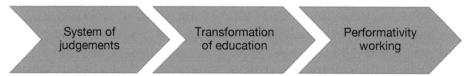

FIGURE 9.2 Adapted from Ball's (1998) three-way performativity implication which we have adapted to the context of early years

monitored and evaluated against to ensure children make progress. In Early Years, this may mean that practice is tailored to ensure that more opportunities are available for teaching phonics and early number in comparison to the other areas of learning, usually on a daily basis. Second, Ball goes on to talk about the transformation of education which is how practices are changed to ensure that children make the required progress. So, in the Early Years this could mean the use of daily flashcards for sounds and numbers, or repetitive songs or daily games involving mental arithmetic or spelling. Essentially this is how education is transformed on a regular basis to ensure that progress in key areas of learning are made. Finally, the third part of the model is about understanding the notion that performativity is actually working in relation to children making the progress required. In the context of Early Years this means that repetitive opportunities and activities are helping children in relation to memory learning, however we argue that perhaps contextual learning also needs greater emphasis as remembered facts may help gain results but links to wider learning especially in relation to mastery of subjects could be weaker as children progress up the primary phase.

This means that performativity can reduce natural teaching strategies and in the moment teaching because it implies that teachers have to teach according to externally placed information because 'the perception is that teachers and the teaching profession are unable to deliver the required standards of schooling' (Forde *et al.*, 2006: 25). In the terms of practice, this implies that Early Years practitioners can be incapable of deciding and implementing the best way of learning for their children unless they have a prescribed ideology.

Critical debate between performativity and the ideology of key Early Years founders

One of the issues associated with performativity is that it tends to favour some areas of learning over others (Macfarlene, 2015), such as literacy and numeracy, which can give the impression that other areas of learning are not important. This goes against many of the ideals from key founders from Chapter 3 that talked about learning naturally through play for all areas of learning rather than just focusing on core areas.

There also seems to be tensions between practice shaped by regulation and practice informed by the ideologies of key founders. Practitioners are held accountable for progress made by children which in turn can overlook the natural ways in which children learn best. The implication being that forced knowledge to gain short term results can sometimes be perceived as more beneficial for the setting rather than identifying childrens' needs and the best approaches of learning for them. This is supported by Ball (2013: 59–60) who has suggested that practitioners feel under so much pressure to perform in order to achieve top results for their setting data through 'inspection criteria, policies, reports and recommendations' that this takes precedence over the needs of children. For children with EAL this implies that their differential language and cultural needs can be overlooked, which in turn goes against the ideologies of key founders such as Vygotsky from Chapter 3.

This heavy emphasis on accountability and evidence collection may imply that practitioners may not have the time or the energy to be as creative with learning as they would like to ensure that they are meeting the needs of the children as demonstrated by the following case study.

Case study 9.2

Nina was a nursery teacher and had been working in the Early Years sector for seven years. Although Nina loved her job and was very passionate about working with young children, at times she felt she did not have the time and space to create learning opportunities that would suit some of her children. This was especially the case for her children with EAL, whereby she always felt under pressure from the feeder primary schools to ensure that her children knew a range of key sounds, words and a range of number bonds. In addition she also felt under pressure to ensure that her children could do some of the basics such as being able to write their name – which proved challenging especially since some of her EAL children had names that were not spelt phonetically. Even if some of her children were able to achieve what was perceived to be the norm, they still had to work harder to ensure that children achieved even more to ensure that the setting was judged to be at least good by Ofsted in the view of the local community. Furthermore, this pressurised feeling was common among all the practitioners within the setting as they felt that primary schools judged them on what the children could not do by the time they entered the reception class rather than what they could do.

This case study shows the effect of performativity on learning opportunities and experiences for children such as those with EAL. Even if children achieved what was required, they had to achieve even more which again goes against the ideologies of key founders in terms of giving young children the time and space to explore and investigate for themselves as suggested by key founders such as Dewey and Montessori.

Another concern with performativity is what Ball calls 'fabrications' which is where 'individuals or institutions describe, in reports and other texts, the work they do using language that demonstrates that they are meeting performative criteria' (2003: 224). This implies that what is being said is more important than the actual practice taking place as summarised by Ball:

> Fabrications are versions of an organization (or person) which does not exist – they are not 'outside the truth' but neither do they render simply

true or direct accounts – they are produced purposefully in order 'to be accountable'. Truthfulness is not the point – the point is their effectiveness.

(Ball, 2003: 224)

The impact of this kind of practice is that performativity is the most important goal to achieve in Early Years. What is perhaps negated is the impact of over-looking childrens' needs on future education and life chances because, on the one hand education is expecting all practitioners to meet the needs of their children like those with EAL from an equality and human rights perspective, but on the other, this seems secondary in relation to the current performative agenda. The main argument being that practitioners may not have the time to follow the ideology of key founders under the umbrella of performativity.

What is the impact of performativity for children with EAL?

The focus on standards and measurement of performance results means that deeper issues associated with early education can go unnoticed (Eisner, 2004). This means children with EAL can be assessed against narrow targets linked to specific areas of learning only, therefore what a child is holistically capable of may not be considered. Furthermore, the philosophy of teaching to the tests means that there could also be a lack of time for creativity in Early Years imply-ing that children with EAL may have less opportunities to showcase their knowledge in different ways because 'education has lost sight of the needs of students and is failing to recognise the broad range of capacities inherent in an increasingly diverse student population' (Slee, 2010, cited in Hennessy and McNamara, 2013: 9). This can be further demonstrated by narrowing childrens' opportunity to become autonomous independent learners if learning and the methods imposed are restricted, which can also mean that not all childrens' needs might be met.

However, as Macfarlene (2015) argues earlier, childrens' performativity is a mirror image of practitioner performativity which implies that some practition-ers will automatically be able to see the needs of their children with EAL and adapt opportunities appropriately. But, we argue that this is not consistent across the Early Years sector, especially where you have isolated children with EAL. Here, children with EAL could be just expected to assimilate within the dominant culture as discussed in Chapter 5.

Critical debate between play and the performative agenda

Even with the emphasis on the importance of play as the key form of learning within the Early Years, there is still a perception in society that young children in Early Years setting do not really learn much as they just play all day. The critical debate here is how do you measure learning in natural play? We say natural play because this is not the same as structured play because play is a complex process with no rules or set processes or set criteria that must be achieved. We argue here that if play is perceived as being a waste of time, then why have key founders like Plato suggested it is the only way for children to learn as discussed in Chapter 3? For children with EAL, it has already been discussed previous in this book that it is essential they have the opportunity to play so that practitioners can observe their knowledge and understanding in any language children chose to use. Play is the only medium through which children are not told by practitioners to do things in a particular way. Furthermore, we also argue that if play is not seen as being of value then why do we give children playtime during the middle of the morning and at lunchtime in both primary and secondary sectors of education today. Surely, if we just wanted to give children access to some fresh air then opening windows is all that is required?

Another issue is if young children are spending time playing then, in the eyes of some, they are not learning what is required to achieve a set of results. Here, the emphasis on achievement of results is seen to be more important than the learning and consolidation of knowledge. This is very evident today when some settings teach to the tests in that all learning opportunities and experiences are geared toward achieving certain results (especially in key areas), this means that in some cases children are being taught to memorise facts (which hold no value according to key founders) to achieve a result, after which there is no recollection as illustrated by the following scenario.

Scenario 1

Vishal was an EAL boy in a reception class with his first language being Urdu. After Christmas his teacher would give all the children three words they would have to learn that week. Vishal knew that if he got his words correct on the Friday, he would get a treat from the snack table. So he memorised the words required to get a treat from the snack table. On parents evening his teacher showed his parents the results associated with how many key words he had go correct on a weekly basis. At this point his mum intervened and said that Vishal had no idea what the key words were or what they meant and more importantly he could never recall or remember any of them after Friday, this was because he knew he had to get them right on a Friday so he could get a treat from the snack table with his friends.

This scenario shows that teaching to the tests or results required maybe beneficial in terms of progression of data in a setting, but in reality if there is no consolidation of knowledge and the opportunity to demonstrate childrens' understanding in play, then there will more situations like that of Vishal. Today this can be illustrated to the rote nature of learning times tables which if not taught correctly, has no resonance with problem solving and mastery.

If childrens' creativity is diminished through the freedom they have in play based learning, then there is a chance that standards achieved could go down. This is because if children are not motivated to achieve because learning is focusing on key areas only, then there is a danger that children will not develop skills in the way they should as mentioned by the ley founders. Finally, in addition to the current focus on neuroscience it is important for children to develop as fully as they can, which is possible through play. If play is reduced or overtaken by the performative agenda, then there is a risk that we are inadvertently inhibiting childrens' development too.

Managing performativity to ensure children with EAL are not disadvantaged

So far this chapter has focused on the performative agenda and some of the associated challenges in terms of managing practice in Early Years settings. One thing is clear, and that is that the performative agenda is here to stay, therefore how we manage this best for all children including those with EAL becomes paramount.

For children with EAL, learning needs to be considered in relation to the ideology of key founders like Vygotsky initially. Vygotsky (1978) has talked about the importance of children learning in a social and cultural context. Alongside this there needs to be a clear understanding of the performance criteria and how the two can be married up to benefit the child and the progress they can make as illustrated by the next scenario.

Scenario 2

Ben was a reception class teacher in a multicultural inner-city primary school. He had many years of experience of working with a diverse community alongside children with EAL. Ben knew the Early Years outcomes that had to be achieved by the end of the reception year. In addition, he was keen for children to have the knowledge and understanding required rather than just isolated facts that he could tick off on his check list. For his children with EAL, Ben used to embed phonics and number knowledge in play through adult led play, followed by opportunities for these children to demonstrate their understanding in free flow play. The practitioners in Ben's setting initially questioned why he was wasting time in play when results needed to be achieved. Here, Ben's view was that young children, especially those with EAL needed as many opportunities as possible to make connections in learning which can only happen if children get a variety of learning opportunities. The way Ben worked meant that although it looked like the children were playing most of the year, by the end of the reception year, most children with EAL had achieved the expected outcome required with some even exceeding expectations.

This scenario shows that Ben was focusing on encouraging children to have a desire to learn rather than focusing on the performativity agenda alone. The result of Ben's strategy in the reception year meant that when children moved up to Year 1, they were more able to apply their knowledge and understanding as the learning was embedded within them. Here, Ben did not believe in learning isolated facts most of the time, which was in support of the ideology of key founders like Plato.

We have suggested a range of strategies to help manage performativity for children with EAL to ensure that they are not disadvantaged in anyway.

1   Invest in spending time getting to know the child as an individual (whether this is by observing them, working with them as part of a group or listening to their conversations)

2   Having a secure understanding of how children learn and the factors that influence this

3   Being aware of the ideologies of key founders that emphasise the importance of learning socially

4   Setting up a range of opportunities in all areas of learning so that children can see how key skills associated with literacy and numeracy can be applied

5   Help children to make connections in learning

6   Training the Early Years team to encourage them to develop higher order questioning to get a deeper understanding of childrens' thinking

7   Encourage as many opportunities for speaking and listening as possible

It is important to say here that many of these strategies are beneficial to all children, not just those with EAL. However, the emphasis should be on ensuring children with EAL develop a love for learning, questioning, exploring and investigating rather than isolated learning which these children have no connections to.

Key reflection points

- The current culture of performativity does have an impact on the practices taking place in Early Years settings.
- For children with EAL, learning needs to be contextual so that connections can be made rather than just learning isolated facts for performance criteria.

Summary

In summary all parents want their children to be high performers. Perhaps what seems to be forgotten in the current standardised Early Years framework is that high performance is different for different children, like those with EAL. Here, perhaps it would be wise to remember that enabling children to achieve for long term is more effective than short term memorisation. We also need to be mindful that maybe if the focus was on the 'unique child', rather than the standard performance deemed to be the norm all the time, then perhaps children would make more progress in different aspects of learning in the long run.

References

Ball, S. J. (1998) Performativity and fragmentation in 'Postmodern Schooling'. In J. Carter (ed.) *Postmodernity and fragmentation of welfare*. London: Routledge. pp. 187–203.

Ball, S. J. (2003). The teacher's soul and the terrors of performativity. *Journal of Education Policy*, 18 *(2):* 215–228.

Ball, S. J. (2013) *Foucault, power and education*. New York: Routledge.

Bartolomé, L. (2009) Beyond the methods fetish: Toward a humanizing pedagogy. In A. Darder, M. B. and Torres, R. D. (eds) *The critical pedagogy reader*. New York: Routledge. pp. 408–429.

Department for Education (DfE) (2017) *Statutory framework for the early years foundation stage: Setting the standards for learning, development and care for children from birth to five*. London: DfE.

Eisner, E. W. (2004) What does it mean to say a school is doing well? In D. J. Flinders and S. J. Thornton (eds) *The curriculum studies reader* New York: Routledge Falmer. pp. 297–306.

Elger, D. (nd) Theory of performance. In *Expectations of faculty in Higher Education*. Retrieved from www.webpages.uidaho.edu/ele/scholars/Results/Workshops/Facilitators_Institute/Theory%20of%20Performance.pdf (Accessed April 2019).

Eun, B. (2008) Making connections: Grounding professional development in the developmental theories of Vygotsky. *The Teacher Educator*, 43: 134–155.

Forde, C., McMahon, M., McPhee, A. D. and Patrick, F. (eds) (2006) *Professional development, reflection and enquiry*. London: Paul Chapman Publishing.

Hennessy, J. and McNamara, P. M. (2013) At the altar of educational efficiency: performativity and the role of the teacher. *English Teaching: Practice and Critique*, 12 (1): 6–22.

Hill, D. (2007) Critical teacher education, new labour, and the global project of neoliberal capital. *Policy Futures in Education*, 5 (2): 204–225.

Macfarlane, B. (2015) Student performativity in higher education: converting learning as a private space into a public performance, *Higher Education Research & Development*, 34 (2): 338–350.

Perryman, J. (2006) Panoptic performativity and school inspection regimes: disciplinary mechanisms and life under special measures. *Journal of Education Policy*, 21 (2): 147–161.

Piaget, J. (1952) *The origins of intelligence in children*. New York: International Universities Press.

Schön, D. (1983) *The reflective practitioner: How professionals think in action.* New York: Basic Books.

Shabani, K. (2016) *Applications of Vygotsky's sociocultural approach for teachers' professional development.* Philadelphia, PA: Cogen Education.

Slee, R. (2010) Political economy, inclusive education and teacher education. In Forlin, C. (ed.) *Teacher education for inclusion. Changing paradigms and innovative approaches.* London: Routledge.

Tan, E. T. and Goldberg, W. A. (2009) Parental school involvement in relation to children's grades and adaptation to school. *Journal of Applied Developmental Psychology,* 30: 442–453.

Vygotsky, L. (1978) *Interaction between learning and development.* (Trans. Cole, M.) Cambridge, MA: Harvard University Press.

10 Leading learning for children with EAL

When you have finished reading this chapter you will

- have a better awareness of how to lead learning in Early Years for children with EAL
- understand the need to prepare and develop Early Years leaders for diverse communities of children
- be aware of why some Early Years practitioners are reluctant to view leadership as a career path
- understand the challenges faced by Black Minority Ethnic (BME) leaders

Overview of the chapter

This chapter explores the importance of the role of Early Years practitioners and leaders for children from birth to age five. The role of leaders is to inspire and create spaces for practitioners, governors and other stakeholders to hold intellectual debate both about what Early Years educational leadership is as a concept, and how you 'do' leadership through a shared vision. We begin this chapter by briefly exploring why the Early Years education sector is vital in developing and supporting learning in young children through conceptualising current Early Years education and what this means for children with EAL as a foundation for leadership. The next focus is briefly looking at what Early Years leadership is and why leadership in this sector is unique. Following this, we explore different ways of leading required for and with diverse communities for children with EAL in order to be successful leaders and how to specifically lead learning for children with EAL. Next, we consider the importance of recruiting practitioners with the right skills and investing in them, not only for their own development as a highly-qualified Early Years workforce but to make sure the service offered is the best it can be in the early stages of learning, followed by how to better prepare and develop these leaders. Then, we analyse the impediments and opportunities in attracting, retaining and developing these practitioners. Next, we look at the challenges faced by Black Minority Ethnic (BME) leaders and the reasons for low numbers of these. Finally, we conclude with a personal reflection on leadership as two BME leaders who have had leadership responsibilities in a variety of different contexts.

Key words: Early Years, leadership, English as Additional Language (EAL), leadership preparation and development, Black Minority Ethnic (BME) leaders

Introduction

The term 'leadership' over 'leader' can be confusing, but we think practitioners can be interchangeably leaders and learners who work to support childrens' learning rather than for personal standing. Early Years practitioners are cautious of the concept of leadership yet arguably, when they converse with their colleagues about teaching and learning, planning and organising, managing the setting, monitoring and assessing, they are undertaking leadership activity, but may not see it as such. However, leading in a complex and turbulent educational sector requires moral courage and resilience to make things happen. Strong leaders challenge the norm through grass-roots conversations to improve lives of all children and their families.

Everyone can be a leader in Early Years if they have the required set of attributes and skills, but there are many styles of leadership so one must be careful not to stereotype an ideal leader. Leadership is personal, a choice, an ambition one has, a want and a passionate desire to make a real difference to adults and children. It is about being good at leading Early Years practice through having 'energy and resilience, creating a learning culture' and having different 'ways of thinking and behaving' (Rodd, 2013: 28). Leaders and practitioners have a moral imperative to ensure all children achieve success. Therefore, everyone in Early Years is accountable through a collaborative culture informed of good professional relationships, with individual responsibility and collective high expectations to do the right thing for children and their families by having excellent 'interpersonal and communication abilities' (ibid.: 34). We believe effective leadership in Early Years is child-centred, all-embracing of people, humanising, liberalising, emotionally invigorating, and equitable to change and improve lives of all children and their families. To promote such values requires a common vision that delivers high quality, world class Early Years education.

Conceptualising current Early Years education for children with EAL

Before we can talk about Early Years leadership for learning, we need to briefly conceptualise Early Years and what this means for children with EAL. This then gives a solid base to understand the different facets of leadership and how it can be perceived to be seamless in this context by experienced leaders.

The Education 2030 Framework for Action (UNESCO, 2015) sets immense importance on quality, inclusiveness and equity. We affirm that education is a public good and this starts from birth or some would say even pre-natal by transforming lives through addressing 'all forms of exclusion and marginalization, disparities and inequalities in access, participation and learning outcomes' (UNESCO, 2015: iv). In this respect, we believe that Early Years educational philosophy of child-centred learning should reach and be accessible to all and should instil values of social justice, human rights, racial and gender equality. This offers a crucial opportunity for practitioners, governors, parents and leaders to work together and across settings/sectors of education towards securing a sustainable future by providing quality education in Early Years. It is clear from the extant literature that Early Years education provides a head start for all children including children with EAL and leaders need to be ready to tailor their provision to promote this (Ofsted, 2018). This is because historically, one of the challenges of Early Years perspectives (discussed in Chapter 3) is that they do not consider the diversity of children. Today, diverse pupil populations together with cultural, social and linguistic variations, alongside the different needs of these children with different ways of working to meet these needs, means it is important to look at the current social and political context. This implies Early Years leadership should now be focusing on the beginning of policy formation on areas like poverty, inequality, discrimination, ethnicity and forced migration.

Early Years leaders need to recognise that the focus should be on pedagogy of learning rather than just following a standardised curriculum. This is also supported by Foucault who implied the curriculum should focus on the 'multiple processes which constitute' how children learn (1981: 60). We suggest leaders and practitioners in Early Years should realise that children with EAL may initially not achieve to their potential. Therefore, deconstructing thinking is necessary to challenge the structures around which curriculum content is framed so children with EAL can achieve (Donaldson, 1978).

Leadership in the Early Years

We define an Early Years leader as someone who is not only a leader of learning, but also of other practitioners, children, resources and the learning environment (both indoors and outdoors). In education, leaders can be a range of individuals including head teacher, senior leader team member, Early Years stage co-ordinator, or subject leader, and sometimes a combination of these. In the Early Years sector we see leadership capabilities spread across all practitioners in the setting and not residing in one specific area only (like one subject area – such as one person being responsible for literacy, another person being responsible for Understanding the World) like current practice in primary schools. This is because current thinking regarding leadership and management in Early Years is that there is a greater focus on collaborative and partnership working, rather than working in isolation. Such an integrated approach is more evident in Early Years where practices are ideologically aligned to child centred education rather than moving to an aspirational vision with a tight curriculum and assessments as seen more generally in education. Today, we are witnessing leadership at all levels in education from Early Years to primary phases and beyond, and this in turn requires leaders to blur traditional boundaries of leadership by building new alliances with each other and beyond to strengthen and build new collaborations.

So, what is unique about Early Years leaders?

Nutbrown says Early Years leaders create 'an enabling environment' in their settings where everyone can work together to make a difference, no matter how small or large (2018: 154). This is unique to the Early Years sector as the learning environment is a key aspect of the EYFS framework (DfE, 2017). This was also supported by research from Mistry and Sood (2012) where they noted that a facilitative culture made people feel valued, and knew from gathering data what made the school 'tick' and used their analytical skills for setting improvement. One reason for this is because these leaders were self-reflective, self-critical and self-conscious of their behaviours towards others and remained focused on how to transform lives of children and their families.

Ways of leading in Early Years

Ideally, Early Years leaders should aspire towards greater equality informed of human rights and justice and to know how to put this into practice for the best interests of all their children through play and other forms of creative learning. Striving for greater equality requires giving all a fairer deal and for leaders to take the lead in working towards a vision of a society we want for everyone (Lumby and Coleman, 2016: 171). May (2016) suggests the following ways of leading that we feel would be useful for leaders to consider.

1   Start from where the energy for change lies
2   Build a coalition within the organisation

3   Seek out pragmatic and entrepreneurial solutions

4   Design the service around the end user

5   Look at what you can influence, not just what you can control – design your solutions with your partners

6   Enable self-adopting behaviours

In the context of Early Years we have adapted May's (2016) ways of leading into three key areas which we feel are important in relation to Early Years leadership.

In Figure 10.1 we show how leadership behaviour and action plays a crucial part to influence and support educational provision for the child and the family. As stated earlier, a leader working in isolation cannot support the child, partnerships and collaborations with inter-agencies is a more effective way. This is particularly relevant in Early Years as leadership is more about meeting the personal educational needs of children, including those with EAL to ensure that they make progress in a holistic way rather than just leading on individual subject areas, or other areas like assessment.

One certainty in education is that change is constant and how to deal with change in a positive way is another leadership skill. Grint (2010) poses the following ideas for successful change using an adaptive work model (which means a practical leadership plan in terms of developing leadership competencies) which we feel is useful for Early Years leaders:

- an accepted need to change;
- a viable vision/alternative state;
- change agents in place;
- sponsorship from above;
- realistic scale and pace change;
- an integrated transition programme;
- a symbolic end to the status quo;
- a plan for likely resistance;
- constant advocacy;
- a locally owned benefits plan.

In Early Years this means that leaders need to have the 'buy in' of the stakeholders of all communities in and out of the setting. Then, it is more likely that the vision for the future starts to develop, systematically, collaboratively and in a realistic manner. Leadership may encounter difficulties that need to be listened to, resolved and conflict minimised. The end product, the vision seen in the mission statement or on the board outside the setting, will represent and

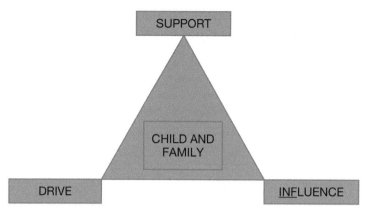

FIGURE 10.1 Our adaptation of May's ideas in relation to Early Years leadership

symbolise what the setting stands for and believes in especially in relation to children's development, learning and improved outcomes.

Leading in Early Years is similar to a head teacher's role in a primary school because head teachers have overall responsibility in their school and in one respect this is the same for Early Years leaders. So, if Early Years leaders have many different ways of leading for phase or setting improvement including positive relationships and partnerships within and beyond the setting, then why is this not recognised in the educational sector? Furthermore, we believe the skills Early Years leaders have and/or develop are much more than leadership for subject areas in a primary school – and yet there seems to be very little recognition for these skills. Successful leaders require the necessary skills and competencies to manage constant change and foster good professional relationships to put in action strategies to enable high quality educational experiences for all.

Being a successful leader for children with EAL

Early Years leadership is people-centred as much as it is child centred. So, managing relational, personal, environmental and social dimensions are important enablers for leadership in addition to their perseverance, respectable personality, appeal and magnetism. Such leaders make a difference to everyone's lives on daily basis because they speak and act to and from lived experiences to adopt appropriate behaviours which is essential for children with EAL. This is because they know their children, families, practitioners, support staff and governors, in terms of their needs and wants, and above all, what good teaching and learning looks like to have a positive impact on children's progress and outcomes. For children with EAL, this kind of leadership knowledge and awareness is essential to ensure that children feel secure enough in the setting for learning to take place.

Research by Mistry and Sood (2011) explored how twenty Early Years and primary leaders in English primary schools helped to narrow the gaps of attainment for children with EAL. They also provided information on practitioners' experiences and what they perceived to be the challenges for change (see Table 10.1).

Although the data presented in Table 10.1 is based in the primary sector of education with some input from Early Years leaders, there are similarities of approaches seen in Early Years settings like for example, focusing more on play-based learning and working closing with other communities. The table also shows there is a strong focus on data collection and analysis of children with EAL in the Early Years which is undertaken more collegially in this phase than the primary sector. So, for example, Early Years leaders are not seeing children with EAL as a problem (as discussed in Chapter 5) and giving away such responsibility to specialist language or specialist special needs practitioners. Instead, these leaders ensure that all practitioners are accountable through

TABLE 10.1 Narrowing gaps of attainment in primary sector for children with EAL

Leaders with teaching responsibility	What do you think the learning gaps are for children who have EAL?	How do you help to close the gap for children who have EAL?	What are the challenges for change?
(Primary including Early Years)	Lack of experiences in play situations as some children are new arrivals.	Provide contextual child and adult initiated play opportunities.	Needs to be embedded in the rest of the school for children who have EAL.
	Lower level of language which has an obvious effect on curriculum learning.	Lots of phonics related work using visual aids.	Money for resources, also encouraging all staff to use phonics in the school.
	Systematic assessments through monitoring and evaluation.	Making sure that all staff are using similar formats for assessments.	Helping staff to understand the importance of carrying out these assessments, and what they actually mean.
	Lack of knowledge of their homeland especially if they are new arrivals.	Making contact with other professionals in the local community who can help.	Difficult to access professionals and resources initially for new arrivals.
	Isolated learners in our school are increasing.	Need to have access to resources and people who can help with new languages.	Not knowing where to get help from for isolated learners of less common languages.
	Lack of data for children who have EAL.	Keep long term records to track progress.	Need whole school specific data.
	Lack of understanding regarding what the data means.	Trying to have some training sessions for staff including support staff.	Issues of time, and money for training.

the creative opportunities presented to promote learning. However, Early Years leaders need to be mindful that the values of some practitioners and the personal values of the children may mask conflict which may constitute obstacles to children with EAL. Above all, leaders must believe that all children are educable and not that they are only educable with great difficulty, like children with EAL. To maintain the continuity of an inclusive ethos in the Early Years means that Early Years leaders need to track children with EAL appropriately and deploy the most qualified and experienced practitioners.

Therefore, Early Years leaders are successful as leaders because they ensure all practitioners are accountable as a team for the progress of all children including those with EAL. Additionally, in our view, success is not just about ensuring children with EAL achieve the outcomes they are supposed to, it is about children feeling happy in the setting and comfortable with all the adults and children around them. It is about children being happy about developing holistically and not just key skills in literacy and numeracy. Furthermore, success is about children being given the opportunities to develop a love for learning and to develop higher order skills such as being able to explore, problem solve and investigate alongside having an awareness of the needs of other children around them to develop traits like compassion, empathy and kindness.

Leadership for learning for children with EAL

Leadership is often about someone with responsibility for seeing and leading on the 'the bigger picture of change and influence' (Mistry and Sood, 2013: 42), like modelling good practice to encouraging language development for children with EAL. Like most leaders, Early Years leaders also influence how learning is tailored to ensure childrens' progress. Wider literature on leadership suggests that with greater emphasis on accountability, leadership has necessitated moving from a pedagogical approach towards more distributed approach mobilising leadership expertise at all levels in the Early Years team (Harris, 2013). We suggest three key strategies that are useful for leaders in leading learning for children with EAL.

The first strategy is that Early Years leaders must understand the context in which their settings are situated and learn to reach out to their diverse communities as demonstrated in the following example.

Example 10.1

In one multicultural urban primary school the head teacher promoted her setting's practice by embracing tradition, custom, values of her EAL children and their families by encouraging her staff to spend time talking to the children in their learning and being visible to parents at the beginning and end of the school day. In addition, she would regularly do a learning walk around the school to challenge and support poor practice and standards of teaching in a supportive way (Mistry and Sood, 2014). She was not afraid to try new ideas which sometimes could be culturally incompatible in relation to what had to be achieved in terms of key outcomes associated with literacy and numeracy. But she encouraged her staff to offer additional challenges to all children in a cognitive way whilst also focusing more on children with EAL because some of them she said were 'generally behind across the city'. She did this sensitively and in consultation with parents, being totally mindful of tradition and respect of customs for a morally driven vision. She valued, respected and cared for all children and knew what excellence in education looked like so that she could strategically look at what she could influence, not just what she could control. This head designed solutions and sought out pragmatic and entrepreneurial solutions with her partners.

This example shows that the head teacher demonstrated her style of leadership through embracing traditions, customs and values of her EAL children and their families because she realised that working with communities is a better way than working alone. In this way she forged stronger relationships with her community, which is also a key factor of building relationships in Early Years (DfE, 2017). Her key philosophy was that the child was at the heart of the learning process and leadership needs to foster how children learn best as individuals and as part of a group.

The second strategy is knowing that adult interaction has the potential to make a huge difference to childrens' development and attainment, but we are aware that some practitioners 'can remain distant' from their children with EAL (NALDIC, 2016). This could be due to a lack of awareness of the home language and customs by some practitioners resulting in difficulties with communication and understanding between the setting and parents. Additionally, monitoring children with EALs' progress is challenging perhaps in part due to their language development but, also in understanding differential patterns of achievement amongst diverse groups of children. Minority ethnic groups are heterogeneous in constitution, thus the outcomes will be different for children from different minority ethnic groups like the Muslims, Hindu, Sikh, Jain or Chinese. For example, although Sunnis make up the majority of Muslims, not every Muslim belongs to the same Islamic sect. Being aware that some practitioners may lack experience in supporting children with EAL and some have no experience of working with them makes it vital for Early Years leaders to support practitioners in enabling these children to access the curriculum through appropriate language development needs.

The third strategy is that Early Years leaders should support learning for children with EAL by giving each child what is needed from their perspective – culturally, ethnically and socio-economically. Fundamentally, leading for equality should matter to us all, therefore leaders need to look for opportunities to up-skill themselves to better understand the experience of minority ethnic groups within their setting, whether characterised by ethnicity, gender, religion, language, sexuality or a range of other factors. These opportunities can be having the opportunity to observe staff in more multicultural settings (in terms of how they deal with parents, how they set up learning for children with EAL, how they ensure cognitive challenge in learning is evident), another way is making time for research so that practice is informed by current research in the field of EAL. The use of language by children with EAL should be observed to prevent labelling as this can be potentially problematic in categorising them into groups. Leaders and practitioners need to develop a challenging curricula and pedagogy to help make settings more inclusive. This means, every effort needs to be made in the settings by leaders to minimise or not exacerbate inequality through vetting their policies and practices aimed to support children with EAL. When employing leaders, outdated gender and racial stereotyping must be avoided and seek out the true capabilities of men and women as Early Years leaders.

Thus, leading for equality in Early Years is fundamentally important to us all. That means giving each child what is needed from their perspective which is not the same for all children with EAL. Giving some children fewer chances than others to live a life rebounds overall on society. For equality, leaders must create a level playing field of access as a necessary foundation for the social and physical health of the entire community and this begins with having a high quality workforce, because only then will learning be led effectively.

Having a high quality Early Years workforce

A skilled, knowledgeable and stable workforce is a key part of Early Years provision and therefore it is an important part of a leader's role to maintain this stability to 'reduce staff turnover' (Nutbrown, 2018: 160). However, we are also aware that stable wages and good working conditions remain an issue for recruiting and retaining these highly qualified individuals. Perceptions by some regarding anyone working in Early Years conjures up images of low skill, underpaid staff, poor pay and conditions, low morale, but in reality, Early Years practitioners and leaders are very committed, passionate and hardworking individuals who shape young childrens' lives and influence how they develop and learn. These key individuals have the potential to help raise aspirations of children and their families out of poverty very early on by giving them the best possible start in life regardless of their family circumstances. This is supported by the Minister for Women, Equalities and Early Years for England, who wrote in her foreword that 'an effective workforce drives high quality provision, which is critical to children's outcomes and is important to parents making childcare choices' (DfE, 2017a: 4).

In this respect, evolving practice in Early Years requires leaders to encourage their workforce to be competent in subject knowledge, pedagogical skills and on how to use technology to innovate. This will necessitate developing new models for leaders based on research and informed dialogue and shared practice. This means forming alliances and partnerships with local, national and international practitioners and leaders that really understand and practice daily the art of pedagogy that engages, informs, excites and improves childrens' lives. In other words, leaders need to be outward looking to improve their own setting's practice further.

Preparation and development of Early Years leaders for diverse communities of children

This section will deconstruct how to better prepare Early Years leaders to lead learning effectively for children with EAL. It begins by looking at the current context in terms of a lack of leadership skills preparation for leading a multicultural child population, which in part stems from a lack of university teacher training. It then breaks professional development into valuing and embracing diversity before briefly looking at some Early Years leadership practices associated with specific approaches including a lack of male leaders in this sector. Finally, we explore the absence of BME leaders along with some of the challenges by them before a personal reflection from the authors' perspective.

Research by Mistry and Sood (2014) on leadership challenges on managing diversity in a primary classroom based in two urban, multicultural schools with over 90 per cent minority ethnic children concluded that some Early Years practitioners and leaders were ill prepared to teach children from diverse backgrounds. This may be due to a lack of cultural and linguistic awareness of a plural society, which is supported by findings from Oliveira-Formosinho and Barros Araújo (2011) whose research demonstrated that practitioners believe children are colour-blind to ethnicity, racial identity and other social and cultural differences. This means diversity management then becomes an important pre-requisite for good Early Years practice, requiring leaders to prepare future practitioners to challenge stereotyping, prejudice and discrimination (Shah, 2006).

Some Early Years leaders are poorly aware of practices linked to poverty, gender, ethnicity, immigrant language or sexuality, which are often aggregated within a general rhetorical commitment to equality especially if they are situated in a monolingual environment. Tokenistic gestures to equality will not do. This is supported by Shields and Mohan (2008) who suggest they need to know how to analyse racial or ethnic conflict to help build positive interethnic communities. This means those who prepare Early Years trainees on courses in the initial teacher training institutions should further equip them with the knowledge and skills for tackling inequalities as related to children with EAL specifically, and more generally, for all and be ready to argue against resistance. This needs to be embedded in all subjects on a teacher training course. Furthermore, policy makers like governors also need proper training on recruitment, retention and progression strategies when looking for the best practitioner to employ in the Early Years sector.

Leaders in Early Years need to critically scrutinise their practice that may promote myths that some children with EAL have lower capacity to learn with poor innate ability. They need to start by unpicking their own unconscious habitual thinking, attitudes and behaviours about gender, ethnicity, language, poverty, class and religion inequality before they begin to tackle poor teaching in Early Years especially if teaching practices are unsuccessful for children with EAL. For example, Shah (2006) provides examples of practice for leaders who have children with EAL in their school which we feel are useful as a starting point especially if practitioners have limited experience of working with this diverse community.

Professional development for Early Years practitioners

The development of professional development programmes for Early Years practitioners at all levels is crucial in order for high quality teaching and learning to take place for children. Coaching and mentoring development have been known to have an impact on personal and settings' effectiveness, but succession planning and building leadership capacity offers different challenges. It is essential to invest professional development in the Early Years team as this is the first step in preparing leaders in action (Schön, 1983). According to the report by Her Majesty's Inspectorate of Education (2007) leadership capacity is built by giving opportunity to exercise leadership through first-hand experience, ensuring role accountability and undertaking staff reviews (p. 62). One challenge is that leadership in Early Years is viewed to be not as important as subject leadership in a primary school. This implies that professional development in Early Years is not as important as core subjects across the school. Early Years leaders have more subject and pedagogic responsibility and therefore they need greater professional development investment in them in order to produce excellent leaders in comparison to lone subject leadership responsibility.

Earlier in this chapter we introduced the notion of adaptive leadership which is a practical leadership framework that helps individuals and settings adapt and thrive in challenging environments as one possible influential model of leadership, as we are mindful that there are many other models too. Here, we argue that the isolated leadership model now seems redundant, replacing distributed leadership approaches requiring a whole school – whole system (school) approach in change management leading to more focus and coherence.

Leadership for and with diversity (after Lumby and Coleman, 2016)

As we know, there are as many diverse settings as there are diverse communities with language diversity and cultural/racial diversity that need to be led and managed. This means leadership for and with diversity becomes both a challenge and an opportunity especially if there is an ethnically diverse child population and white monolingual practitioners. This poses an interesting political, philosophical and moral issue. We believe that the minimum pre-requisite qualities and attitudes for leaders to embrace diversity required to lead in such settings are empathy, sensitivity, recognition of respect for difference and 'personal authenticity informed of consistency of beliefs, language and behaviour' (West-Burnham, 2016: 4). This is because we see such leaders needing to integrate diversity into all of the processes of their organisation. Only then will diversity become a lens for looking at, identifying, developing and advancing talent, and a culture where everyone has a single vision to embrace and celebrate diversity.

Valuing and embracing diversity

Lumby and Coleman (2016) observed that some leaders found it difficult to manage student diversity when the ethnic origins of practitioners (mainly white) to large BME student population was not representative. In addition, practitioners and leaders have to manage complexities such diversity brings with it, like helping to narrow the attainment gap in areas of multiple deprivation; addressing the poor outcomes for some of our most vulnerable young children, particularly those who are looked after; and supporting children and families for black and other minority ethnic background and those children affected by social change and health inequalities. This means individual leaders have to think and act differently to manage such complexities, requiring both resilience and vision to make things happen for the child and the family. Early Years leaders need to ensure everyone's voice is heard as it is essential to experiment and learn from a fusion of cultures to remove stigmatisation, exclusion and domination in relation to minority ethnic groups, otherwise there is a danger that we will get more of what we have always had. However, we are aware that there are indications in literature (Lumby and Coleman, 2016) that some leaders may prefer to have less diversity because it is too difficult to manage it in the current performance driven culture.

Lessons from some leadership approaches from around the world

We can learn much from international practices associated with Early Years education. We believe there is much to do in developing and adopting a cross-cultural approach to Early Years practice often seen in Eastern countries – for example, the practice based on the philosophy of Confucianism, Montessori, Te Whariki or Ubuntu. Confucianism has its influence on moral obligation valuing Chinese traditions. Montessori is a method of education that is based on self-directed activity, hands-on learning and collaborative play. In a Te Whariki setting, there is promotion of values of honesty, respect and kindness based on the Mauri culture which clearly shows how local diversity is embedded in current practice. The philosophy of Ubuntu derives from a South African word Nguni, with ubuntu meaning the quality of being human. The Reggio Emilia approach, interpreted through different forms of leadership is practiced involving a whole team, holistic approach in working with young children. Different countries may hold different philosophies and ideology important in terms of their Early Years approach, which in turn influences how leaders lead. Perhaps leaders in Early Years and Primary settings in England need to take a closer to look at international Early Years perspectives in early education to see which good ideas of practice can be adapted from a leadership perspective.

Reluctance to become Early Years leaders

We believe most Early Years practitioners have the potential, capability and control to progress in their career path to a senior leadership role. During an informal conversation with teaching assistants undertaking an undergraduate degree in education and with initial teacher trainees on an undergraduate Early Years course, the authors separately investigated the reluctance of Early Years practitioners to take on whole school leadership role. They found the groups were confused regarding what leadership meant; lacked self-belief about being a leader; had low confidence in their capabilities about managing people and conflict in KS1/2; and were worried about their lack of skills and experience in financial management.

Furthermore, some practitioners even said they did not want to be a leader (about taking on fulfilling whole school role and responsibilities) because they felt uncomfortable and out of their comfort zone. They felt confident and secure as Early Years practitioners, but not under the term 'leader'. Unfortunately, this also inferred there were far fewer good Early Years leader role models to aspire to. We are suggesting that although the Early Years leadership role may not be for everyone as an aspirational career path and that is a reasonable and acceptable choice to make, but there needs to be an avenue where they can discuss such matters.

Lovett (2018) undertook a study with fifty seven primary and secondary teachers from their third to their seventh year of teaching in New Zealand, which supported some of our empirical findings. She found there was confusion amongst teachers of what they thought a leader is and what they do.

Typically, their understanding of a leader was someone with a named positional role. Furthermore, Lovett (2018) found that 'there was reluctance amongst teachers to be leaders … a realisation that leadership involves personal risk taking, courage, and supportive colleagues' (p. 2) which can be challenges in an Early Years context where the emphasis is on a level tiered team. Although her study was undertaken with primary and secondary teachers, there is close resonance to attitudes and practice of how Early Years practitioners felt. In summary, there was a feeling that many practitioners do not recognise the link between leading childrens' learning and 'doing' leadership which is why many are reluctant to take on leadership positions.

Developing practitioner leadership

To develop teacher leadership, May's (2016) research undertaken with leaders of children's services recognised the following factors as important leadership attributes:

- creativity, ingenuity and skills of collaboration;
- entrepreneurial/business planning skills;
- ability to marshal resources and make best use of professional expertise; and
- confidence and courage to challenge orthodox solutions and to implement change in the face of opposition from the professional establishment.

We would add that it is equally important when working with people in a team situation to have the skill of managing conflict. There are now more opportunities to overcome the reluctance of the few to become Early Year leaders by building leadership capacity through creating a culture of self-belief, and a can-do approach by individuals. This means focusing on what is important and knowing what makes a difference for all children, and unambiguously to those with EAL. We need to focus on 'releasing the talents and energies of the leaders of the future' (HMI, 2007: 21). Furthermore, there is a discernible challenge of recruiting men into Early Years as there is for attracting BME practitioners to provide good role models to all children, but especially those with EAL.

Lack of male leaders in Early Years

It is common knowledge that there is a lack of male leaders in the Early Years sector (Mistry and Sood, 2013). This is supported by the National Review of the Early Years and Childcare Workforce Report and Consultation (2006) which was based on a large sample of practitioners across all sectors that found 'men are severely under-represented in this sector … and that they provide a positive role model to children and young people' (p. 35). This can be particularly important to children with EAL especially if they have a patriarchal type of family environment. This report looked at how males and other under-represented groups can be attracted into the sector. The main responses were to increase wages of practitioners which accurately reflected the qualifications, roles and responsibilities and address society's attitudes towards men working in the early years and childcare sector. Other recurring themes were that men would be more attracted if there were more full-time posts available and more favourable attitudes by employers towards taking men onto their staff. One example of a changing attitude was that perhaps there needed to be a consideration of changing job titles as men do not want to be referred to as 'nursery nurses', which was an interesting suggestion. These findings further support some of the research evidence of Mistry and Sood (2013) – which suggest perpetuations of negative stereotypes, attitudes, values and beliefs held by some. In addition, Mistry and Sood (ibid.) went on to say many head teachers are looking for the right person for the job in Early Years regardless of whether they were male or female, which is challenging if males do not apply for the job in the first place due to perceived stereotypes.

The absence of Black Minority Ethnic (BME) leaders

BME leaders are greatly under-represented in English schools and Early Years settings compared with the number of BME children. Research by Bush *et al.* (2006), showed that BME teachers experience many barriers in developing their careers, including family and community attitudes, unfair recruitment and selection processes, and both covert and overt discrimination. The participants in this research demonstrated qualities of determination, resilience and hard work in overcoming these barriers, leading to the conclusion that these pioneers are 'exceptional' people. But personal attributes and capabilities are not enough as there are deeper reasons why there are so few BME leaders especially in the context of Early Years. This is illustrated in Education Today (2015) by the fact that there are currently only 104 secondary school head teachers from Black Minority Ethnic (BME) backgrounds in the UK. With some schools seeing 70 per cent of students from a BME background, this means that the staff make-up simply does not reflect the student body. Whilst numbers of BME head teachers in England are slowly growing – from 5.6 per cent in 2012 to 6.1 per cent in 2013, this picture differs hugely regionally. The north west, for example, has only twenty seven BME head teachers in comparison to 99,910 BME children (Education Today, 2015).

In the Early Years sector, these kind of statistics are rare to find, as there are simply not enough BME practitioners joining the profession in the first place and very few seem to progress to leadership and headship. Keates, General Secretary of the NASUWT, notes that BME teachers still face discrimination, bullying and harassment which hold them back from career progression and may be a factor in the low take-up into the profession (Educational International, 2017). Having BME practitioners and leaders in Early Years settings encourages children to value people from different backgrounds, colour, faith and culture, leading to greater tolerance. Role-models are essential in inspiring children to aim high and to view school as a place that welcomes them and where they could be successful.

Practical suggestions to increase BME numbers

Universities have a key role to play in recruiting more BME students on to their courses. Government figures show the proportion of BME teachers in England rose from 11.6 per cent in 2012, to 13.4 per cent in 2016 (Rhodes, 2017). Hermitt (2015) thinks that BME leaders' can use their experiences to engage more with BME students by challenging racial stereotypes and making changes throughout the school to address any issues of discrimination harming students. This, he argues, will make students feel that their school leaders are looking out for them.

The government's trial of the scheme aiming to increase the number of BME head teachers, like Leadership, Equality and Diversity Fund, had some success (DfE, 2019). This trial under the equality and diversity fund support schools to develop local solutions that help teachers covered by at least one of the protected characteristics as defined in the Equality Act 2010 progress into leadership – and race was one such factor. However, we argue that what is required more in a systematic way is mentoring and practical training like concrete actions to address discrimination for aspiring BME leaders. This in turn will give them increased confidence and improved leadership skills to plan their next career move. Leaders of schools worldwide find that unconscious and conscious bias may affect BME applicants when applying for leadership positions (Ethnic Dimension Research and Consultancy, 2014).

We believe more BME people's stories need to be heard to help understand discriminatory experiences that recruiters (head teachers, governors and parents) have never had to confront themselves to help with their decentred thinking (Donaldson, 1978). As well as listening to staff, the governing body should be questioning themselves regularly about the culture of their organisation and how inclusion is demonstrated within that organisation. It is at the governor level we begin to challenge negative stereotypes and restrictive career paths for the BME community within the setting and beyond.

Research reported in the *Guardian* (2011) identified a number of barriers for BME applicants for leadership from non-education sector which we feel are useful in understanding some of the reasons as to why there are lack of BME practitioners and leaders in education:

- Inconsistent approaches to develop talent
- A lack of perceived transparency in the recruitment process

- Selection panels appointing in their own image
- BME candidates having less access to significant networking opportunities
- A recurrent lack of commitment from leaders in many organisations on diverse recruitment
- Inconsistent approaches to developing talent

In the context of education, these barriers are probably mirrored and more specifically in Early Years it means the leadership quickly identifies, nurtures, mentors and gives every opportunity to grow their own leaders. Additionally, some possible strategies advanced by the *Guardian* report include:

- Recognition of the business case for greater diversity in top jobs, with visible role models, more balanced teams and greater alignment with community needs
- More champions, white and BME, who keep this issue to the fore
- Recognising the BME managerial talent which does exist and being less risk averse in senior appointments
- BME managers working to gain greater exposure and networking

There are many similarities from this list that can be applied to the education sector to advance the career opportunities for aspiring BME leaders in Early Years. One way this can happen is through 'building capacity in staff by offering leadership opportunities and trusting their abilities' (Lumby and Coleman, 2016: 184).

Challenges faced by BME leaders

Like any leader, Early Years leaders face many challenges and opportunities against a tide of change after change, with little chance of stability, time to reflect and space to stimulate debate that informs and develops leadership practice. One main challenge is to continue to build community cohesion for stable society, requiring leadership to work closely with the communities where their children attend the school. An interview with an experienced and influential Muslim head teacher in the Midlands explained some of the challenges faced (Mistry and Sood, 2011). These being:

- some staff do not have connection with their local communities that they work in so have little understanding of their children;
- attracting suitable staff which reflected the diversity of the school;
- ensuring all staff and children were tolerant of each other and each other's religions, faiths and cultures required constant vigilance;

- ensuring everyone in the setting (children, staff, leadership, governors, parents, administrative staff) carefully considered their use of language to ensure that no offence was given in dealing with contentious issues about attitudes to lesbian, gay, bisexual, transgender and queer (Lumby and MacRuairc, 2018).

This is further supported from research by Lumby and MacRuairc (2018) on school leadership and religion in twelve multifaith schools across England, Wales and Republic of Ireland which found leaders dealt with deeply embedded perceptions of sexuality, faith, ethnicity (visible or non-visible), gender in many different ways and 'grappled with the language of social justice' (Executive summary). This means, the challenge for leadership practice is to enter into debate about inclusion in both diverse and non-diverse settings as Britain's society becomes more increasingly diverse.

Authors' personal reflections

Both authors of this book have been middle leaders and senior leaders in schools (including Early Years) and have encountered first hand prejudice, stereotyping and consequent discrimination and racism/sexism. This has deeply affected their experiences of Early Years, primary school, secondary school and University because at times they felt stigmatised, maybe unconsciously (Moule, 2009) and at times felt they were seen as alien/other especially from parents of a monolingual community. Here, all they wanted was to be accepted as individuals with their own identity and be part of the setting life. Goffman (2009) develops the concept of a stigmatised identity further. So, eradicating prejudice and racism in all its forms remains a major challenge for all leaders. But, arguably, the challenge for minority ethnic leaders is how best to support individual BME men and women from marginalisation and stigmatised identities as these may impact their life chances. This requires all leaders to focus on and address the blind spot of discriminatory practice and be equally supportive of the learning and development of all children and staff.

Whether such challenges are a regular occurrence in Early Years remains debatable, but lessons learned from literature suggests the need for teaching, learning and talking about global perspectives in the curriculum; talking about diverse views and beliefs, including those with faith beliefs or not, discussing fairness and inequality; creating a culture of respect and understanding that reflects their locale; talking about different faiths and cultures to draw out the similarities; creating a culture to develop a deep and respectful understanding of people and developing the children as critical, confident thinkers. If the setting does not reflect child/practitioner diversity, then this is particularly a critical challenge.

Key reflection points

- Leadership in Early Years is about knowing how to lead learning for children of all faiths/non faiths, cultures, sexuality, and those with EAL. This requires strong leadership that enables children to develop deep and respectful understanding of other groups. These children need critical skills that will enable them to confidently challenge prejudice and discrimination by knowing and learning with and from children with EAL.

- Going forward, we need the Early Years sector to have culturally responsive leadership; promote anti-racist leadership, address head on the challenges faced by BME leaders; to proactively look at the reasons for the absence of BME leaders; and look at new models on leadership drawing on spirituality, creativity, ethics and aesthetic.

Summary

The current concept of what leadership looks like in Early Years settings is either confusing or contested. If leadership is about enabling vision implementation in a setting and in a systemic holistic way, then there is some confusion arising about whose voices should be heard in developing such an Early Years vision. In essence, who might be the central players and who might be excluded in developing policies, practice and accountability towards children with EAL and their families? This contested idea requires strong leadership to remould what has always been done in the Early Years. It requires leaders, governors and practitioners to look to future by reflecting on lessons from around the world, mobilising and sustaining individual competencies, sharing, adapting and developing practice based on individual contexts and communities that Early Years serves.

References

Bush, T., Glover, D. and Sood, K. (2006) Black and minority ethnic leaders in England: a portrait. *School Leadership & Management*. 26 (3): 289–305.

Department for Education (DfE) (2017) *Statutory framework for the early years foundation stage: Setting the standards for learning, development and care for children from birth to five.* London: DfE.

Department for Education (DfE) (2017a) *Early years workforce strategy* (March 2017) https://assets.publishing.service.gov.uk/government/uploads/system/uploads/attachment_data/file/596884/Workforce_strategy_02-03-2017.pdf (Accessed January 2019).

Department for Education (DfE) (2019) *Guidance – Equality and diversity fund: for school-led projects.* www.gov.uk/guidance/equality-and-diversity-funding-for-school-led-projects (Accessed March 2019).

Donaldson, M. (1978) *Children's minds*. London: Harper Collins.

Education International (2017) *UK: Racial discrimination is a reality in schools and classroom*. https://ei-ie.org/en/detail/15446/uk-racial-discrimination-is-a-reality-in-schools-and-classrooms. 11.10.2017 (Accessed March 2019).

Education Today (2015) Helping BME teachers into leadership roles. www.education-today.co.uk/helping-bme-teachers-into-leadership-roles/ 1 June 2015 (Accessed March 2019).

Ethnic Dimension Research and Consultancy (2014, Online). *Identifying and removing barriers to talented BAME staff progression in the civil service*. https://assets.publishing.service.gov.uk/government/uploads/system/uploads/attachment_data/file/417250/EthnicDimensionBlockagestoTalentedBAMEstaffProgressionintheCivilServiceFinal16.12.141.pdf (Accessed March 2019).

Foucault, M. (1981) The order of discourse. In R. Young (ed.) (1981). *Untying the text: A post-structural anthology*. Boston: Routledge and Kegan Paul. pp. 48–78.

Goffman, E. (2009) *Stigma: Notes on the management of spoiled identity*. New York, London, Toronto: Simon and Schuster.

Grint, K. (2010) *Leadership: A very short introduction*. Oxford: Oxford University Press.

Guardian (2011) *Why are there so few BME managers at the top?* www.the guardian.com/social-care-network/2011/dec/07/why-so-few-bme-managers (Accessed March 2019).

Harris, A. (2013) *Distributed leadership matters*. London: Corwin Press.

Her Majesty's Inspectorate of Education (HMI) (2007) National Review of the Early Years and Childcare Workforce: Analysis of Written Consultation and Workshop Responses. (2007) Scottish Executive Social Research, March 2007. www2.gov.scot/Publications/2007/03/21090538/0 (Accessed January 2019).

Hermitt, D. (2015) Improving diversity among leaders. *SecEd*. www.sec-ed.co.uk/best-practice/improving-diversity-among-leaders/ (Accessed March 2019).

Lovett, S. (2018) *Advocacy for teacher leadership: Opportunity, preparation, support, and pathways*. pp: 1–138. http://dx.doi.org/10.1007/978-3-319-74430-8 (Accessed February 2019).

Lumby, J. and Coleman, M. (2016) *Leading for equality: Making schools fairer*. London: Sage.

Lumby, J. and MacRuairc, G. (2018) *All faiths and none: School leadership and religion in multifaith societies*. Southampton, UK: University of Southampton.

May, A. (2016) Tomorrow will not be the same as today. Power-Point presentation by the Corporate Director for Children and Young People. ALICSE programme, Nottinghamshire County Council. Nottingham: SDSA.

Mistry, M. and Sood, K. (2011) Rethinking educational leadership to transform pedagogical practice to help improve the attainment of minority ethnic pupils: The need for leadership dialogue. *Management in Education*, 25 (3): 125–130.

Mistry, M. and Sood, K. (2012) Challenges of early years leadership preparation: A comparison between early and experienced early years practitioners in England. *Management in Education*, 26 (1): 28–37. https://doi.org/10.1177/0892020611427068 (Accessed January 2019).

Mistry, M. and Sood, K. (2013) Why are there still so few men within early years in primary schools: Views from male trainee teachers and male leaders? *Education 3–13: International Journal of Primary, Elementary and Early Years Education*, 43 (2): 115–127. http://dx.doi.org/10.1080/03004279.2012.759607 (Accessed February 2019).

Mistry, M. and Sood, K. (2014) Permeating the social justice ideals of equality and equity within the context of early years: Challenges for leadership in multicultural and mono-cultural primary schools. *Education 3–13: International Journal of Primary, Elementary and Early Years Education*. Online. www.tandfonline.com/doi/full/10.1080/03004279.2013.837944. (Accessed February 2019).

Moule, J. (2009) Understanding unconscious bias and unintentional racism. *Phi Delta Kappan*, 90 (5): 320–326.

National Association for Language Development in the Curriculum (NALDIC) (2016) *Assessing EAL: Learning and Teaching*. 23rd Annual Conference, 14 November 2016, King's College London.

Nutbrown, C. (2018) *Early childhood educational research: International perspectives*. London: Sage.

Office for Standards in Education (Ofsted) (2018) *Early Years inspection handbook*. London: Ofsted.

Oliveira-Formosinho, J. and Barros Araújo, S. (2011) Early education for diversity: Starting from birth. *European Early Childhood Education Research Journal*, 19 (2): 223–235.

Rodd, J. (2013) *Leadership in early childhood*. 4th edn. Maidenhead, UK: McGraw Hill/Open University Press.

Rhodes. D. (2017) Schools need 68,000 extra BME teachers to reflect population. BBC News. www.bbc.co.uk/news/uk-england-40568987. 13 July 2017. (Accessed March 2019).

Schön, D. (1983) *The reflective practitioner: How professionals think in action*. New York: Basic Books.

Shah, S. (2006) Leading multi-ethnic schools: A new understanding of Muslim youth identity. *Educational Management, Administration and Leadership*, 34 (2): 215–237.

Shields, C. and Mohan, E. J. (2008) High-quality education for all students: Putting social justice at its heart. *Teacher Development*, 12 (4): 289–300. November 2008.

The National Review of the Early Years and Childcare Workforce Report and Consultation. (2006) Scotland: Scottish Executive, August 2006.

UNESCO (2015) *Education 2030 Incheon Declaration towards inclusive and equitable quality education and lifelong learning for all*. www.unesco.org/new/fileadmin/MULTIMEDIA/HQ/ED/ED_new/pdf/FFA-ENG-27Oct15.pdf (Accessed January 2019).

West-Burnham, J. (2016) Leadership for diversity: securing equity, inclusion and social justice. *Educational Leadership Development*. www.johnwest-burnham.co.uk/index.php/leadership-for-diversity (Accessed February 2019).

Index

Page numbers in **bold** denote tables, those in *italics* denote figures.

Leedham, D. 71
Lewthwaite. B. 118
linguistic diversity 47, 50, 65, 67, **75**, 92, 102–103, 109, 121, 135, 173; *see also* multilingualism
linguistic identity 120–121
Linguistic Relativism 93–95
linguistics 79, 80, 83–84, 88, 95–96
literacy 9, 25, 26, 36, 40–41, 73–74, 86, 88, 169; as core subject 50, 132, 139, 140, 142, 149, 153, 154, 158; *see also* phonics; reading
Lizardo, O. 129
local authorities 44, 45, 131, 132
Locke, J. **20**, 22, 23, 25, 27, 80, 81, 112
looked after children 173
Lovett, S. 174–175
Lumby, J. 114, 116, 173, 179

Macfarlane, B. 155
MacRuairc, G. 116, 179
male leaders and practitioners 113, 171, 175–176
Mallows, D. 73
Mandarin 7, 8–9, 67
marketisation 6, 13, 24, 42, 129–130
Martins, L.L. 112
May, A. 164, *166*, 175
McAlpine, L. 120
McMillan, M. **20**, 33, 34, 133
McMillan, R. 33, 34, 133
meaning-making 96, 105
mediation 103, 151
memorising knowledge 22, 25, 97, 132, 156
migration *see* (im)migration
Milliken, F.J. 112
Mistry, M. 57, 107–108, 113, 118, 136, 164, 167, 171, 176
MKO (More Knowledgeable Others) 26
modelling 9, 30, 34, **75**, 87, 93, 95, 103
Mohan, E.J. 171
Moll, L. **20**, 23, 28, 30, 35
monolingualism 50, 91, 93, 97, 171, 179; of practitioners 22, 47, 61, 65, 82–83, 135, 173; of students 8, 11, 24, 40, 44, 45, 46, 47, 48, **62**, 68, 72, 82, 83, 84, 94, 140–141
Montessori, M. **20**, 32, 34, 130, 133, 134, 154, 173–174

moral education 22
multilingualism 1, 10, 60–61, 62–63, **62**, 65, 67–70, 76, 86
Murphy, V. 71, 73

NALDIC (National Association of Language Development in the Curriculum) 63, 70, 82, 118
names 56
NASUWT 176–177
national identity 40–41, 102, 103
NC (National Curriculum) 2, 24, 41, 132, 140–141
Ndhlovu, F. 102–103, 121
neo-liberalism 24, 146
neuroscience 25, 90, 157
New Zealand 135, 174–175
Newbold Report (1921) 41
'normalising' children with EAL 40, 41, 48
Norwich, B. 13
numeracy/number skills 9, 10, 25, 29, 158, 169; as core subject 13, 23, 36, 131, 132, 139, 140, 146, 149, 151–152, 153, 154; learning through play 24, 136, 153, 157, 158
nurseries 1, 8, **130**, 131, 176; case studies in 11, 55, 81, 110, 139, 154; earliest **20**, 32, 33, 133
Nutbrown, C. 164

Ofsted (Office of Standards in Education) 3, 70, 92–93, 137, 148, 154
Oliveira-Formosinho, J. 171
operant conditioning 81
Osborne, J. 96
outdoor environments 24, 32, 33, 133, 135, 136, 139, **150**
Owen, R. **20**, 32, 34, 133

Pakistan 7
Paradis, J. 68
parents 65, 68, 70, 95, 118–119, 138, 139, 148, 156, 177, 179; relationships with 54, 55, 92, 115, 120, 136, 149, 168–169; *see also* communities, working with; families
participatory justice 117
performativity 3, 6, 13, 18, 19, 36, 57, 129, 145–159, *152*; definition of 146–147; theory of performance 145, 148–151, *149*, **150**

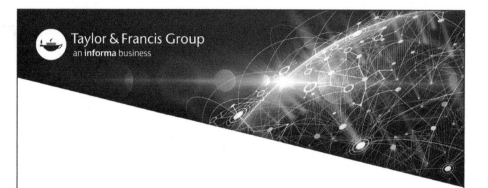